NASTY
WOMEN

NASTY WOMEN

FEMINISM, RESISTANCE, AND REVOLUTION IN TRUMP'S AMERICA

EDITED BY

SAMHITA MUKHOPADHYAY
AND KATE HARDING

PICADOR

NEW YORK

picadorusa.com • picadorbookroom.tumblr.com
twitter.com/picadorusa • facebook.com/picadorusa

Picador® is a U.S. registered trademark and is used by Macmillan Publishing Group, LLC, under license from Pan Books Limited.

For book club information, please visit facebook.com/picadorbookclub or email marketing@picadorusa.com.

"How to Build a Movement" by Alicia Garza was previously published in *Mic*.

"A Nation Groomed and Battered" by Rebecca Solnit was previously published as "From Lying to Leering: Penis Power" in *The London Review of Books*, January 19, 2017.

Designed by Steven Seighman

The Library of Congress Cataloging-in-Publication Data is available upon request.

ISBN 978-1-250-15550-4 (trade paperback)
ISBN 978-1-250-15551-1 (ebook)

Our books may be purchased in bulk for promotional, educational, or business use. Please contact your local bookseller or the Macmillan Corporate and Premium Sales Department at 1-800-221-7945, extension 5442, or by email at MacmillanSpecialMarkets@macmillan.com.

First Edition: October 2017

10 9 8 7 6 5 4 3 2 1

CONTENTS

vi   CONTENTS

NASTY
WOMEN

"I'M A WOMAN, VOTE FOR ME"
Why We Need Identity Politics

Samhita Mukhopadhyay

UNDERNEATH THE LARGEST GLASS CEILING in New York City, Hillary Clinton's campaign planned to celebrate victory at the Javits Center, on election night 2016. I gathered there along with thousands of others to witness Clinton make history as the first female president of the United States.

In the lead-up to the election, polls had the former senator and secretary of state leading reality-TV star Donald Trump by at least 4 to 6 percentage points. *The New York Times* gave Clinton an 85 percent chance of winning. As an editorial director at *Mic,* an online news and culture website for millennials, I had also planned for a Clinton victory, assigning a dozen or so stories, and had written and revised a two-thousand-word piece about this big, albeit fraught, moment in feminist history.

We all know how this story goes. At around 10 p.m., CNN called Ohio for Trump. The mood at Javits turned grim, but viewers held out hope. Idaho and North Carolina followed, and then the tipping point: Florida. By now, small groups of women were sitting on the ground crying; hundreds left the building in droves. Amid the chaos,

I realized I had to make my way back to the office. We had to rewrite everything. Donald Trump was going to be president.

The intact glass ceiling at the Javits Center turned out to be a metaphor even more apt than the Clinton campaign could have imagined.

The 2016 election wasn't just a loss for Clinton, it was a loss for feminism. Not only did the first female candidate from either major party lose, she lost to an open misogynist—someone who called a former Latina beauty queen fat and was caught on the record bragging about grabbing women by the pussy. Despite that the election played out like a morality tale gone wrong, in which the smart girl who had done her homework loses to the class clown who barely shows up for school, in its wake progressives seemed to bristle at discussing the role sexism and racism played in it. Instead, they openly debated whether the campaign—and the left more generally—had focused too much on "identity politics": on Clinton being the first viable woman candidate for president and catering to minorities and their concerns, instead of speaking to the economic anxieties of the white working class.

Born of the civil and women's-rights activism of the 1970s, identity politics seeks to recognize and organize around the complex and interwoven ways race, class, gender, immigration status, and sexuality, among other factors, impact how life is lived in America—and who has access to the American dream. Both a political and intellectual movement, identity politics offers a critique of privilege and the ways it is meted out. It has been pilloried by critics on the right and left who say its focus on difference is divisive. At the heart of the debate is the fundamental question of how we conceive of ourselves as a country: Do we recognize that different groups of people experience unique challenges based on their identity and organize around and embrace those differences, or do we ignore them in service of a more universal, uniform understanding of Americanness?

Clinton's campaign banked on the former, speaking directly to the interests of women, people of color, sexual minorities, and the disabled. Her campaign's rallying cry—"I'm with her"—was a clear reminder that she was the first woman presidential candidate for a major party. In what would come to be regarded as a tactical faux pas, Clinton dared to refer to Trump's supporters as "deplorables" for their regressive views on race and sexuality. In the third presidential debate, she ardently supported the right to an abortion: "I will defend Planned Parenthood. I will defend *Roe v. Wade,* and I will defend women's rights to make their own health care decisions," she said. In a powerful ad, she juxtaposed shots of women, people of color, and people with disabilities with footage of Trump denigrating these groups. The campaign included women and people of color in senior positions, and the mothers of Trayvon Martin, Tamir Rice, and Eric Garner appeared at several campaign stops, after Clinton personally met with the women and promised to advocate on their behalf.

This is not to say that Clinton had always done right by the communities she courted during the election. When her husband was president, she supported the passage of NAFTA, which some have argued exported well-paying American jobs; the 1994 Violent Crime Control Act, which is credited with fueling the mass incarceration epidemic that disproportionately impacts black men; and the 1996 Personal Responsibility and Work Opportunity Reconciliation Act, Bill Clinton's attempt at welfare reform, which is known for leading the way to criminalizing and stigmatizing welfare recipients. Her own ties to Wall Street—whose subprime lending practices caused the housing crisis, which disproportionately impacted the black community and its decades of progress in financial growth—dogged her as a candidate.[1]

After Clinton lost the election, criticism of her campaign's approach came swiftly. In a much discussed op-ed for *The New York Times,* Mark Lilla argued that "American liberalism has slipped into a kind of moral panic about racial, gender and sexual identity that has distorted liberalism's message and prevented it from becoming a uni-fying force capable of governing." Lilla's views were reinforced by lib-erals also warning of the electoral consequences of following Clinton's strategy. In a *Washington Post* op-ed, John B. Judis wrote that the left "overestimated the strength of a coalition based on identity politics."

Echoing similar sentiments, Senator Bernie Sanders regularly crit-icized Clinton for failing to focus on issues of class. "We need a Democratic Party that is not a party of the liberal elite but of the working class of this country," Sanders said in March. "It's not good enough for someone to say, 'I'm a woman! Vote for me!'" he said at a rally in Boston after the election. "What we need is a woman who has the guts to stand up to Wall Street, to the insurance companies, to the drug companies, to the fossil fuel industry."

Sanders is right in suggesting we need more than token references to identity to galvanize authentic support from voters, but it is impor-tant to remember that most identity politics are about class. And Clinton did talk about class during her campaign—about equal pay for women, paid family leave, increasing the minimum wage, a fair tax system, and revitalizing American manufacturing. She proposed a $10 billion investment fund to encourage companies to produce goods in America as well as tax credits to help revitalize areas devas-tated by deindustrialization. "Manufacturing is coming back," she said during the campaign. "My job as your president will be to do everything I can to create more good-paying jobs, to get wages rising again for American workers and families."

Exit polls also failed to substantiate the claim that Clinton's cam-paign didn't speak to economic anxieties in the electorate. Black women—the poorest demographic in the country—voted for Clinton at a rate of 94 percent. According to an analysis of exit polls by *The New York Times*, 53 percent of Americans making less than $30,000 per year voted for Clinton versus 41 percent for Trump. In those same exit polls, 52 percent of voters who listed the economy as their top political issue of concern voted for Clinton (as opposed to 42 percent who voted for Trump).

To suggest that progressives move away from identity politics, in the service of a broader "American" narrative, is also to suggest that we ignore the heavy-handed role that sexism played in Clinton's loss. In both her 2008 and 2016 presidential campaigns, people critiqued her voice, her demeanor, and her appearance. She was considered "untrustworthy," while her opponent, who wouldn't release his tax returns—the first candidate ever to refuse to do so—was supposedly a straight-talking, no-bull breath of fresh air. The press and the public became fascinated with Clinton's private server and leaked emails, both used to bolster the argument that she played by her own rules. Meanwhile, Trump was caught on the record repeatedly lying about everything from the unemployment rate, to his own tax plan to ultimately refusing to disclose his own tax documents. But Clinton's critics persisted—*they just didn't like her.*

Lost in the hubbub of debate on the left over identity politics was that Trump, too, ran a campaign based on identity, but it was white identity and white fears. During the election cycle, he deflected criticism of racialized language as unnecessary "political correctness"—a derisive term used to describe liberals' attempts to express sensitivity toward minorities. An outgrowth of identity politics, political correctness has become an obsession of thinkers on the right and left who are focused on the impact of "PC culture"—or rather, on students running amok on college campuses demanding gender-appropriate terminology who have simply hamstrung the progressive movement. Left-leaning writers like Greg Lukianoff and Jonathan Haidt have caricatured, prior to the 2016 election, "safe spaces" and "trigger warnings" as evidence that today's college students are intellectually coddled. *New York* magazine columnist Jonathan Chait called PC culture "exhausting," that being held to the standards of political correctness is difficult and ineffective and therefore tiresome.

These critiques first came from staunch conservatives: in his 1998 *Illiberal Education*, author Dinesh D'Souza argued that political correctness impairs free speech, preventing society from talking openly about "brutal truths."

Trump built his campaign around speaking those "brutal truths," which gave way to the rise of the alt-right and other white ethnonationalist sentiments in the 2016 election cycle. He stoked fear of the "other" when he proposed a ban on Muslims entering the United States. He aggravated class anxieties by insinuating "illegals" would take jobs and used that fear to push forward the idea that we need a bigger, taller wall to keep Mexicans out of the country. As Laila Lalami argued in *The New York Times*, Trump won the votes of the white majority on a campaign that "explicitly and consistently appealed to white identity and anxiety."

Senator Sanders made the claim that not all Trump supporters are "racists and sexists and homophobes and deplorable folks." Yet a series of studies suggests that they share a fear of and antipathy for the "other." In *The Nation*, Sean McElwee and Jason McDaniel published an analysis of a survey from the Cooperative Congressional Analysis Project and found that fear of diversity made voters more likely to vote for Trump. In an analysis of data from American National Election Studies, political scientist Philip Klinkner found racial resentment was a key motivator in voting for Trump. He told Mehdi Hasan at *The Intercept*, "whether it's good politics to say so or not, the evidence from the 2016 election is very clear that attitudes about blacks, immigrants, and Muslims were a key component of Trump's appeal." Trump galvanized existing racial animus by stoking fear of America's increased diversity to bring out white voters in droves.

That Trump's explicit appeals to white identity and resentment were considered legitimate rallying cries that supposedly united an unheard working-class base, while Clinton was called divisive, suggests that calls for "universality" generally mean centralizing white, male experience. Whereas the experiences of people of color are marked as nonstandard, white identity—white concerns, sensitivities, anxieties—is taken as representative of the whole; anything that deviates from that identity is "diversity" or "difference." In practice, it is impossible to have a liberal politics devoid of identity: to eschew identity politics is to ignore the experiences and concerns of a vast segment of American society. Take, for example, how we conceptualize the plight of the working class—politicians are focused on coal miners and factory-line jobs, not the retail, fast-food, or health care industries, which employ predominantly working-class people of color.

From a tactical standpoint, identity politics may be alienating to working-class voters who see their privilege as earned and that the cause of their economic stagnation is due to competition with other lower classes, such as working-class people of color or immigrants, as opposed to a system that privileges the rich. But the answer is not to shy away from uncomfortable truths about race, gender, class, sexuality, and disability. As the country grows more diverse—by 2050, whites may well become a minority of the population—these truths become harder and harder to ignore.[2]

Beyond the necessity of grappling with identity on the left, much of the successful political organizing in recent years has been rooted in identity. The robust, extensive, and complex Movement for Black Lives' rallying cry is based on identity: "Black lives matter." Not only have activists been successful in changing the public conversation on race and the criminal justice system, they got the presidential candidates to talk about policing practices and have brought out protesters against racially motivated violence in droves. Immigrant-rights organizers have focused their efforts on communities targeted by racial profiling. These coordinated efforts led to record-high turnout at protests, like the one at New York's Kennedy airport when Trump issued the Muslim ban and the May Day protests in 2017. And of the many "isms" impacted after the Trump election, sexism was the target and the organizing principle for millions of women around the world who participated in the Women's March protests the day after the inauguration.

Identity-based organizing is our best tool in the fight for equality. Granted, it's not always easy. Within each of these communities there are robust, sometimes difficult, and sometimes agonizing discussions about the fickle borders of identity. What issues should be included? How can we include all of these issues and still stay focused on a common goal? How do we prioritize our agendas with so many different factions involved? But those questions shouldn't divide the left; instead they pressure-test beliefs and ensure the fight for justice and equality is expansive, creative, and inclusive. For example, considering how the fight for trans rights is an important part of the feminist movement doesn't weaken the feminist movement but instead strengthens it, forces it to be more comprehensive and truly inclusive.

And it is exactly those conversations that need to enter the mainstream political discourse rather than our hiding from them in the service of a false narrative about America. How do we navigate a world that gives us Beyoncé's groundbreaking album *Lemonade,* a tribute to black women's sexuality, and the rise of the alt-right? We live in complex, sometimes mind-numbingly confounding times and the only way to understand them is to understand each other: the good, the bad, and the sometimes extremely ugly.

It is in service to these complex conversations that Kate and I put together this anthology. In the chapters ahead we have curated some of the strongest voices writing at the intersection of feminism, identity, and personal experience with their own identity to meditate on what we lost that fateful night in November 2016 and what lessons we can take from it. In "Country Crock" Sam Irby writes beautifully on being a queer, working-class woman of color who moves to Trump country. Reflecting on her travels in Ghana, Jill Filipovic shares a gut-wrenching story about a young woman she meets in her travels and how her life may be impacted by Trump's unleashing of the global gag order. In "Beyond the Pussy Hats" Katha Pollitt makes it plain how we can lose our abortion rights in Trump's America. Zerlina Maxwell reflects on her time as a black woman working on the Clinton campaign in "Trust Black Women." Jessica Valenti shares her feelings the day after the election in "Permission to Vote for a Monster: Ivanka Trump and Faux Feminism," and the inimitable Cheryl Strayed, in "She Will," discusses how she felt after Clinton lost. Meredith Talusan, in "We've Always Been Nasty: Why the Feminist Movement Needs Trans Women and Gender-Nonconforming Femmes," makes the case for how we have an opportunity to redefine gender in the women's movement and we should absolutely take it.

In the end, diversity is embedded in America's social fabric. Hillary Clinton might have lost the election by way of the electoral college, but she won the popular vote—so more people across the country supported her vision of America than Trump's. And Barack Obama, our first black president, won twice. We may not see eye to eye on the political positions of these candidates or how the details of identity politics play out on the national stage, but coalitional politics—recognizing and fighting for the diverse needs of many—are our best shot at building a progressive future. It will be our ability to draw from, incorporate, and celebrate our differences that will truly make America great.

---

1. For additional information on the impact of subprime lending on black wealth, see Nathalie Baptiste, "Them That's Got Shall Get," *American Prospect*, October 14, 2014. Accessed at http://prospect.org/article/staggering-loss-black-wealth-due-sub prime-scandal-continues-unabated.

2. Bill Chappell, "For U.S. Children, Minorities Will Be the Majority by 2020, Census Says," "The Two-Way," March 4 2015. Accessed at http://www.npr.org /sections/thetwo-way/2015/03/04/390672196/for-u-s-children-minorities-will -be-the-majority-by-2020-census-says.

ARE WOMEN PERSONS?

Kate Harding

"The history of mankind is a history of repeated injuries and usurpations on the part of man toward woman, having in direct object the establishment of an absolute tyranny over her."
—FROM THE *DECLARATION OF SENTIMENTS*, SIGNED AT THE FIRST WOMEN'S RIGHTS CONVENTION, SENECA FALLS, NEW YORK, 1848

I AM AN ATHEIST, a pragmatist, and a staunch proponent of better living through chemistry, but the 2016 presidential election made me downright superstitious. Especially about dead women.

The morning of November 8, I arrived at my polling place wearing a suffragette-white pantsuit, my hands bedecked with rings belonging to my late mother, mother-in-law, and grandmother. Not all of them were fans of my politics or outspokenness, let alone Hillary Clinton's, but I still wanted, arguably *needed,* them all in the booth as I voted for her. Having given up the faith I was raised in long ago, I no longer believe in the Holy Spirit, the holy Catholic Church, the resurrection of the body, or even, on a bad day, the forgiveness of sins.

But the communion of saints—the idea that the dead remain more or less available to take your anguished calls—has always been the hardest part of the Apostle's Creed for me to let go.

Another thing you should know about me: I am not an easy crier. Generally speaking, my brain alchemizes strong emotions into excessive stomach acid, insomnia, and decades-long grudges rather than tears. But the 2016 election, bizarre and unprecedented in so many ways, made me cry early and cry often. Periodically throughout the daylight hours of November 8, I tortured myself by checking the live feed of Susan B. Anthony's grave in Rochester, New York, where lines of pilgrims snaked around headstones, waiting to place their I VOTED stickers on hers. Every time I checked the live feed, I came utterly undone.

I cried thinking about all the original owners of the jewelry I wore; about Susan B. Anthony and Elizabeth Cady Stanton and Matilda Joslyn Gage; about Ida B. Wells and Mary Ann Shadd Cary and Frances Ellen Watkins Harper; about Sarah Winnemucca, Mrs. S. K. Chan, Jeannette Rankin, Adelina Otero-Warren, Shirley Chisholm, and every other dead American woman who publicly insisted that live American women deserve full political equality. Every time I thought about Dorothy Howell Rodham—born the year before women got the vote—dying just a few years before her daughter become the first female nominee for president from a major party, I sobbed.

I cried as I voted, of course. After casting my ballot, I adorned one white lapel with my I VOTED sticker and the other with a trio of Hillary Clinton campaign buttons that extolled her nerdy virtues: *SHE* USES BIG WORDS. *SHE* BELIEVES IN SCIENCE. *SHE* DOES HER HOMEWORK.

She *is running against Donald-Fucking-Trump*, I kept telling myself as I reloaded the feed of Anthony's grave; cried; checked Facebook for pictures, of other pantsuits, and stickers, and hopeful smiling children in Hillary shirts; cried more; and generally did everything but concentrate on work for even one hot minute. *She is going to be president.*

In 1873, Susan B. Anthony was tried and convicted for casting a vote in the previous year's presidential election.

Anthony's attorney, Judge Henry Selden, cross-examined election inspector Beverly W. Jones, who testified that he and other members of the Board of Registry were ultimately persuaded that Anthony was entitled to register to vote. They did have some misgivings about it, though.

"What was the defect in her right to vote as a citizen?" asked Judge Selden.

"She was not a male citizen," Mr. Jones testified.

Refusing to pay the $100 fine levied against her, Anthony argued that the U.S. Constitution already guaranteed her right to vote under the Fourteenth Amendment, the first clause of which defined citizens as "all persons born or naturalized in the United States." Never mind the second clause, which referred specifically to the right of "male citizens" to vote. The language that instructed states to count former slaves as full citizens (or go without representation for that portion of the population) seemed broad enough to elevate born or naturalized women of almost every race and ethnicity[1] to voting citizens. *All persons*, it said.

"The only question left to be settled now," said Susan B. Anthony, "is: Are women persons?"

It wasn't a new or original argument. Three years earlier, Victoria Woodhull—the first woman ever to claim to run for president[2]—had delivered a memorial to Congress on this very subject. Whereas women are citizens, and whereas the Constitution prohibits abridging the privileges and immunities of citizens, and whereas the Constitution also takes precedence over state laws when the two are in conflict, women already have the right to vote, QE-motherfucking-D.

It was a clever argument, but one only necessitated by the failure of the feminist movement's earlier plea to lawmakers: "Please, please don't write the word 'male' into the U.S. Constitution."

Having supported Hillary Clinton in both 2008 and 2016, and having been politically sentient (if only just) during Bill Clinton's presidency, I am well aware that enormous chunks of the left—let alone the rusted-out, heavily armed, no-fucks-to-give right—loathe her beyond all reason.

Oh, they'll tell you there are reasons, and they'll list those reasons, the same ones, again and again, ad infinitum. Post the mildest praise of Hillary in any public forum, and you might as well have voiced an incantation from a dusty old grimoire—the spirits you've unwittingly summoned will immediately descend upon your Twitter, Facebook, comments section, blog, lunch table, local pub, or office. They will explain that Hillary Clinton is a warmongering neoliberal liar who gave speeches to Goldman Sachs executives, and she can't connect with the average voter, and she doesn't care about the white working class, but she also doesn't care about people of color. In fact, she doesn't care about anyone except herself, and once she cried and once she had cleavage, and her butt and ankles are too big, and her laugh is too loud, and her face is too expressive, or else impassive, and she couldn't keep her husband satisfied, and she's probably a lesbian, and don't you think she looks a bit peaked and NONE OF THIS IS SEXIST WHY DO YOU KEEP TRYING TO BRING SEXISM INTO IT WHEN THE RATIONAL, NONEMOTIONAL POLITICAL POINT I'M TRYING TO MAKE IS SHE'S A ROTTEN CUNT.

But even if all of that were true—hell, even if she killed Vince Foster[3]—she was still running against Donald Trump! Could the left really not get it together to vote for her on those grounds alone?

Of course not. To ask the question was to invoke a new horde of trolls whose guiding principle is that the American president exists to provide individual customer service. "She hasn't done anything to convince me that she deserves to be president," they'd say, as though reading her website, attending one of her gazillion events, or, say, checking Wikipedia was too much to expect of a voter wondering what the most famous woman on earth was *really* about. "She can't base a whole campaign on not being Donald Trump!"

Really? Why not? "If I win, Donald Trump will not be president" is a fucking *great* campaign slogan, if you ask me.

When I consider those who disagree, I'm tempted to throw in a rhetorical, indignantly italicized "Who *are* these people?" But the thing is, we know who they are. They're white men. They're white women who will do anything to maintain the protection of white men. They're a few sexist men of color. They're stone-cold racists. They're people who would never say and maybe don't even think that they're racist. They're people who would back anyone who says, "If I win, Hillary Clinton will not be president."

That's how much they hate her.

How much they hate us.

How much they hate, in some cases, themselves.

Donald Trump is how much.

This didn't come as a surprise to me, exactly. I've been a public feminist going on ten years now, so I have some experience with being publicly despised. Steve Bannon, Milo Yiannopoulos, Richard Spencer—did you just hear of those guys for the first time during the period of endlessly dawning horror that followed Trump's victory? Because they've been harassing outspoken women for ages, not to mention outspoken people of color, trans people, Muslims, and Jews, whether or not they're women. Men on the left can be nearly as relentless in their petulant demands for attention if you make a political choice they disapprove of, such as supporting an imperfect female candidate. So I'm not going to give you some "This isn't the America I know" bullshit. This is absolutely the America I know.

If you're an intellectually honest American, at some point you have to find a way to live with the knowledge that this country was founded on genocide, slavery, and misogyny. Every majestic national park was stolen from a murdered and exiled people. Some of our most beautiful historic buildings were constructed by the hands of human beings brought here in bondage. Nearly every "Great Man" we celebrate was raised by a woman working for free, then married to another woman who kept his house and raised his kids for free. This is the America we all know.

It's okay to admit that. Like a harried mother, you can feel a bone-deep attachment to this country of ours and be furious at it simultaneously. *I love you, America, but I do not like your behavior one bit.*

I've been a U.S. citizen for forty-two years, during which time I watched in horror as George W. Bush was elected by a vote of the Supreme Court; as we invaded Iraq and Afghanistan; as the religious right clawed away at reproductive freedom, state by state; as the Tea Party became a serious force in Republican politics. By now, I have seen so many videos of African Americans being extrajudicially executed by people sworn to serve and protect, I don't even know what the point of filming them is anymore. Evidence? What are the chances that the murderers will even be indicted, let alone tried and convicted?

I've come to believe that the real purpose those videos will one day serve is to show future generations how violently racist we were. As history, their existence, and the overall lack of resulting change, will make sense. Our descendants will tell a story about us: in the olden days, Americans were deeply invested in white supremacy. In the olden days, the police could beat black people to death and never be held accountable. In the olden days, there was resistance—people marched on Washington and on their own city halls, people wrote scathing op-eds and carried handmade signs and called their representatives and tried to be a little kinder to their neighbors. But it was never quite enough, because America was just so racist, just so violent, in the olden days.

They won't be wrong, any more than we are about Manifest Destiny, about the Trail of Tears, about slavery, about the Chinese Exclusion Act, about the Three-Fifths Compromise, about Jim Crow laws, about "separate but equal," about the Bisbee Deportation, about the National Origins Formula, about lynching, about the Mexican Repatriation movement, about Japanese internment camps, about the Zoot Suit Riots, about redlining, about Operation Wetback, about murdered civil rights leaders, about everything our parents and grandparents and founding fathers either committed or suffered under before we were born.

They won't be wrong. They will just be too slow to connect the dots, to remember Faulkner's famous line from *Requiem for a Nun*: "The past is never dead. It's not even past."

"To women this government is not a democracy," wrote Susan B. Anthony.

> *It is not a republic; it is an odious aristocracy—a hateful oligarchy of sex; the most hateful aristocracy ever established on the face of the globe. An oligarchy of wealth, where the rich govern the poor; an oligarchy of learning, where the educated govern the ignorant; or even an oligarchy of race, where the Saxon rules the African, might be endured; but this oligarchy of sex, which makes father, brother, husband, son, the oligarchs over the mother and sister, the wife and daughter, of every household—which ordains all men sovereigns, all women subjects, carries dissension, discord, and rebellion into every home of the nation.*

The astute reader will note that an "oligarchy of race" as described would be rather more endurable for the Saxon than the African. This is the problem with reading most white "first-wave" American feminists: even the ones who, like Anthony, began their activist careers in the abolition movement are prone to such casual, thoughtless racism.

And the generation that came after Anthony wasn't even casual about it. Whatever progress Carrie Chapman Catt helped make toward securing the ballot for women, she will always be the person who argued—in hopes of persuading Southern states to ratify the Nineteenth Amendment—"White supremacy will be strengthened, not weakened, by women's suffrage." That is not a real fuckin' ambiguous statement. (Nor, sadly, was it necessarily wrong.) And it makes me distinctly uninterested in preserving Chapman Catt's legacy in any way other than exercising the franchise.

I understand why many feel similarly about Susan B. Anthony, who took money from the white supremacist George Francis Train to found a radical newspaper, believing the ends for which she used it were more important than the windfall's provenance. She advocated, at times, for basing the right to vote on education, suggesting that those too poor, or poorly connected, to access opportunities for formal learning were less deserving of a voice in our democracy. And her lifelong bestie was Elizabeth Cady Stanton, who famously wrote, "Think of Patrick and Sambo and Hans and Yung Tung, who do not know the difference between a Monarchy and a Republic, who never read the Declaration of Independence . . . making laws for [white feminists] Lydia Maria Child, Lucretia Mott, or Fanny Kemble." There wasn't a lot of concern in the feminist movement then about throwing immigrants and uneducated black men under the bus to promote a certain class of white woman. Many would argue there still isn't today.

Still, I have an enduring soft spot for Anthony, in part because I'm skeptical of attempts to separate ourselves so cleanly from *the olden days* of feminist history, and in part because she's often maligned by today's feminists for things she *didn't* actually screw up. At least, not entirely.[4]

In 1869, leadership of the American women's rights movement split into opposing camps over their response to the Fifteenth Amendment. (You know, the one right after the one where a bunch of men wrote "male" into the U.S. Constitution.) The camp that would become the American Women's Suffrage Association, led by Lucy Stone, argued that the urgency of passing a Fifteenth Amendment to guarantee men the right to vote regardless "of race, color, or previous condition of servitude" was too great to keep arguing whether "sex" should be added to the list. They chose to support the amendment as written, and work on a state-by-state strategy for ensuring women's right to vote. But the camp that would become the National Woman Suffrage Association, led by Anthony and Stanton, refused to withdraw their demand that the amendment guarantee *universal* suffrage. They guessed, correctly, that if they couldn't pass it then, it would be decades before women's franchise was secured in the Constitution.

At some point during this contentious period, Susan B. Anthony said and/or wrote: "I will cut off this right arm of mine before I will ever work or demand the ballot for the Negro and not the woman." I'm not sure where she said that—it's hard to find a citation with a Google search, because the first several pages of results are all articles and blog posts about how Anthony was essentially an irredeemable racist who shouldn't be honored or celebrated in the twenty-first century. They all seem to lead back to a passage from the book *Divided Sisters: Bridging the Gap Between Black Women and White Women* by Midge Wilson and Kathy Russell, excerpted on a page about black women and the suffrage movement, hosted by Wesleyan University. I'm sure the printed book has a citation, but the website does not, and my editor is eager for me to finish this essay, so I'll simply stipulate the point: Yep, that sounds like Anthony! But the key words in that quote are: "and not the woman."

Susan B. Anthony loved women with all her heart. (Yes, probably in bed, but also everywhere else.) The motto of the radical newspaper she would found with that dirty white-supremacist money was "Men, their rights and nothing more; women, their rights and nothing less." In *A Brief Biography of Susan B. Anthony*, Stanton recounts her friend's stock answer to nosy questions about her romantic life:

> *She has often playfully said, when questioned on this point, that she could not consent that the man she loved, described in the constitution as a white male, native-born, American citizen, possessed of the right of self-government, eligible to the office of President of the great Republic, should unite his destinies in marriage with a political slave and pariah. "No, no; when I am crowned with all the rights, privileges, and immunities of a citizen, I may give some consideration to these social problems; but until then I must concentrate all my energies on the enfranchisement of my own sex."*

The comparison of married white women's lot to slavery is one more thing that endears few contemporary feminists to Anthony (or to the lengthy list of nineteenth-century white women who also made that analogy). It is the plain truth that nothing but slavery is like slavery, nothing but lynching is like lynching, nothing but genocide is like genocide. Some things should never be diminished to the status of metaphor.

Similarly, white women's problems in the nineteenth century should never be diminished to the status of white women's problems in the twenty-first. One can acknowledge an unbroken line of white supremacy through the feminist movement, as through all of American history, without pretending that white feminist concerns have remained static. Married women in the nineteenth century were legally the property of their husbands, who could beat and rape them without consequences. If they tried to leave, they would likely not be awarded custody of their children (who were also their husbands' property). They would have few job opportunities and zero social status if they managed to obtain a divorce, which was extremely difficult.

If you were white and married a kind man—as Elizabeth Cady Stanton did, by her own account—your suffering was reduced substantially. But you still might die giving birth to one of your many babies, and you still did not enjoy the rights, privileges, and immunities of the white men you married or the ones you raised from infancy. Meanwhile, if you married an abusive man, you were trapped in a home with no autonomy over your own body, constant fear of physical and mental anguish, an expectation of 24-7 unpaid labor, no legal recourse whatsoever, and no means of escape.

This was the context in which Susan B. Anthony developed her feminist principles: *Men, their rights and nothing more; women, their rights and nothing less.* To her, accepting the Fifteenth Amendment as written meant accepting, for the umpteenth time, that women's rights were not as important as men's—including, crucially, black women's rights.

The History of Woman Suffrage, a project initiated by Anthony, Stanton, and Matilda Joslyn Gage in 1876, is a six-volume, 5,700-page attempt to document the journey from the Seneca Falls Convention in 1848 to the ratification of the Nineteenth Amendment in 1920—fourteen years after Anthony's death. Working from their own memories, journals, letters, articles, and boxes of papers donated by their contemporaries, these women set down the arguments and agreements, setbacks and triumphs, that drove the movement they devoted their lives to. There were omissions, to be sure: notably any contribution from Lucy Stone, who declined to offer one when asked.

But reading the *History,* one is struck by the authors' apparent good-faith effort to create a comprehensive, painstakingly nuanced document. The fight over the Fifteenth Amendment is told in transcripts of heated convention discussions and letters representing multiple viewpoints, as well as a collective narrative mostly written by Stanton.

Consider this excerpt from that narrative's explanation for the NWSA's refusal to support the Fifteenth Amendment unless it guaranteed universal suffrage:

> *Having served the Government during the war in such varied capacities, and taken an active part in the discussion of its vital principles on so many reform platforms, women naturally felt that in reconstruction their rights as citizens should be protected and secured. They who had so diligently rolled up petitions for the emancipation and enfranchisement of the slaves now demanded the same liberties, not only for the white women of the nation, but for the newly made freed-women from Southern plantations, who had borne more grievous burdens and endured keener sufferings in the flesh and far more aggravating humiliations in spirit, than the man slave could ever know. And yet Abolitionists who had drawn their most eloquent appeals for emancipation from the hopeless degradation of woman in slavery, ignored alike the African and the Saxon in reconstruction, and refused to sign the petition for "woman suffrage."*

These are not women who were pissed off at black people getting rights before they did. These were women who were pissed off at *white men.* Specifically, progressive white men. Progressive white men who soapboxed about the plight of women under slavery but did nothing to help those women advocate for themselves once freed. Progressive white men who convinced progressive white women to put all talk of women's rights on hold during the war, who promised that later, they would fight tirelessly for their sisters', wives', and daughters' deserts as citizens, then kept moving back the date at which they'd get right on that. Progressive white men who did the political math and figured out that adding 2 million former slaves to the rolls likely meant adding 2 million voters loyal to the party of Lincoln, but enfranchising women would risk canceling out their own votes.

I know those progressive white men. I called them down every time I voiced my support of Hillary Clinton, first in 2008 and then in 2016. They were the ones who insisted that Bernie Sanders was a "more feminist" candidate than Clinton, who explained with exasperated condescension that they were eager to elect the first woman president, *just not her*. They were the progressive white men who swore they would vote for Elizabeth Warren—perceived to be an ideologically correct woman—right up until she voiced her support of Hillary Clinton. After that, Sanders-supporting protesters began demonstrating against her, and graffiti reading "#JudasWarren Sellout" appeared in the famously feminist town of Northampton, Massachusetts.[5] I know that to this sort of progressive white man, the right time for women is always some day in the future, and the right woman candidate is always the hypothetical one.

I can't stand those guys, and I have a full complement of voting and property rights. I can only imagine the fury that must have roiled in Anthony's guts every time one of them told her to wait her turn.

Susan B. Anthony and Elizabeth Cady Stanton were racist. So were Lucy Stone and the members of the AWSA. So were all the progressive white men of the time. So was Frederick Douglass, who cheated on the dark-skinned, illiterate wife who helped him escape slavery and bore his five children, with a white, European intellectual. So am I. So are you, if you're American. Systemic racism isn't something you can opt out of; it's only something you can consciously resist.

Noting the overt racism of people lionized for their contributions to American liberty is one form of resistance, and by no means do I wish to discourage that. I only want to encourage two other things alongside it: First, noting equally the sexism of both our forebears and our contemporaries, the patriarchal system from which none of us can fully opt out. And second, resisting oversimplification as strenuously as we resist hatred.

I didn't sob watching people put I VOTED stickers on Anthony's grave because I wish to hand-wave away a legacy of hatred in order to enjoy an intergenerational white-girl-power moment. I sobbed watching that because whatever else Susan B. Anthony fucked up, she tried *so* hard, for *so* long, to secure equal rights for women. And more than a hundred years after her death, so-called progressive white men are still telling women we need to step back and take direction, telling us we're lousy at movement leadership, telling us to vote with our brains instead of our vaginas. I sobbed because so-called progressive white men, whenever they decide to cede a tiny bit of power, always seem to make black men and white women fight each other to the death over that scrap of influence—from the Fifteenth Amendment battle to the 2008 Democratic primary. As long as they keep those two groups in competition with each other, trapping black women in between them and erasing all other people of color, they will never have to cede more than that tiny bit.

Being an intellectually honest American means finding a way to live with the knowledge that every generation through the present day has relied on unpaid and underpaid labor, the self-sacrificing *love* of women, to keep this country upright.

In her 2015 book, *Who Cooked Adam Smith's Dinner?*, Swedish journalist Katrine Marçal describes Western society's prevailing wisdom about economies: to wit, that their engine is always and only self-interest. The baker bakes, the brewer brews, because that's how they get people to pay them money, so they can buy the things they want. Conveniently elided from this butcher-baker narrative are the caregivers, the cooks, the cleaners. The mothers. The wives.

> *For the butcher, the baker, and the brewer to be able to go to work, at the time Adam Smith was writing, their wives, mothers, or sisters had to spend hour after hour, day after day minding the children, cleaning the house, cooking the food, washing the clothes, drying tears and squabbling with the neighbors. However you look at the market, it is always built on another economy. An economy that we rarely discuss.*

That hidden economy, which still exists today, is one of love. There is self-interest, certainly, in all of these women's endeavors; for their trouble, they get shelter and food. But you don't do any of that—the mind-numbing care of small children, the endless repetition of cooking and laundry, the indignity of having a mind as fine as any man's and no opportunity to exercise it—without love. Either love for the owners of the dirty underwear and the sticky little hands, or love for people whose survival depends on the pittance you make for doing it.

Almost three hundred years after Adam Smith was born, women still dominate the "caring professions"—teaching, nursing, social work—and are scarce in positions of financial or political power. Married women who work full-time still do substantially more cleaning, food preparation, and child-engagement tasks than their male partners. And when professional women's work becomes too time-consuming, the care of children and the household isn't shared more equally with male partners, but outsourced to other women, frequently poor women of color. It is men who are raised to participate in a strict economy of self-interest. Most women could never afford that.

In a long interview with *BuzzFeed*'s Ruby Cramer that ran ten months before the 2016 presidential election, Hillary Clinton—in her usual maddeningly nuanced, sound bite–unfriendly way—tried to explain what consistently drives her, regardless of political vicissitudes. Writes Cramer:

> *Her words are slow and deliberate and she takes the conversation to this discussion she's been trying to talk about, to bring up on the trail, as she is again ensnared in a campaign that's more difficult than expected, in an election dominated by the language of anger and fear.*
> *"I am talking about love and kindness," she says.*

I believed her.

A lot of us believed her.

Progressive white men, summoned time and again by the mere mention of her name, never did. Hillary Clinton was a cold fish, a war hawk, and a hateful liar. Their objection to her wasn't sexist—unlike progressive white men of yore, these men deplored sexism! They would never repeat the oppressive mistakes of the olden days.

They just *did not care for* that woman. Is all.

On the evening of November 8, while we waited for election results to roll in, I drove to Seneca Falls with my husband. I had promised to file a response for *The Guardian* within three hours of the networks calling it, and I was going bonkers trying to fill the time before then. I am a reasonable enough person to understand that Rochester, ninety miles northeast of my central New York home, is too far to drive on a weeknight to visit a stranger's grave in the dark. But I am not too reasonable to demand a forty-mile journey to honor the ancestors. Even if I couldn't make it to Anthony's grave, I was determined to put my I VOTED sticker somewhere more meaningful than a garbage can or the bottom of my purse.

As I stood outside the small, unassuming Wesleyan Chapel, where the Seneca Falls Convention took place, a strange woman came up and threw an arm around my shoulder. She was with two girlfriends, all of them around fifty. They'd been planning this night for months, driven by the same desire I had to pay homage to women who never lived to vote legally, who never could have imagined such a thing as a female president. A light rain blemished our white jackets and blurred our faces, but none of us could stop smiling. We radiated love.

"It's really happening, isn't it?" the woman with her arm around me said, and before I knew what I was doing I turned to give her a full-on hug. Or really, to take one—the hug I couldn't get from my mother or my grandmother or mother-in-law or Susan B. Anthony. The communion of saints I no longer believed in.

"It's really happening," I agreed.

When I got back home, I changed out of my pantsuit to gear up for watching the final election results. One by one, I dropped my feminist talismans back in the jewelry box.

Bye, Mom.

Bye, Grandma.

Bye, Kathy.

Bye, SHE USES BIG WORDS.

Bye, SHE BELIEVES IN SCIENCE.

Bye, SHE DOES HER HOMEWORK.

I put on yoga pants and my Hillary sweatshirt, and continued writing the essay I'd already started, about what it meant that we finally elected our first woman president. All I had to do was wait for the official announcement, so I could file my piece and go to bed.

A couple of hours later, I was sobbing harder and more hysterically—I use the term advisedly—than I had since my mother died.

We had not elected our first woman president. Hillary Rodham Clinton, I realized with fresh sobs, would never hold the position she worked so hard to achieve, the position she deserved infinitely more than her opponent. Worse (*sob, blubber, snot*), there was no obvious woman on deck to run next time. Sure, there were a few female contenders for 2020, but no one with even half of Clinton's experience, no one vetted even half as thoroughly. As with the passage of the Fifteenth Amendment, women might now wait generations before our shot would come around again.

I began writing a new essay for *The Guardian*. It began: "My country hates women, which is bad enough, and pretends it doesn't, which is worse."

In the car on the way back from Seneca Falls, before the unthinkable went *thunk*, I asked my husband if he had learned anything from this election about how our country treats women.

He thought for a moment, then said, "Anyone other than Hillary would have given up ages ago, rather than take that kind of abuse. That's why there's never been a woman."

He wasn't wrong. To date, there's never been an American woman who could fully transcend the relentless, crushing resistance that comes with wanting more for herself, or for her country. But there have been many who, out of deep respect for themselves and love for their fellow women, grew old and died trying. Susan B. Anthony was one of them. Hillary Clinton will be one of them. If I have to, I guess I will, too.

I'll do it for love.

---

1. With the notable and predictable exception of "Indians not taxed."

2. I say "claim" because Woodhull's run chiefly consisted of advertising in *Woodhull & Claflin's Weekly*, the paper she ran with her sister Tennessee, that she had received the nomination of the Equal Rights Party, with Frederick Douglass as her running mate. But it is not clear that the Equal Rights Party was much more than Tennessee and Victoria's closest friends, nor that Douglass ever accepted the nomination.

(See Myra MacPherson's excellent *The Scarlet Sisters: Sex, Suffrage, and Scandal in the Gilded Age* [New York: Twelve, 2014].) It is perhaps worth noting that Susan B. Anthony cast her illegal vote for Ulysses S. Grant, not Woodhull.

3. She did not kill Vince Foster.

4. Also in part because her memory has been co-opted by anti-choice women, who believe her writings indicate that she would be against abortion if she were alive today. My read is that she was mostly against men knocking up naive girls who were then forced to make painful choices in a society that rejected illegitimate children and their sullied mothers, a hundred years before the Pill. Tomayto, tomahto.

5. Dan Glaun, "Northampton Graffiti Calls Sen. Elizabeth Warren Sellout After Hillary Clinton Endorsement." Masslive.com, June 17, 2016. Accessed on June 6, 2017, at http://www.masslive.com/news/index.ssf/2016/06/northampton_graffiti _calls_sen.html.

SHE WILL

Cheryl Strayed

MY KIDS DIDN'T HAVE SCHOOL the day after Donald Trump won the presidential election and eventually, near noon, they came into my room to see what was wrong with me. Perhaps they'd come to me at their father's prompting. Perhaps they'd heard me weeping. They'd never seen me this way before. Inconsolable.

"Hillary didn't lose!" I insisted, as they sat on the bed around me, even as Hillary's voice drifted into the room—her concession speech, on the radio downstairs, my husband shouting up, "Honey, you should come listen to this!"

I would not listen. I would never listen. The sound of Hillary Clinton conceding to Donald Trump is what compelled me to rise at last, if only to shut my bedroom door.

"It can't be true," I said to my kids, back in my bed encampment. "It can't be. It *can't*!"

"I know," said my daughter with real sorrow in her voice.

"Is Trump going to ruin our lives?" asked my son, with real worry.

Hillary Clinton wasn't, to them, a distant and unknown figure. They'd met her six months before, when I'd been invited to introduce her at an event in San Francisco. We'd flown there from Portland for the occasion. My husband and kids and I got to hang out with Hillary in a room backstage before the event began. When my son asked Hillary what she thought of Donald Trump, she didn't answer. She turned the question around and instead asked him what he thought of Donald Trump.

"I think he's very disrespectful," he said.

"I agree with you about that," she replied.

His disrespect was the reason I'd repeatedly assured my children in the months leading up to the election that Donald Trump could not win. He slandered Muslims and immigrants and those of Mexican heritage. He referred to women as pigs and dogs. He repeatedly criticized the grieving parents of a young soldier who'd been killed in the line of duty. He mocked a disabled man in front of cameras and denied having done so. He failed to disavow the white supremacists who campaigned for him. He cheated those he'd employed out of money. He bragged about not paying his taxes. He laughed when his supporters threatened journalists with violence. He said he could grab women "by the pussy" if he felt like it because he was a "star." He did and said so many horrible things I couldn't any longer keep a list in my head.

He had no shame. He had no grace. He had no dignity. He had no moral code. Never mind whether you were conservative or liberal, Republican or Democrat, with the evidence mounting by the day, it seemed apparent to me—and many—that Trump was characterologically unfit for the office. Countless members of his own party, both prominent and not, abandoned him in droves. They announced they could not vote for a man who had so little respect—for others, for the bounds of decorum, for the rule of law, for the office of the presidency, for the fundamental principles of American democracy itself. Many of them didn't much care for Hillary or her political views, but they loathed Trump so deeply, they'd vote for her instead. Newspapers that had never in their history endorsed a Democratic candidate for president did. Among the few who endorsed Trump, one was *The Crusader,* the official newspaper of the Ku Klux Klan.

Week by week through the late summer and autumn, my certainty that he could not win deepened. I knew the American electorate was divided politically, but I also knew something else: for all our flaws, we were not a people who'd choose a man to be our president who was so plainly, so essentially, so completely, a disrespectful brute.

I was wrong.

The fact of my wrongness felt like a blunt-force blow. I wasn't naive. I'd long known there were misogynists and racists and people who voted against their own economic interests. I knew that some people voted out of their fear and rage and ignorance, but I didn't know how deep and wide it was in America until November 9, 2016. I believed we, as a people, were better than we turned out to be.

On that day after the election, after I finally pulled myself out of bed, I walked around in a state of numb shock. My numbness was interrupted only by two extremes of emotion: more jags of crying—*this can't be true!*—and an ever-heightening state of outrage—*she won by nearly three million votes!*

In this manic zombie/teary/rager dream state, I somehow managed to go to the grocery store, where I managed to figure out what to make for dinner and then, at home, made it. All through this managing, a memory kept floating into my mind of a conversation I'd had with my maternal grandfather when I was eleven or so and I'd asked him who he planned to vote for in a political race in his city of Huntsville, Alabama—for what office, I do not recall. We were in the car, him at the wheel, me in the front passenger seat. Moments before I asked my question, we'd driven past a campaign sign that caught my eye because emblazoned on it was the name of a woman, a fairly rare occurrence in 1979.

My grandfather replied he hadn't yet decided who he'd be voting for but he knew for certain it would not be the woman. When I asked why, he told me it was because women were not qualified to lead and therefore should not hold elected office. He did not say this unkindly. He didn't become defensive or angry when I vehemently disagreed with him. He only chuckled and explained I'd someday understand that there are certain things men are better at than women, and making important decisions was one of them.

I admired my grandfather and I loved him, too. He was a good man in that way men get to be thought of as good even though they do not believe in the basic human rights of women and girls. Around the time that he told me he would not be voting for the woman because she was a woman, he'd also observed over lunch one day what a shame it was that I was the one who'd "gotten the brains" among my siblings and my brother (according to him) had not. Why was it a shame? Because my alleged brains would only be "wasted" on me since I was a girl.

But of course it wasn't only my grandfather who thought this way. By the time I argued with him in the front seat of the car about the political race in his town, by the time I was told my intelligence was a useless asset, I was well aware that he was not alone in his opinion that women were inherently inferior to men. I knew that in arguing with him, I was arguing with the entire culture—one that had told me what I could not and should not and would not be because I was a girl.

I get asked a lot in interviews when I first became a feminist and why, and though my answer has remained the same since the election, the way I feel about it has changed. I've been a feminist since my earliest understanding that what it means to be female is to be limited by society in ways that males are not. And though I've never been under the illusion that sexism had vanished, before Trump was elected there was a history-lesson element to the stories I told of my first consciousness about what it meant to be female in America, a quality that had made the sexism I experienced as a girl seem antiquated and nearly extinct. The message was: *This is the way it used to be! Isn't that amazing?* In witnessing the presidential race and Trump's eventual win, I've concluded that I had it wrong. This isn't how it used to be. It is the way it is. It amazes me still.

Perhaps that's the reason I felt Hillary's loss on a physical level— like someone had actually delivered a blow to my body—and perhaps, too, it's the reason that long-ago conversation with my grandfather came circling repeatedly into my mind the day after the election. Hillary Clinton's victory would've in some measure healed the lifelong wounds that patriarchy has made on my heart. When people accused me of "voting with my vagina," I laughed. I was proud to do it. President Hillary Clinton would've been repudiation, finally, of all those people who'd said women were not fit to lead (or vote or be doctors or write great books or . . . well, you fill in the blank). Her defeat was personal to me. This election wasn't simply a political contest. It was a referendum on how much America still hates women.

I never have listened to her concession speech and I probably never will. I didn't watch because I've already seen it: the woman who works fifty times harder than the man who got the job. It isn't a story I don't know. I've heard she was strong and dignified and inspiring. I've heard she rose to the humiliating occasion with astounding grace. None of that surprises me. Hillary Clinton grew up in the world I grew up in, only in one that was even harder for girls and women because she's a generation older. She—like so many whose very humanity has been questioned because of race or sexuality or gender identity or physical ability—has had to make her way forward steeped in a culture that usually told her no. One that said: *We will punish you if you try and we will applaud when you fail.* And did.

In San Francisco, when I was introducing Hillary before a thousand or so people six months before the election, the line that got the biggest applause was this: "Hillary Clinton made the world ready for

Hillary Clinton." It was the line she thanked me for specifically when she walked onstage and we embraced while the audience went wild. "No one has ever said that about me," she said into my ear. "Thank you."

What I meant when I said that Hillary Clinton had made the world ready for Hillary Clinton is that I recognized her as a woman who had whacked the weeds to blaze her own trail, who had always stood up again after she was told to sit down, who had persisted, and persisted, and persisted, nevertheless. What I meant is that a woman like this was finally going to win.

Someday she will.

AS LONG AS IT'S HEALTHY

Sarah Michael Hollenbeck

WHEN I WAS TWENTY-FIVE, I was surrounded by women wanting babies. A thirty-seven-year-old friend of mine told me she laid awake at
night calculating the viability of her eggs. Nearly every thirtysome-
thing woman I knew had a number in her head—a number she'd had
since childhood—of how many kids she wanted and when—*two,
three, four for me!* I couldn't help thinking, Shouldn't you wait and
see how the first one goes? Even the first time I scheduled a bikini
wax I only scheduled one. I wanted to monitor the repercussions before I made any long-term commitments, and I'd like to think that
living children are more high-stakes than ingrown pubic hairs.

I thought these women were ridiculous and irrational. When I
checked the ticking of my own biological clock, I was smug—pleased
to hear silence.

When I was twenty-eight, a friend of mine gave birth to a baby
boy who weighed just one pound, five ounces. The day after I heard
the news, I found myself fixated on the weight of everything I lifted—a
cup of ice water, a jug of laundry detergent, a mango.

Two weeks later, while taking a walk with my mom, she asked

about my friend's tiny baby. I told her that they had been able to remove his breathing tubes and that the nurses had taken to calling him "Little Man."

Mom grew quiet. I could tell she was remembering the birth of my older sister Annie, who spent her first months of life in the NICU, only able to be touched through two openings in her Isolette. Annie was diagnosed with Moebius syndrome, a birth defect wherein certain cranial nerves are underdeveloped, resulting in partial paralysis of the facial muscles. Five years after Annie was born, I was born. And although Moebius has no clear pattern of inheritance, my face and Annie's were nearly identical.

The medical definition of my face is "mask-like." I have two flat plains where cheekbones should be. My eyes naturally drift to half-mast, but do not completely close. My mouth doesn't close either. My lips hang loose like fabric on an uncinched drawstring, framing my permanently exposed teeth. The roof of my mouth has the high arch of a cathedral ceiling, swallowing the sharp edges of my words. And while I feel as if I'm smiling all the time, it's a bit of a gamble whether anyone beyond my friends and family can feel it, too.

After we'd walked in silence for a moment, I said to Mom, "It seems weird that the right thing for an expectant mother to say when she's asked if she wants a boy or a girl is 'as long as it's healthy.'"

I cringed at how ridiculous my words seemed spoken aloud. But Mom nodded. She knew exactly what I meant. She had had two "unhealthy" babies; I had been the second of the two. For both of us, the conditional phrase "as long as" sounded like a threat.

When I was twenty-eight, I said "I love you" for the first time to the man I would marry when I was thirty-one. From the moment I met Andy, I knew he would be a good dad. I once watched my nieces and nephew play a game that consisted entirely of seeing how many pick-up sticks they could securely stick in Andy's thick, dark beard. His laughter throughout this game awakened something in me that said, "Maybe."

It was not that being with him kick-started my biological clock as people once told me it would. I still believed that no one would have babies if they thought about it too much, but with Andy, baby-making was something I felt I could dare to do for love. I shared this news with some of my friends and family, but I didn't tell them all of it.

I didn't tell anyone how I got a powerful thrill when I imagined walking around with a big round, pregnant belly bobbing below my disabled face; how I daydreamed of staring defiantly back at those who would inevitably stare at me. I secretly wanted to use my body to shred the notion that only able, normative bodies are allowed to be pregnant. But when I tried imagining my baby born, my fantasy hiccupped. I couldn't imagine her face.

When I was six, a friend and I were sitting side by side in a sandbox on the edge of a neighborhood playground. This particular playground was new to me. Without a tree in sight, the sand was hot to the touch. But the heat was not the reason I felt uncomfortable.

Because I can't close my mouth, I generate more saliva than the average noninfant human. Over the years, I've learned to control my drooling, but at age five a dark circle dampened the chests of all of my T-shirts. That day on the playground, though, is the first time I remember being ashamed of it. In the sandbox, there was a boy I didn't know sitting across from my friend and me. He asked a question and when I started to respond, he said to my friend, "I wasn't asking the retard." I didn't know who he was referring to until I saw my friend's eyes nervously dart in my direction.

I knew that word from the gesture that the older boys at school would use when they would tease others. They would bend their arms at the elbow and bring their hands, limp at the wrists, up toward their faces. Smacking their floppy hands against their chests, they'd shriek, "Retard!" with their mouths open and slack and their eyes rolling.

That same year, there was a boy who would stand beside me in the carpool line, bring his face close to mine, and breathe heavily through his mouth. At first, I thought he liked me. Then I thought he was maybe impersonating Darth Vader. Finally, I realized he was teaching me what it sounds like when I breathe.

As an adult, I'm still occasionally told to shut my mouth, to get more sleep, to stop yawning, or to smile, because either Jesus loves me or "it doesn't cost a thing."

My experience of being a disabled woman is discovering in small, sharp explosions what I look like through the feedback of strangers. Whenever I leave the safety of my home, I am alert—anxious yet curious—for what new ways able-bodied strangers will reflect my body back at me. It took me many years to learn that these exchanges are as much about them and their power as they are about me and the loss of mine.

When I was growing up, our family never talked about Annie's face or my own, and in the few times that I broached the topic with friends, I was told "No one notices" or "It doesn't matter."

In my experience of disability, the people closest to me have always expressed their love by telling me that they, almost magically, cannot see it—that this thing that has both directly and indirectly shaped so much of my life doesn't matter. Instead, it has been the callous strangers and the bullies who have been the ones to say, *I notice. It matters.*

When I was thirty, Andy and I were sitting side by side drinking our morning coffee when he said, "I really want a baby."

And I said, "Me, too."

The speed with which I agreed felt reckless and true.

Andy's eyes crinkled, as he squeezed my hand and said, "That makes me so happy to hear you say that. You're going to be such a good mom."

I kept thinking about what would make me "good" and how that "good" would change if the baby were to look like me.

When I was thirty-two, Andy and I talked more and more often about our future child. It started with little stuff: names, neighborhoods, and the feasibility of using cloth diapers without an in-unit washer/dryer. But eventually, we faced the big stuff: our low-paying jobs, our health insurance, and my body of unknowns. Andy said he just wanted a baby; whether we adopted or had one naturally, that was up to me.

As I tried to make this decision, the phrase "as long as it's healthy" pulsed in my head. If I chose to have a baby biologically, and my baby were to look up at me and see her face reflected, she would know that I knew how hard this would be and that I did it anyway.

When I was in middle school, I'd stare in the mirror and pull the corners of my mouth up into the neighborhood of a smile. I'd pinch my lips together and count to ten because sometimes—sometimes—this maneuver (with just the right amount of spit and Chapstick) would seal my mouth closed for one ecstatic moment. I've spent so much of my life measuring my quality of life not by my acceptance of my disability, but the erasure of it.

So, when my husband, an able-bodied man, gazed directly at my disabled face and said he wanted to have a baby with me, it felt like the final test, and that I'd passed. I knew that secretly I wanted my baby to be normal in order to prove that I was, too. And I knew that wasn't fair to her.

In the summer of 2016, I told Andy that I thought we should adopt. That same summer the country was skidding toward its decision of who would be the next president.

I had never heard a major political candidate use the phrase "people with disabilities" as often as Hillary Clinton. Some of her ads were exclusively dedicated to the issue of disability. She recognized us as a voting bloc. But some advocates flinched at her campaign speech's stiff, sentimental stories of people with disabilities. And some claimed that she was only courting us because of what The Bully had done.

If you Google The Bully's name plus the word "disability," your search will instantly populate with think pieces about the now infamous video of The Bully impersonating Serge Kovaleski. Kovaleski is a *New York Times* reporter with a congenital joint condition. When I saw the video, The Bully's gestures were stingingly familiar—elbows bent, forearms raised, wrists limp, hands flailing, eyes rolling, mouth stuck open.

In the summer before the election, a Bloomberg poll reported: "[m]ore than six in 10 say they are bothered a lot that Trump mocked a reporter's physical disability."[1]

Bothered—like a hangnail or an itch. And almost four out of ten could not even commit to "bothered."

When I was thirty-one, I became the co-owner of a nationally recognized bookstore, launching me into the public arena. Since then, my face, with all of its peculiarities, has been featured in newspaper articles and on the local news. My voice with its pronounced speech impediment has been recorded on podcasts and introduced authors onstage in front of more than a thousand audience members. Feeling safe in this role requires telling myself firmly and frequently, *You belong here.*

I knew that the video of The Bully mocking Kovaleski was a year old. I knew it was a distraction from much bigger issues facing the disability community. I knew that this was a lost opportunity, that finally disability was at the center of a national conversation, but we weren't discussing substantive issues like equal pay, accessibility of public space, and health care. But I couldn't stop watching that video. Kovaleski is a Pulitzer Prize–winning reporter who has worked at some of the most prestigious newspapers in the world. I felt humiliated with every viewing, shoved back to that hot sandbox, the word "retard!" freshly launched in my direction. The laughter and cheers of The Bully's audience, letting me know this: *Your worst fears of how we see you is precisely how you are seen. How you will always be seen.*

As the election season marched on, I listened to interviews with voters who loved The Bully's candor—voters who said, "He's not afraid to say what we're all thinking."

When Annie was a toddler, Mom and Dad took her to a speech pathologist who asked Mom, "What do you want?" Mom, having at that point been to dozens of appointments with dozens of specialists, cried, "I want the world to be nicer. Annie's perfect. She's perfect. *She's perfect.* It's the world that needs to change."

On November 9, 2016, I woke up with my eyes and throat raw, having sobbed myself to sleep.

Activists and artists, many of them people of color, reminded me on Facebook that plenty of past presidents didn't give a damn about the voices of the marginalized—that this wasn't anything new in the history of this country. But it felt new to me. My own privilege and complacency led me to overestimate how much my fellow citizens care about people whose lives differ from their own. Waking up to the election results was like looking down to find thousands of cracks in a floor that, seconds ago, I'd thought solid and smooth. Every day since election day, I wake up an angrier, more radical activist, forced to see the floor for what it was this whole time.

In her campaign speeches, the woman who I assumed would be our current president often quoted the proverb "It takes a village to raise a child." I'd cringe whenever she'd said this. I found the phrase sappy. But the other day I came across that proverb and was startled to feel warm tears prickle the back of my throat. I didn't know I needed that village until—with each state painted red on November 8 and each able-bodied, straight, cisgender white person calling for "unity" on November 9—I felt the loss of it.

I never expected anything from The Bully. But I expected more from us. My faith in the possibility of us as a collective, a village, was shaken by the 53 percent of white women who voted for The Bully, by the people who hugged me at my wedding who voted for him, by those who were not, as it turns out, really that "bothered" after all.

When I was two and Annie was seven, Annie would go to school and I would spend the whole day waiting for her to come back. I'd dress up in her clothes, layer after layer, until I could barely bend my small arms. At the end of the day when, finally, Annie walked through the front door, I'd run to her shrieking with delight. I'd look up at her face—a face so much like my own—and grab her hand and refuse to let go.

Even after Andy and I began the first steps in the adoption process, I'd sometimes rest a hand on the flatness of my stomach and feel longing. Part of me still wondered about a baby who looked like me. Part of me believed that I could have convinced her *and* me that, yes, it would be hard, but it would also be worth it.

But not anymore.

With every fearmongering executive order issued by The Bully and every human being who applauds or fails to condemn these actions, my longing for a biological baby dims. In its place grows a fury of mama bear proportions.

I am now thirty-three years old—in the age range of all of the baby-crazy women I judged so harshly when I was twenty-five—and babies keep me up at night. I'm furious watching The Bully and his family, and how they move in the world with the effortlessness of those who have never once had to question their place in it. I am furious when I think about all of the black, brown, refugee, and queer babies, and the "unhealthy" ones like me, like Annie, being born into a world that feels unequivocally less nice now than it was more than thirty years ago when my mother shouted at a stunned speech pathologist.

For the last several months, the only thing that has felt good to me is hate. This confirms that The Bully is very good at doing what bullies do—cowardly standing on the sidelines, making sure that we know that there are sides and which one we are on.

For me, what is new about this era is a top-down unkindness. It is the bracing reality that there is no one but us taking care of us. Instead of making a new human, I feel a responsibility to be a better caretaker for the humans who are already here. Those of us who can must stand up for the most vulnerable among us: the black, the brown, the refugee, the queer and trans, the people with disabilities, and so many others whose lives are increasingly at risk. But I'm also beginning to swivel my head toward the object of my hate, the other side, and to see the vulnerability of those who stacked their hopes on the craven shoulders of a man who cares about them like a snake cares about a frozen mouse. We, the vulnerable, we're everywhere. We're the village.

---

1. John McCormick, "Clinton Up 6 on Trump in Two-Way Race in Bloomberg National Poll," *Bloomberg*, August 10, 2016.

WE HAVE A HEROINE PROBLEM

Carina Chocano

THE FIRST TIME IT HAPPENED, I thought it was a joke.

I don't remember what I'd posted, exactly. Some inspiring story about some half-forgotten historical accomplishment. How Hillary Clinton helped desegregate Arkansas schools, or helped make public schools accessible to disabled children, or fought for women's rights around the world. I'd started to make it my mission to post positive stories about Hillary Clinton, because her media coverage was so consistently narrow and negative. I was preaching to the choir, but I didn't entirely realize it until the first time someone attacked her on my page.

I don't remember what he wrote, just how bad it made me feel. Whatever it was, it was swift and ferocious, a toxic blend of brute-force rancor and contempt. The guy who wrote it was not a guy I had expected to hold these views, let alone talk to me, or about Clinton, in this way. So, of course, I disregarded my feelings. He was a Democrat, after all. A creative professional about a decade my senior who I'd worked for a few times in San Francisco. I barely knew him, but it didn't cross my mind to think he might be an asshole, so I took responsibility for his assholeness. I was instantly awash in guilt and shame. Perhaps I'd misunderstood him. Maybe he was ironically impersonating an asshole for comic effect. Maybe he was impervious to the DEFCON 11–level of vitriol he was leveling at me. Maybe he'd unleashed all that verbal and emotional violence by accident and would feel just terrible if he knew how traumatic the interaction had been for me. So I gave him the benefit of the doubt. I responded to his comments with civility and humor. The first time I typed "Quit trolling me!" I thought it was funny, because *no way was this guy actually trolling me.* But it wasn't funny, and he didn't stop. Every time I posted a positive Hillary story, he clogged the comments with vitriol, conspiracy theories, and derogatory memes. I deleted them and asked him not to post anymore; he did it again. His rage was out of control and relentless. It turned him into another person, or revealed a person I hadn't known was there. He didn't care what I thought or felt. He was there to play an epic game of whack-a-mole against every pro-Clinton statement on earth, and anyone who came between his target and his mallet could fuck right off.

I've said the experience was disorienting, but it was also familiar, though it was only in retrospect that I recognized it as a trauma response. He ignored my boundaries, and I absorbed his annihilating rage. Like a soon-to-be-hospitalized tourist on a London street, I'd been so focused on the right that I'd missed the oncoming truck from the left, which had taken Hillary Clinton, attacked as a radical feminist by the right for decades, and made her into a symbol of conservative, white-feminist, "neoliberalism." Eventually, I blocked him, as I later blocked the former friend who posted pictures of vampire Hillary eating kittens on my wall, who crowed about how he wasn't sexist because he was voting for Jill Stein, and the reasonable-sounding Bernie supporter, who kept his comments polite and bemused in public and saved the really ugly stuff for private messages. He was from

Brooklyn and made environmental videos. He started off by saying it was obvious that I identified with Hillary for some reason, but that I shouldn't let it cloud my judgment. Then he said it was obvious that I hated men. Then he said he guessed I was divorced, and when I said I wasn't, he guessed that my husband wished he was. He messaged me early the following morning to ask if I'd had a chance to reflect on my mistakes. I blocked him after that. Watching men I'd liked, admired, and instinctively trusted reveal themselves as secret misogynists felt like stepping into a horror movie. They were in denial, of course. But it was the hatred that gave them away.

Hillary Clinton has always had her share of detractors, but her image took a hit when Bernie Sanders started to run not as her genial colleague but as the socialist savior to her friend of Wall Street. He used her connection and her experience against her, just as lack of experience and lack of connections would have been used against her had she not had them. Bernie was never above doing both, calling her, at his most desperate and grasping, unqualified for a job he himself was far less qualified for. Though he pretended otherwise, Sanders—as a white man—had the home-court advantage and could consequently avail himself of all the tricks, even when they contradicted each other. When he started running a fulminating, fire-and-brimstone campaign in which he railed against the moneylenders, all but knocking over podiums during debates, a familiar dualism came into view. It was a story we could wrap our heads around. It became a story of good versus evil, of light versus darkness, of lovable old men versus witchy old women. The stories the Bernie Bros told about Hillary Clinton were horror stories—dark fairy tales about a monstrous woman who would not be contained or repressed. They hinged on Gothic themes—hidden pasts, long-buried secrets, ancestral curses, generational decay, gender instability. To hear the Bernie Bros tell it, she was not a Democrat but a grotesque revenant, an aristocratic vampire thirsty for the blood of virgins. She was corrupt, venal, duplicitous, a succubus Lady Macbeth. Over time, in the echo chamber of the Internet, these stories became, if not true, then somehow *realer* than true: not just more familiar and recognizable than the truth but more authentically raw. Their outrageousness wasn't the problem—Hillary's authority was the problem. Her authorship was the problem. Her speech was the problem. The fact that she spoke at all. What did people focus on? Emails, speeches, Benghazi. Emails, speeches, Benghazi. Emails, speeches, Benghazi. What did she say? How did she lie? *Who did she kill?* The Bernie cultists did not simply prefer their candidate. They didn't just disagree with Clinton on policy—which, after all, along with her voting record, was not all that different from Sanders's. (Other than in that she had actual plans.) They didn't just want Bernie to win; they wanted Clinton to lose to Bernie. And if she wouldn't lose to Bernie, or let him win, they wanted her to lose everything. They wanted to prove that *she deserved to lose.*

Why did this take me by surprise? Was it because I hadn't worked in a corporate office for six years? Although I do share a workspace with other writers, roughly 80 percent of them are women with kids. So was it because I no longer really inhabit male spaces on a daily basis? Because I've aged out of being harassed on the street? I suppose it's possible this allowed me to forget, during the first part of the race, that I still live in a man's world, but I don't think that's it, entirely. I think it was denial. It was a couple of decades of postfeminism telling us we'd come far enough. It allowed me to forget that there's no more despised figure on earth than a woman who seeks power. In the United States, it's fine for a woman to claim equality, as long as she cheerfully opts out of it.

In *A Room of One's Own,* Virginia Woolf wrote about astonishing extremes a woman is made to represent in the stories written by men. "One would never imagine her a person," she wrote. And in fact, very often, one doesn't. One is conditioned by visual and symbolic culture to think of her as the sexy embodiment of noble ideals. Real women, with their flaws, only get in the way of that. The Hillary Clinton that emerged in the early 1990s was young, but as a married woman with a child, she had already aged out of the damsel bracket and into the wifely, motherly role that requires, as with the *Odyssey*'s Penelope, great displays of patience, self-abnegation, passivity, and silence—none of them her strong suits. Bill was a hero in the classic mold, but Hillary was not young, demure, or bashful enough to be mistaken for a heroine. What was she? She might appear in *The New York Times* one day, photographed in pants, on the Hill, and then again a few days later, wearing a dress and talking about place settings. She was mocked for wearing a headband, then for ditching the headband and trying new hairstyles, then for each subsequent hairstyle—for so much as thinking that she could counter the structural hatred she was confronting with a different coiffure. She was pilloried for dismissing Tammy Wynette's "Stand by Your Man" lyrics, but then briefly loved for being cheated on and standing by her man anyway, then hated again for the same. This was much later, after she'd aged into wealth, power, experience, and influence—which could only make her the wicked witch, the evil stepmother, the malevolent fairy.

In an old documentary I found on YouTube, people on the street talked about their extreme feelings for her, feelings that were hard (the more negative they were) to express. A *Washington Post* reporter remarked on how poorly defined and amorphous the role of First Lady is, and how Hillary's stepping into it had only brought its strangeness to the fore. Hillary becoming the First Lady had shed an uncomfortably bright light on the distinction our culture makes between the archetypal "independent woman" and the archetypal "wife." Hillary made people crazy because she scrambled their schemas. She was a mash-up of two symbolic opposites. She was an "independent wife."

A heroic thing to me, but not to everyone, it turns out.

Throughout the election, I was working on a book about the stories culture tells us about women. I was focusing on the dominant narrative, the story that shapes most Hollywood storytelling, commercial fiction, advertising, and other tales rooted in patriarchal capitalism, which obscures commodification and exploitation into what get called "traditional" gender roles. We're familiar with the story of the hero who has a girl—or an ideal represented by a woman—to fight for and rescue. If the hero were a girl, then who would stand for the values that need defending and avenging? If a woman became president, who would we cast as the defender of hearth, nation, republic, and home? *Who would decorate the White House, or be decorative in the White House?* ("Maybe I'll get a decorating show," Clinton joked on the *Today* show when asked her plans after stepping down from office as secretary of state.) *Who would stand for the republic, reason, liberty, and justice with her tits out?* We're less familiar with the story of the righteously angry woman, the woman who wants to avenge wrongs, or aspires to power, or knows or says too much. We don't know how to tell the story of a woman like Clinton—experienced, powerful, authoritative. Competent, entitled, outspoken women have always threatened the patriarchal structure because their very existence subverts it. To cast her in the hero role is to smash the world. So we recognize her as the villain. Perhaps Pat Robertson was thinking of Hillary Clinton when he wrote, in a 1992 Iowa fund-raising letter opposing a state equal-rights amendment, that feminism "encourages women to leave their husbands, kill their children, practice witchcraft, destroy capitalism, and become lesbians."[1] Perhaps Bernie and his Band of Bros had cast her in the inverse and opposite, but just as cartoonishly deviant, role.

Not long after the second presidential debate, the sociolinguist and gender theorist Robin Lakoff posted a blog post on her website titled "On Language, Gender, and Politics" that began with this riddle:

What does a woman running for president have to do to be likable?

Not run for president.

The joke was funny because it was true and also because it wasn't funny—although it had yet to acquire the tragic overtones it would later be burdened with. Hillary Clinton, the most qualified candidate ever to run, lost the presidency to an unhinged, unqualified thug. And yet, almost immediately, the stories about how Clinton went wrong appeared, and continue appearing to this day. How she failed to read the room, how she failed to inspire, how she represented the wrong interests. My private message troll changed his profile picture to a Hillary campaign logo emblazoned with the slogan SHE DID THIS.

Which you really have to want to believe to believe.

But this election was always about faith: It was about disbelieving what was right in front of you in order to believe in what was presumably hidden. It was, as they say, a religious experience—only, for most of us, in the worst possible way. A Sanders supporter wrote on *Medium* "An Open Letter to #BernieOrBust Voters from a Die-Hard Bernie Supporter" urging them to support Clinton if she got the nomination despite everything they'd done: "You've caucused, made phone calls, marched in demonstrations, and spent long hours into the night coming up with the dankest meme-to-end-all-memes to post in the stash," he wrote.[2] "You've *faithfully defended His infallible name* [italics mine] to your racist, Trump-supporting uncle and even that filthy Hillary supporter at work. ('Come on, how could she still support Hillary after all you've told her about Bernie?!')" Not everybody took to capitalizing the pronoun, but the conflation of the word of a white-haired old man (an old Jewish man, even, bonus!) with reality is not a concept that is new to us in the Judeo-Christian West. Bernie's word was gospel. And if Bernie was God (in the context of a relentlessly binary, mercilessly zero-sum system of beliefs endlessly replicated across media platforms in which even toys are categorically gendered and must be kept on separate shelves at Target), then Hillary can only be Satan. We had a problem, but it was never a candidate problem, or a personality problem, or an inspiration problem. It was a narrative problem.

We have a serious heroine problem. It's ingrained in the culture at every level—symbolic, narrative, visual. It goes all the way back to the start, to the emergence of the hero cult in ancient Greece. A hero was a warrior in the Trojan War. Later, a hero was a dead warrior to be venerated. He ranked, in the Homeric pecking order, above men but beneath gods. He had magical powers, but not necessarily superpowers. Most heroes were male, though some women were considered heroic as well. Penelope, for instance, whose heroism involved warding off suitors while being modest, chaste, and wise. The kind of avenging anger that forged a mortal into a hero was not encouraged in women, lest they act out, like Clytemnestra. Nobody cheers for the avenging lady, unless she is fighting the bitch-monster who threatens her babies.

Greek hero worship differed from previous ancestor worship in that the hero was a political figure, a man of the polis, the city-state, which eventually co-opted heroes and institutionalized them. This pattern was adopted by French revolutionaries, for whom the political hero—the hero of the polis—served as a useful symbol under which to consolidate power, dictate ideology, and preserve hegemony. He's a flexible figure, too. Gumby-like, he can be molded to stand for just about anything, which is why in 2016 we had populist heroes in the shapes of Bernie Sanders and Donald Trump, both of whom managed to position themselves as anti-establishment rebels against Hillary Clinton, whom they positioned, as if by sexist magic, as the establishment candidate. This is not the first time this has happened. In pre-revolutionary France, the Greek hero Hercules represented the power and authority of the monarchy until the monarchy was toppled by the French Revolution—and he was dusted off as a symbol of revolutionary ideals. Napoleon was a hero of the revolution until he became the emperor. The "father" of the state was replaced, then, with the fraternity, *avec fraternité*—with egalitarian "band of brothers," or bros. In this neoclassical ethos, masculinity was assigned all active protagonism. Revolutions go around and come around. Images of women were everywhere, though, as female allegories of liberty, justice, the republic itself. Women were ideal, and ideals were female. With her noble brow and her bared breast, and her raised standard, she made patriotism sexy and political engagement hot, and played a pivotal role in transitioning France from the old regime to modern society.

The classical and neoclassical hero gave way to the Romantic rebel-artist-hero of the nineteenth century, embodied by the Italian nationalist and South American freedom fighter Giuseppe Garibaldi—poet, artist, rebel, mass media superstar. Garibaldi was born in Nice, participated in an insurrection in Piedmont, and ended up in exile in Latin America, where he became a fixture in a succession of wars of independence. In Brazil and Uruguay, he picked up the habit of dressing like a gaucho, donning a red shirt, poncho, and sombrero—very radical chic. His fame was aided by the emergence of the cult of celebrity fueled by newspapers and photography, and a concurrent interest in biography. A new kind of charismatic popular figure in popular politics, Garibaldi became emblematic across Europe, North America, and South America as a man of the people and a champion of democracy and liberal ideals. He was the model of the "poet-revolutionary," the anti-authoritarian bohemian, the anarchist bomb-thrower, and the charismatic nationalist/populist guerrilla leader turned dictator/t-shirt icon of the twentieth and twenty-first centuries, along with Pancho Villa, Ché Guevara, and Bernie Sanders.

There were women like them along the way, too, but you're less likely to have heard of them, or to have purchased their silk-screened image. Here's an excerpt from a review of a book about the myth of the revolutionary hero and its uses that rings some bells:

> *O'Malley uses concepts of myth derived from Roland Barthe's My-*
> *thologies (1972) to analyze the institutionalization of the Mexi-*
> *can Revolution of 1910. Basic to this idea is the assumption that*
> *mystification produces myth, which is not a fable, but instead a*
> *confusion of the way one thinks about facts. O'Malley contends*
> *that the revolution was guided through this mystification by the*
> *government in order to perpetuate the bourgeois character of the*
> *regime. He explains the emergence of the myth through an analy-*
> *sis of hero cults for Francisco Madero, Venustiano Carranza,*
> *Emiliano Zapata, and Pancho Villa. Propaganda surrounding*
> *these four heroes had several common traits: the claim that the*
> *government was revolutionary; the promotion of nationalism; the*
> *obfuscation of history; the denigration of politics; Christian im-*
> *agery and the promotion of Catholic values; and patriarchal val-*
> *ues.' All of these traits were used, according to O'Malley, to co-*
> *opt opposition to the middle class revolution.[3]*

According to this logic—logic of the system that is already established—Hillary Clinton, who had to fight centuries-old, incredibly fortified barriers to be allowed into the establishment, got labeled "establishment" by a man who was established since before it was possible to imagine that a woman might someday be president, or come close enough to have the presidency stolen from her with the enthusiastic aid of revolutionaries; a woman who, had she been a man, would have had the presidency at hello.

My run-ins with Bernie Bros were more painful and frustrating than any encounter with a Trump voter ever was, because they felt like the rug being pulled out from under, like sabotage. Revolutions—it's right there in the word—tend toward circularity. As often as not, they are followed by counterrevolutions, reigns of terror, Thermidorian Reactions; or they cycle straight into totalitarian dictatorships, regimes indistinguishable from the ones they toppled. One of the biggest "tells" of women's unique gender-based inequality is that our revolutions never result in women taking power. A powerful woman will always be attacked on one side for being powerful and on the other for being a woman. The psychologists Carol Tavris and Carole Wade wrote about what they called pedestal–gutter syndrome, which defines ambivalent sexism as a conflict between polarized attitudes about women—as in, you're perfect, "flawless," or else a worthless monster. When, during the 2016 election, people said that Hillary Clinton was a flawed candidate, what they were really saying was that Hillary Clinton was a woman, rather than an idea about women. She was too multifaceted, too experienced, too old. Clinton haters assiduously disavowed sexism, of course, tirelessly pointing to their courtly adoration of Elizabeth Warren (my troll liked to say he'd "lay down in front of a train for that woman," which was so very white knight of him, and so very condescending to that woman, who is an oncoming train), or their bizarre tolerance for that walking human cognitive impairment, Jill Stein, as proof of their feminism. But Warren wasn't running, and Stein had about as much of a shot at winning the presidency as a tree stump, whereas Clinton was both uniquely qualified for the job and projected to win. What made her a "flawed candidate" was that she wasn't some hypothetical platonic ideal. She was an unclipped toenail away from turning potentiality into actuality. We didn't do it. Again. Instead, we continue to cycle from feminist insurgence to balkanization to "post-feminism" to backlash, always with a little help from our friends. The problem with Hillary was never that she wasn't a good enough candidate. The problem was always the story. And until we change the story, the revolution will not be feminized.

1. "Robertson Letter Attacks Feminists," *The New York Times*, August 25, 1992. Accessed June 11, 2017, http://www.nytimes.com/1992/08/26/us/robertson-letter -attacks-feminists.html.

2. Jordan Stephens, "An Open Letter to #BernieOrBust Voters from a Die-Hard Bernie Supporter," *Medium,* February 25, 2016. Accessed June 11, 2017, https:// medium.com/@jsteph17/an-open-letter-to-bernieorbust-voters-from-a-die-hard -bernie-supporter-7491b3d67b8a.

3. Ilene O'Malley, *The Myth of Revolution: Hero Cults and the Institutionalization of the Mexican State, 1920–1940* (New York: Greenwood Press, 1986).

ADVICE TO GRACE IN GHANA
Trump, the Global Gag Rule, and the Terror of Misinformation

Jill Filipovic

THE DAY AFTER President Donald Trump signed an executive order barring refugees from entering the United States, I'm crammed in the backseat of an early-2000s Toyota Camry, careening down a long dirt road in rural Ghana, a few kilometers outside of a town called Mando. Sandwiched on my left is Nicki, the photographer I'm traveling with to cover a story for *Foreign Policy* magazine on the devastating impact of Trump's foreign aid policies on women in this part of the world; to my right (and nearly on my lap) is Grace, an eighteen-year-old girl with a round face and close-cropped hair who lives outside of this town, and who is in turn squeezed in next to her older sister and mother. Grace wants to be a journalist, too. "I *love* being Ghanaian," she says, but she also wants to travel and report abroad—she's just not sure she'll be able to and doesn't really know how to start. So for now, she finds escape in the local library, where she reads anything she can get her hands on. "I read one book about America," she says. "Abraham Lincoln: the father of democracy."

When Grace asks Nicki and me for career advice, we tell her: Keep doing what you're doing. Work hard in school. Ask a lot of questions. Read your local paper, and if you find an article you like, see if you can get in touch with the person who wrote it and ask for their advice. Work at a newspaper when you finish school—start at the lowest job and learn.

What we don't say: Be careful. You don't know it yet, but the world just became a harder place for you.

In Ghana, about one in seven girls Grace's age—adolescents fifteen to nineteen—has already given birth at least once.[1] According to one region-specific study, about a third of adolescent girls have also had abortions.[2] According to another study that evaluated autopsy data from a large teaching hospital in Accra, Ghana's capital, complications from abortion were the primary cause of mortality for pregnant adolescent girls.

Abortion remains illegal or inaccessible for most women across sub-Saharan Africa, but that doesn't translate into fewer abortions. Instead, women simply try their own hand at abortion, or go to a traditional healer, or secure some abortion-inducing medication from a friend. As a result, this region has the highest death rate from unsafe abortion in the world, and the procedure remains a major cause of death and injury to women and girls.

One of the first things Donald Trump did in office was reinstate and then expand the global gag rule, an executive memorandum that pulls U.S. funding from any foreign organization abroad that provides abortions with non-U.S. money, refers women for safe abortion services, advocates for abortion rights, or even tells women their legal options. Previous iterations of the gag rule under Republican presidents have limited it to USAID (U.S. Agency for International Development) family-planning funding; Trump's version expands it to include all foreign-aid funding, even money allocated for HIV/AIDS, malaria treatment, Ebola, and childhood vaccinations. Organizations abroad are slated to lose millions of dollars, none of which

are going to abortion but toward modern contraception, HIV treatment, vaccines, and other basic health care. Contraception will be hit
especially hard. And without contraception, women get pregnant
when they don't want to be. When women get pregnant when they
don't want to be, some of them have abortions—legal or not, safe or
not. The overwhelming majority of women in sub-Saharan Africa
live firmly in this "or not."

I met Grace in the front yard of an older man's house, a squat,
square home facing a half dozen other squat, square homes, all several
kilometers away from the nearest town. The older man is Kofi Noma,
a fifty-seven-year-old herbalist and healer, the person villagers come
to when they have a boil that needs soothing or diabetes that needs
regulating or even cancer that needs curing. He's been doing this
for thirty-six years, just like his father before him. Grace has rheuma-
tism, a painful inflammation of her joints, and she comes for Noma's
medicine: an herbal liquid he's made that halfway fills a repurposed
jug of Frytol cooking oil, which she drinks from twice a day until it's
finished. She's been to a modern hospital and taken prescription
drugs, but they wear off quickly. This, she says, works better.

In a decade reporting on women's rights and reproductive health,
from the U.S. to India to Brazil to Indonesia to my current home in
Kenya and half a dozen other countries in sub-Saharan Africa, I have
been in a lot of front yards and backyards and living rooms and health
clinics, invited to create a literary snapshot of someone's life after
spending a few minutes or a few hours observing and asking questions
about their most intimate moments. I have stood in the workshops of
men who show me how they hand-brew abortifacient concoctions. I
have flexed my fingers to fight the impulse to hold a woman's hand
as I sit with her, her feet in stirrups and her head turned to the side, as
a doctor ends her pregnancy. I've met midwives who deliver babies in
rooms with little more than a metal table and a washbasin, who wipe
their patients' sweat and stroke their hair and remind them that they

are fierce and brave mamas. I've sat with a woman glassy-eyed and listless, too sick to breastfeed or bathe her year-old infant, pregnant with her ninth child while her husband works in a neighboring country as a migrant laborer, and praying to God to grant her a little mercy. I've listened to a woman describe the tears that came like a river for months after she was raped by soldiers, now dry-eyed as she holds the baby that came from that rape and pacifying him with her breast.

And I have met a lot of bright, talented girls like Grace—girls whose entire futures depend on a complex set of puzzle pieces falling exactly into place, who have little room for error, whose lives are indelibly, invisibly shaped by forces half a world away in a country they only imagine from books in the library. Girls whose lives, I suspect, Donald Trump has never even tried to imagine.

Much has been made in the U.S. press of the role of "fake news" and the proliferation of misinformation (potentially from a hostile foreign nation) in tipping the electoral scales in President Trump's favor. Much, too, has been made of Trump's position as an anti–politically correct crusader, someone who uses his First Amendment freedom of speech to say ugly and offensive things; his defenders often claim they don't totally agree with him, but they're just glad someone has the guts to say the previously verboten.

Information, the cliché goes, is power: bad information can shape elections; new information can change the course of one's life. Words, too, have power—to wound, to spread new ideas, to draw millions to a rally, to instigate violence, to combat oppression, to oppress.

In these protected debates about what "truth" even means and the power of speech and the impact of words, less attention has been paid to how the American government shapes access to information and manipulates speech across its borders. The U.S. isn't the only place with a misinformation problem; despite the ubiquity of smartphones, the corners of the world where education is limited, where one's daily interactions are mostly confined to the other residents of a small town or village, and where cell phone data may cost more than one has to spend don't have the privilege of three local newspapers on the stands, an onslaught of twenty-four-hour cable news, or even a trained doctor nearby. Information travels from mouth to ear, over front fences and kiosks selling bagged water, from the woman next to you at the well and the man sitting beside you to watch the football match at the local shop turned sports bar. One way governments and NGOs have improved the health of a great number of people around the world is by putting trained medical providers as well as educators and outreach workers into this information chain—maybe bringing in a midwife to live and work in a village, as the Ghana Health Service did in the town in which Graces lives, or identifying the most trusted woman in the community and arming her with information about the importance of childhood vaccinations, prenatal care, and family planning. It doesn't disrupt this organic information chain so much as make the information that travels through it more reliable. And it's one piece of a much more complex effort that has, over the past three decades, reduced maternal and infant deaths by half.

Still, a woman in sub-Saharan Africa has a one in thirty-six chance of dying in childbirth. For a woman in the U.K., it's one in 5,800.[3]

Most of this is about health care itself—trained medical professionals, medications that are actually in stock, money to pay for procedures. But it's also about information. Does a woman know where to go to get the care she needs? Does she trust the care will be better than what she could get in her own home? Does she have the information about the benefits and costs of the care on offer so she can make an informed choice?

This all sounds quite simple, but it's what President Trump's gag rule disrupts. The rule prevents not just medical providers but anyone working at a foreign-aid organization from telling women the truth about their health care options if those options include abortion. It prevents them from referring women to a facility that provides abortions—even if that's the best place to get an IUD or seek treatment for infertility or get screening for cervical cancer. It prevents these same employees, many of whom work in reproductive health or provide services to adolescents and teenagers, from bringing their expertise to national debates about abortion rights, and from fully engaging in their own democratic systems. It's notable that the gag rule only applies to foreign organizations. It can't apply to American ones, because it violates our First Amendment.

Organizations that refuse to sign the gag rule will lose all U.S. funding, none of which was funding abortion. This amounts to tens of millions of dollars, much of which was going to bring modern contraception and prenatal and well-baby care to some of the poorest and most underserved areas on the planet: places like Niger, where women average seven children each, and where the international women's health organization Marie Stopes will have its USAID-funded family-planning project gutted, despite the fact that it doesn't provide abortions there.

The question most opponents of the gag rule try to answer is, How does this harm women? The answers from advocacy groups are stunning: 6.5 million unintended pregnancies, 2.1 million unsafe abortions, 600 health care facilities losing family-planning tools.[4]

Talking to Grace in the backseat of that bouncing, hot car, I had a different question: What does a girl like Grace get to know?

This is the quieter impact of the gag rule, the one you don't see on the body of a woman walking into a hospital bleeding and septic. In the name of promoting "life," policies like the gag rule shrink the universe of information for girls like Grace. The whole point of this policy is to curtail the spread of information, to silence the people working most intimately on concerns that may be "issues" on Capitol Hill but could mean life or death for a girl who lives in a village on the outskirts of Mando, Ghana. If she gets pregnant when she doesn't want to be, and like 56 million other women every year decides to end her pregnancy, will the leader of the local youth health education group, which has gotten USAID funding on and off over the years, be able to refer her to a legal clinic that will give her a safe procedure? Or will they be afraid of losing U.S. funds and say nothing, leaving Grace with what she knows—the herbalist down the street?

Forget getting pregnant. Will Grace, who wants to be a journalist, be able to fully engage in her country's ongoing debates around abortion rights and access? She will certainly be able to hear the views of church leaders and religious nonprofits; will she be able to hear from abortion providers, social workers who advocate for the rights of young people, researchers who quantify the impact of unsafe abortion and lack of family planning?

The U.S. government is trying to ensure that the answers to all of those questions are no.

We don't drive with Grace for very long; maybe fifteen or twenty minutes. She tells us what she knows about Abraham Lincoln, the information she's gleaned from the books she's read, her mom and sister nodding because they've heard this all before. In the background, Kendrick Lamar plays on the radio.

Into this little Ghanaian town, America has exported its very best, the same bits of art and information and history that resonate with the kind of smart, ambitious young American women who, when luck and opportunity allow, go on to find jobs on Capitol Hill or in communal workspaces in Brooklyn or in glass offices in the high-tech stronghold of Mountain View.

But here in Mando, America has also started to impose its very worst: treating information as illicit and dangerous, the same way Donald Trump seems to view the news media—as the "opposition."

And so when Grace says she wants to be a journalist, my photographer friend and I don't tell her the things we talk about privately with our colleagues: the security measures we take to keep our bodies and our information as protected as possible; the sense of utter helplessness we feel when we hear the term "refugee ban," knowing it's nothing compared to the devastation gutting the people we've met in refugee camps and immigrant pockets of urban slums; how we're all coping, or not, in our own dysfunctional ways, drinking too much or sleeping with people we shouldn't be or not sleeping at all. We don't tell her that it's draining, a lot of the time, doing this job on a continent few outside its edges seem to care about.

Instead, we tell her the better part of the whole truth: that this is the greatest job in the world, because words and the information they impart are so important. That she should do it. That she will be great.

1. "Ghana: 2014 Demographic and Health Survey, Key Findings." Accessed at http://dhsprogram.com/pubs/pdf/sr224/sr224.pdf.

2. Sarah D. Rominski and Jody R. Lori, "Review: Abortion Care in Ghana: A Critical Review of the Literature," *African Journal of Reproductive Health* 18, no. 3 (September 2014): 17–35. Accessed at https://www.ncbi.nlm.nih.gov/pmc/articles/PMC4465587/.

3. Nicola Davis, "Maternal Deaths Worldwide Drop by Half, Yet Shocking Disparities Remain," *The Guardian*, September 15, 2016. Accessed at https://www.theguardian.com/science/2016/sep/15/maternal-deaths-worldwide-drop-by-half-yet-shocking-disparities-remain.

4. Center for Health and Gender Equity, "Impact of Trump's Global Gag Rule on Women's Health," updated May 2017. Accessed at http://www.genderhealth.org/files/uploads/change/publications/GGR_Fact_Sheet_Jan_2017_1.pdf.

BEYOND THE PUSSY HATS

Katha Pollitt

THE 1950S CALLED. THEY WANT YOUR UTERUS BACK.

Almost from the moment *Roe v. Wade* was decided, in 1973, activists warned that reproductive rights were at risk. They weren't far off—the Hyde Amendment barring federal Medicaid funds for abortion went into effect in 1976—but too few people wanted to hear it. Abortion was legal, after all, and sort of affordable, and sort of accessible if you lived in a blue state or a big city or a university town. It was easy to overlook the way abortion rights and access were being chipped away for underage girls, low-income women, women in rural areas where clinics were sparse. Even among feminists, it gradually became a niche cause: of passionate concern to some, worthy but ho-hum to the rest. Older women complained the young were forgetting history; younger women complained their elders were stuck in the past: *Mom, stop waving the bloody coat hanger already, okay? We get it!* On campus and in the blogosphere the hot issues were becoming LGBTQ rights, rape, sexual harassment, sex work, porn. Much more exciting.

Progressives were even more complacent, especially the men. The conventional wisdom was that the GOP would never overturn *Roe v.*

Wade, because that would set off battles in every state and waken the sleeping giant that is the pro-choice majority. Republicans just toss that threat out there every election cycle to get donations and volunteers and votes from abortion opponents too dumb to realize they are being played by their corporate overlords. Subtext: *Calm down, ladies, and pay attention to the Big Economic Picture, which we will now explain to you.*

Unfortunately, the coat-hanger-waving Cassandras were right. Especially since 2010, when Republicans swept state and federal elections, hundreds of laws have been passed to make abortion harder to get and harder to provide, more humiliating, more infantilizing, more expensive, more stressful, and, in effect, more dangerous.[1] Millions of dollars in state and federal aid have gone to so-called crisis pregnancy centers, many of which use misinformation (*abortion will give you breast cancer and make you infertile*) and manipulation (*why not wait, you'll probably have a miscarriage anyway*) to keep women from getting to a clinic in time.[2] Dozens of clinics have closed. Violence against providers has ratcheted up: multiple arsons, incidents of extreme vandalism, murder. Two thousand sixteen was the worst year yet; according to the Feminist Majority Foundation, 34.2 percent of abortion providers reported "severe violence or threats of violence" in the first half of the year.[3]

Had Hillary Clinton won the 2016 election, reproductive rights would have been preserved as a legal matter and perhaps even expanded at the federal level for many years, with a pro-choice Supreme Court and federal bench, cabinet and agency appointments, executive orders, and regulations. Now, with Donald Trump in the White House, the anti-choice storm long brewing in the states and in Congress is about to break over our heads. Whether or not Republican Party strategists would prefer to dangle a ban or near-ban on abortion just beyond the reach of anti-choice voters forever, that possibility grows less likely by the day. Evangelical voters overwhelmingly supported Trump, with many citing his vow to appoint Supreme Court justices who would overturn *Roe v. Wade*. This is one political debt that has now come due.

As I write this, Donald Trump has been president for four months. With his virulently anti-choice vice president Mike Pence by his side, he has moved swiftly to implement the anti-choice agenda he promised his evangelical Christian and conservative Catholic supporters. He's reinstated the global gag rule barring international and foreign health care organizations that receive U.S. funds from so much as mentioning abortion—in fact, he expanded it. He's nominated a string of abortion and contraception opponents to high positions: Tom Price at Health and Human Services, Betsy DeVos as secretary of education, Jeff Sessions as attorney general, Ben Carson at Housing and Urban Development. FDA head Scott Gottlieb opposed the birth-control provisions of the ACA. Title X head Teresa Manning once said that "contraception doesn't work." Katy Talento, health-policy aide to the White House Domestic Policy Council, claims contraception leads to infertility and miscarriages. Charmaine Yoest, former head of Americans United for Life and now an assistant HHS secretary, thinks the IUD and emergency contraception are abortifacients.

As his first Supreme Court pick, Trump has chosen Neil Gorsuch, who strongly supported the right of employers in the Hobby Lobby and Little Sisters of the Poor cases to refuse to provide insurance coverage for employees' birth control and—twice!—supported Utah's attempt to defund Planned Parenthood.

Meanwhile, the House voted to make the Hyde Amendment, which bars federal Medicaid payments for poor women's abortions, permanent. The House also voted to prevent people using the health exchanges to get coverage under the Affordable Care Act (ACA) from using government subsidies to purchase plans that cover abortion. Coming up: a proposal for a federal ban on post-twenty-week abortions on the bogus grounds that a fetus at that stage of development can feel pain. As of this writing, the American Health Care Act (AHCA), the GOP replacement proposal for the ACA, would allow states to opt out of "essential care," which includes the very popular no-copay birth-control provision of the ACA. But since the AHCA defunds Planned Parenthood, cuts Medicaid, and will throw an estimated 24 million people off health insurance, women will find it harder to obtain and afford contraception even if the no-copay provision remains. The Trump administration can also restrict the birth-control benefit by expanding the right of employers to refuse to cover contraception on religious or "moral" grounds, and through regulations. Tom Price has said that he's never met a woman who couldn't afford to pay for contraception, so what's the problem?

Things aren't looking better in the states. Republicans are deluging legislatures with anti-abortion proposals: banning abortion after twenty weeks, which is when many fetal abnormalities can be detected; imposing mandatory pre-abortion ultrasound.[4] A confusing new law in Arkansas bans dilation and extraction (D&E) procedures, essentially criminalizing abortion after fourteen weeks, and allows a woman's husband or legal guardian to sue a doctor who performs a D&E or plans to perform one. Texas is poised to ban D&E and also require burial or cremation of aborted embryos and fetuses. Iowa is defunding Planned Parenthood by rejecting $3 million in federal Medicaid funds. And so on.

Here is the paradox: the reproductive rights movement has never been more enthusiastic, more creative, and better organized. It's got fantastic lawyers—nothing new there—plenty of young activists, new organizations, new strategies like personal storytelling aimed at overcoming stigma, and skillful use of social media. It has a new (well, actually twenty years old but just recently breaking into the mainstream) analytical framework, reproductive justice, that puts low-income women and women of color (the majority of abortion patients) at the center and ties reproductive rights to making it possible for women who want to have children to raise them safely and well, which means fighting racism and poverty. It even has celebrity spokeswomen: Margaret Cho, Chelsea Handler, Jemima Kirke.

If only this had all happened a little sooner, or with more of a focus on political ground games. Because unfortunately, even as our movement got stronger and connected with more people, opponents were aimed like a laser on winning state power. Anti-choicers are much more likely than pro-choicers to be single-issue voters and it shows: as of now, Republicans control the White House, the Senate, Congress, thirty-three governor's mansions, and all branches of twenty-five state governments.

Here's another paradox. This state of affairs did not come about because Americans were turning against legal abortion. More people than ever support women's reproductive rights. According to a Pew Research Poll, 69 percent support *Roe*. Planned Parenthood is popular, with 75 percent of Americans agreeing it should get federal funds. Even 48 percent of Trump voters support Planned Parenthood. But apparently some of those same pro-choice people, in their capacity as voters, have elected, or allowed to be elected, all those anti-choicers. What happened?

Some voters cared, but not as much as they cared about lower taxes or gun rights or the imaginary jobs the Republicans promised them or building that Wall. Some thought abortion rights were safe (or at least safe for themselves). Then there were the 92 million eligible Americans who didn't vote at all. The Democrats bear responsibility, too: they let local politics slide, especially after the grand gerrymander of 2010, when Republican legislative majorities reconfigured their state's maps to dilute the strength of Democrats and favor their party outrageously. The result: according to the Guttmacher

Institute, 57 percent of all women of reproductive age now live in states that are hostile or extremely hostile to abortion rights. In 2000, it was 31 percent.

You can see why abortion opponents are jubilant. It won't be possible to overturn *Roe v. Wade* for several years—after Gorsuch, Trump will have to replace at least one of the pro-choice justices on the Supreme Court to have a shot at the five needed votes, and a case will have to wend its way from the lower courts. But even if the court preserves *Roe,* it can whittle abortion access down to a nubbin by upholding laws that restrict it, withdrawing protections from clinics, expanding "conscience" laws to cover more medical professionals and more situations and so on. Abortion opponents are nothing if not creative.

WHAT CAN YOU DO NOW?

I've always resisted talking about abortion as if it were already almost unavailable. It gives too much power to anti-abortion proponents and, also, it's false. After all, around 926,200 women terminated their pregnancies in 2014—down 12 percent from 2011 but still a lot of people—and the majority were poor or low income.[5] In a few states—California, for example—access is actually increasing. Clearly, though, the barriers for underage women, low-income women, undocumented women, and women who live far from a clinic are rising dramatically.

How can you help? Supporters of abortion rights tend to be clustered in pro-choice areas: blue states, cities, college towns. That can breed a false sense of security: if you live in New York City, you can take the subway to your choice of providers, while a woman in Texas or North Dakota or Alabama might have to drive for many hours, stay overnight due to mandatory waiting periods, and jump through all sorts of hoops, like unnecessary ultrasounds and listening to their doctor read a required script intended to discourage them. Maybe you can afford an abortion easily, or can put it on your Visa. But what about women who don't have cash or credit cards? Here are a few ways to help women less lucky than yourself:

DONATE. Giving to NARAL and Planned Parenthood is excellent, but don't stop there. Most abortions are performed in independent clinics; send them some love at https://www.abortioncarenetwork.org/. Abortion funds are volunteer groups that raise money to help low-income women in their state or area pay for their abortion care and related costs, and they also need support. Even a small grant to any of the roughly seventy funds that belong to the National Network of Abortion Funds can mean all the difference for a poor woman. Imagine being forced to stay pregnant because you can't afford transportation to the only clinic in your state. Or having to keep postponing your abortion when the later it gets, the higher the price. Abortion funds not only help women pay the fee, they help them with the arrangements and logistics, too. Check them out at www.nnaf.org.

VOLUNTEER. Could you join up with clinic escorts, who protect incoming patients from aggressive and intimidating anti-abortion picketers? Would you be willing to drive a woman to her appointment? Some funds and some clinics in rural areas are setting up groups to do that. If you have a car, use it.

What about hosting in your home a woman who has traveled to your city or town for her abortion care? As clinics shut their doors and new laws require ever longer waiting periods before a woman can actually receive her procedure, patients' hotel and motel bills are skyrocketing. Some women even end up sleeping at the bus station or curling up in their car. No one should have to go through that, especially when they're having a medical procedure. The Haven Coalition in New York City is one group of women who welcome these travelers; there's also ARC-Southeast in Atlanta, the Midwest Access Coalition in Chicago, and volunteer groups associated with some abortion funds. If there's no such group in your area, call the nearest clinic or fund and ask if they'd like you to start one. Providing women travelers a spare room is ideal, but a sofa will do: no matter how lumpy, it's bound to be comfier—and safer—than a molded plastic chair at the bus station or the backseat of a car. If having someone sleep over won't work for you, here's a less taxing proposal. For some abortion procedures, clinics won't let a woman leave on her own afterward. For women going through it alone, that's a problem. Consider volunteering with a home-hosting group to pick patients up at the clinic and escort them back to where they're staying. In the time it takes you to have lunch and check your email, you could be helping a woman and a provider.

SPEAK UP. Roughly one in three American women will have at least one abortion before menopause. (Anti-choicers point out that the number is based on older data, but let's not quibble: if updated figures show that it's one in four or one in five it would still be a very common experience.) Yet women rarely speak about their own abortion experiences, and that lets people believe the stereotype that women end pregnancies because they are selfish and immoral, nothing like the nice women they work with or see at the PTA meeting or across the dinner table. You might not be able to talk about your own abortion—women are silent for a reason. But then again, you might. Not ready for a face-to-face conversation? You can write about your abortion anonymously on http://www.1in3campaign.org/ or shoutyourabortion.com or https://wetestify.org/stories/. Use your words to show other women they are not alone while showing the world that there are no typical abortion patients, just lots and lots of women.

GET INVOLVED IN LOCAL POLITICS. Wearing a pink hat is great. Marching is also great. So is calling your congresspeople every day and sending snarky postcards to Paul Ryan. But have you thought about getting active in your local Democratic club, many of which barely exist? Volunteering to work on a pro-choice political campaign or even running for office yourself? The anti-abortion movement is fueled by thousands and thousands of local activists who energetically participate in civic life. They're on school boards, town councils, planning commissions, and community boards, and that allows them both to seize opportunities and to create them. Zoning boards, for example, can allow an abortion clinic to open—or prevent it.

Beyond electoral politics, there is lots of room to get involved. Are you currently attending an anti-abortion church—Catholic, evangelical, or Greek or Russian or Jewish Orthodox? Well, never mind how nostalgic you feel for your childhood and how nice the priest or rabbi is, stop it. Polish women walked out of church to protest abortion restrictions, and so should you. If you want to go to services, join a pro-choice denomination and put your money in a collection plate that will not be used to hurt women.

A note for those of you who are raising children: Do you know what kind of sex education your kids are getting? Is it fact-based or is it Christian-conservative propaganda? Even if you live in a liberal area, you might be surprised at what's happening in the schools. The writer and scholar Alice Dreger found to her vast surprise that her son, a ninth grader, was in an "abstinence-based" class taught by anti-abortion Christian proselytizers. And this was in a university town! If you are active in the schools, you can help make sure kids get accurate, nonshaming, science-based sex education, not sexist lectures in which girls who so much as kiss a boy are compared to unwrapped, grubby candies and students are not permitted to ask about birth control, abortion, or LGBTQ issues.

PROTECT YOURSELF. Reproductive rights and justice are social issues; fighting for them requires social action. But as potentially pregnant individuals, women should have a plan for how to help themselves in the coming years. I don't want to hear one more woman say, *I never thought it could happen to me.* Why not? You have sex, sex causes pregnancy, birth control has a failure rate, voila! Speaking of failure rates, the pull-out method, surprisingly popular today, has a failure rate of 20 percent. That means that among one hundred women using it for a year, twenty will get pregnant. Long-acting contraception, by contrast, has a failure rate of less than 1 percent, so if it suits your body, get that IUD or implant while the Affordable Care Act still pays for it. Buy emergency contraception in advance so that if the condom breaks or you forget your pill you don't need to scurry around searching for a pharmacy that actually carries it. Build a reserve fund in case you need to end a pregnancy. Even if you can only put aside five dollars a week, in two years you'd have enough for a first-trimester abortion, even if your partner didn't share the cost, which of course he should. (In fact he should pay the whole thing, since you are the one going through that not-fun day.) If you got pregnant before then, you would at least have a head start on raising what you needed. Interesting historical fact: in the Great Depression, some women had savings circles for abortions. Each woman put in a small amount of money every month, and if one of them needed to end a pregnancy, she could take out the price. Abortion was completely illegal, of course, but that didn't prevent women from thinking ahead.

WHAT HAPPENS NEXT? Trump's election has given rise to a huge increase in political activism. The Women's March led to Huddles, small groups (all genders invited) that meet locally and do political work together. There's Indivisible, and SwingLeft, and the Sister District Project, which help you work on winnable political races in other states. The ACLU, bolstered by millions in post-election donations, has started People Power to mobilize opposition to Trump in cities. There are email lists and apps that will give you a daily task. There are multiple marches and rallies every week. At the same time, we need to make sure reproductive rights stay at the forefront of this growing progressive movement. We can't let them be traded away in political prioritizing, as has happened before. Legal and accessible abortion is not "identity politics." It is health care. It is not a battle in the "culture wars." It's an economic issue, crucial to women's ability to support themselves and their families. It's a fundamental matter of human rights.

Of one thing you can be sure: the assault on reproductive rights is just the beginning of an expanded war on women. The politicians and judges, cabinet secretaries and officials, who proudly declare themselves pro-life are not exactly fans of equal pay, paid parental leave, laws against sex discrimination, protections from violence against women, and health care. Earlier this year, Representative John Shimkus (R-IL) wondered out loud in a congressional discussion of the Affordable Care Act why men should have to pay for prenatal care.[6] Um, because men make women pregnant? (Representative Shimkus has three children.) Because every man came into this world through a woman's body? Because insurance means risk sharing? You'll notice that none of the geniuses in Congress have suggested that women not have to pay for men's prostate surgery and Viagra.

If ever there was a time to focus on the big picture, this is that moment.

Feminists have much more important work to do than bashing

Lena Dunham or calling out other feminists on Twitter for some minor thought crime no one will even remember in a day or two.

We can get back to all that later, and I'm sure we will. But the immediate future consists of at minimum four long years of organized assault on the feminist gains of the last fifty years, to say nothing of attacks on the social safety net, civil rights, civil liberties, workers' rights, voting rights, and the environment. Basically, anything government does that helps poor and low-income people, people of color, immigrants, LGBTQ people, and women is going to be on the chopping block. That's their plan.

What's yours?

---

1. "The 334 Abortion Restrictions Enacted by States from 2011 to July 2016 Account for 30% of All Abortion Restrictions since Roe v. Wade," Guttmacher Institute, July 21, 2016. Accessed at https://www.guttmacher.org/infographic/2016/334-abortion-restrictions-enacted-states-2011-july-2016-account-30-all-abortion.

2. "The Truth About Crisis Pregnancy Centers," NARAL: Pro-Choice America. Accessed at https://www.prochoiceamerica.org/wp-content/uploads/2016/12/6.-The-Truth-About-Crisis-Pregnancy-Centers.pdf.

3. Mary Emily O'Hara, "Abortion Clinics Report Threats of Violence on the Rise," NBC News, February 14, 2017. Accessed at http://www.nbcnews.com/news/us-news/abortion-clinics-report-threats-violence-rise-n719426.

4. See: Steve Barnes, "Arkansas Governor Signs Abortion Law Banning Common Procedure," Reuters, January 27, 2017, accessed at http://www.reuters.com/article/us-arkansas-abortion-idUSKBN15B0KF; Doug Criss, "New Law Lets Husbands Sue to Stop Wives Having Abortion," CNN, February 7, 2017, accessed at http://www.cnn.com/2017/02/07/health/arkansas-rape-law-trnd/; and Stephen Young, "Breaking Down Senate Bill 8, Texas' Newest Anti-Abortion Law," Dallas Observer, May 30, 2017, accessed at http://www.dallasobserver.com/news/a-guide-to-undertsanfing-sb-8-the-2017-abortion-law-at-the-texas-legislature-9506932.

5. "Induced Abortion in the United States," Guttmacher Institute, January 2017. Accessed at https://www.guttmacher.org/fact-sheet/induced-abortion-united-states.

6. Elise Viebeck, " 'Is that not correct?': Male GOP Lawmaker Asks Why Men Should Pay for Prenatal Coverage," *Washington Post*, March 9, 2017. Accessed at https://www.washingtonpost.com/news/powerpost/wp/2017/03/09/is-that-not -correct-male-gop-lawmaker-asks-why-men-should-pay-for-prenatal-coverage/ ?utmterm=.058f65c2eb79.

IS THERE EVER A RIGHT TIME TO TALK TO YOUR CHILDREN ABOUT FASCISM?

Kera Bolonik

THERE'S A SORT OF JOKE I used to tell my friends—a joke that's not such an exaggeration—to succinctly describe my mother, about how she taught my younger sister and me European geography by recounting the way each country persecuted the Jews during World War II. (*Austria? Birthplace of Hitler. Germany? The home of the Nazi Party, and the country he led—anti-Semitism central. Poland? Place of the extermination camps that helped to annihilate most of the Jewish population.* And on.) My other not-exactly-a-joke I'd share: If *Shoah* had been on TV in the early 1970s, we'd have watched it right after *Sesame Street.* My mother left out few details when telling us about the Holocaust, and there really was never a wrong time to regale us with these gruesome stories. Which is to say, I can't remember the first time I learned about anti-Semitism or Nazis or even bigotry, because I've always known about it—she hardwired it into my brain. I thought this was what it meant to be a Jew in the world, that this is how she was teaching us. I wasn't wrong, exactly.

My mother was not a survivor of the Holocaust, but rather a survivor of survivors—her Polish mother spent her youth hiding from

Nazis with her family in Siberia, subsisting on weeds and berries; her blond-haired, blue-eyed father mostly hid in plain sight, passing as a gentile, first fighting with the Polish army until they lost, then in the Russian army—until he made a subversive remark that landed him in a Gulag, working in a mine where he almost died. He lost both parents and seven of his nine siblings (his father and a sister before the war). My grandparents met on a Polish train platform after the war, married quickly, and moved to a displaced-persons camp in Germany, where they had my aunt Aylin, and eventually took an illegal boat bound for Israel to start their new life—and instead landed in Cyprus. Their second attempt was successful—they ended up in Haifa, where they had my mother, in 1948, and stayed in Israel for nine years. Ultimately, though, they settled in Portsmouth, Virginia, in the late 1950s, much to my mother's chagrin. Imagine the culture shock: a family of four Jewish, Yiddish-speaking immigrants living in a provincial, Southern, predominantly Christian American naval town. My mom told me a curious classmate, who'd never met a Jew before her, asked whether she had horns. Life with her parents was so insular—she and her sister didn't have sleepovers or otherwise invite friends over—that she had no reason to know that other people's families weren't haunted by visceral nightmares, nightmares that were less dreams than unspeakably devastating flashbacks to their very real past.

Like my mother, my sister and I were raised in predominantly gentile neighborhoods—though, growing up in Chicago and, later, a liberal suburb, our environment was far less provincial than Portsmouth, and life at home, a bit less insular—my parents spent time with their friends (all young Jewish families they'd met from our nearby synagogue) and we regularly enjoyed cultural outings. But my mother zealously vetted our friends—that's what the geography lessons were about: Chicago is a richly multicultural city, a refuge for, among other immigrants, Eastern Europeans, and some of my closest classmates' parents hailed from Germany, Lithuania, and Poland. Those nations were, as she'd remind my sister and me, bad to the Jews. "Mom," I'd say, defending one of my friends, "stop calling her dad the Führer, he fled *before* the war." And: "Who is her mom going to rat me out to? My math teacher? We're just doing homework!" (These "geography lessons" were partly my mother's cynical sense of humor—she was being funny—but also a manifestation of a jealous streak: since she didn't get to cultivate friendships as a kid, neither would we.)

When my mother married my father at nineteen and gave birth to me at twenty-two and my sister three years later, how could she not pass this mindset on to us? I believe there is truth to the studies about how traumas like the Holocaust and slavery are woven into our DNA, passed down for generations. Being such a young parent, sprung straight from a household like hers, at a time when people rarely if ever unpacked family traumas on a therapist's couch or even pored over parenting books besides Dr. Spock's, my mother wasn't raised to have a filter. No one to rein her in or tell her that maybe you should wait to discuss such matters with your children until they're a little older. This is how you raise Jewish children in America, no? To make sure they never forget?

Or is there nothing to forget because it never went away? I think about what James Baldwin said at the National Press Club in 1986, a year before he died, words seared into my brain because now more than ever I am reminded of how true they are: "History is not the past," he said. "It is the present. We carry our history. We are our history."

Because here's where my mother succeeded, though there were times when I was growing up I found her to be overly dramatic, self-serving, even myopic: she impressed upon me that hatred never goes away—its manifestations may lie dormant but still it enacts itself in a number of ways—like microaggressions and casual bigotry, though we didn't have those terms in our lexicon at the time. It wasn't all epithets and graffiti on houses of worship, or physical harassment or worse. It could be subtle—euphemisms, jokes, condescension, cultural erasure, general invisibility. I remember using terms like "out Jews" (to refer to my family) and "closet Jews" to refer to classmates—language I'd rediscover when I came out as queer in college—because very few of my Jewish classmates were as eager to identify themselves as I was. My mother repeatedly told me that when the economy tanks, scapegoating has an awful tendency to creep back, and that in fascist-run or -infested nations, citizens become complicit—and that they have to be.

It was terrifying to imagine that people I knew, people I was related to and loved, could be so loathed that they had to flee or go into hiding, that they were treated like chattel, slaves, lab rats, that they were starved. That their families and friends didn't all make it, that some were gassed to death en masse. But, I admit, it lacked an urgency in my mind no matter how much my mother drilled it into me: it wasn't now, it was two generations earlier. Because I had both parents who didn't have that direct experience, and I was living in the suburbs with creature comforts, it seemed like we were past that, that it was a lesson learned, impossible to repeat. I had, I admit, a level of privilege that my immediate ancestors did not. I had no accent, I could decide whether or not to identify. I could move freely in the world.

But this summer, I watched in horror the Trump rallies—the first warning. And no sooner was this American Führer elected then we saw a spike in hate crimes. From the moment he was inaugurated this nightmare has quickly become realized with a barrage of vicious executive orders and treasonous, sinister, deliberately incompetent appointments. I should have never doubted my mother's warnings that what happened in Europe in the 1930s and '40s could happen again, that it could happen here, a nation where so many sought refuge from fascist regimes (and so many were turned away). And so soon.

As I write this, it's been barely two months into this administration, and my wife, Meredith, and I are bearing witness to this nightmare with our five-year-old black son, Theo: to travel bans and bullet holes through homes and synagogues. Cold-blooded murders of

Muslims, and those presumed to be Muslims. ICE agents rounding up Latinx immigrants for deportation, often separating them from their children. Adults and kids tormenting people of color because they feel they've been given license to yell "Build That Wall" to Mexican people, to rip hijabs off Muslim women's heads, to tell black and brown people—fellow citizens, even—to go back to their country of origin, to threaten Jews that they'll cast them into ovens. We are bearing witness to near-daily bomb threats at synagogues and JCCs. Mosque burnings. Desecrations of Jewish cemeteries. Swastikas on synagogues, playgrounds, people's houses. Recruitment flyers on college campuses by Aryan and Nazi groups. Lawmakers proposing bills to starve public housing and schools of billions of dollars of funding. And complete silence from the president, with his Judenrat son-in-law and daughter, and his anti-Semitic, Islamophobic, xenophobic, racist, Nazi-affiliated senior advisers. I'm too scared to ask how much worse it can get, because it can and will get worse.

I'm not shocked that we've arrived at this place. For so many communities this has always been America—if you're black, or Muslim, or Latinx, or an immigrant. Or a woman. Or LGBTQ. Because we as a nation have never reckoned with our white Christian male supremacy, the stage has been set for the current racist-in-chief (slash traitor slash rapist slash grifter slash pathological liar slash illiterate sociopathic narcissist) to come along. But just because many of us know how it happened doesn't make it any less frightening.

So, no, my mother wasn't wrong to start this conversation so early (though I'm thinking she could have eased into it). It's more that I am trying to figure all of this out now, as Meredith and I raise Theo in a country built from forced labor, on stolen land, one whose history has always been brutal for those who are not privileged white or Christian or cis-male or heterosexual. And now it has been made exponentially worse with the election of a fascist making good on every ugly campaign promise.

Even before we spoke of him, our son already knew Trump's name, recognized his mug—he lurks in the air like smog. He told us, "Trump is a really bad guy"—as if he were the Joker, or some other villain out of a comic book. At the time, our son was in his second year of preschool—the year before kindergarten—and he and his friends were enamored of the good guy–bad guy dichotomy as they had just discovered superheroes and *Star Wars.* Now, as then, Theo doesn't fully grasp what makes Trump despicable, nor does he know what led him to the Oval Office—the racism and racial resentment of a huge faction of white Americans who felt so threatened by a black man in power for eight years that they stocked their arsenals with semiautomatic weapons, openly carrying them in malls and restaurants, and launched the Tea Party movement, which has metastasized from school boards and statehouses all the way to Washington. So when and how do we start that conversation?

I sought the advice of other mothers of black sons when the "bad guy" play at preschool heightened and the kids were putting their toys in jail, building jails with Magna-Tiles and blocks, turning jungle gyms at the playground into "jail"—which the teachers found as disturbing as some of the parents, like us, not least of all because nearly every day, another person of color was being brutally beaten or murdered by police. My friend Kirsten West Savali, who is the mother of three boys, gave me advice that sounded the most familiar to me: "I think being proud and confident of blackness is linked to understanding racism. The framework of racism and privilege are already there. It's important for them to know that they are enough, even when the world tells them they're not."

I take what she says to heart—I think she's right, and it essentially echoes what my mother believes. But I haven't brought myself to enact it quite yet. In part because it's more frightening—what my mother told me, and when she told it, felt abstract, like past tense, because I wasn't seeing anti-Semitism play out before my eyes. But racism is ever present. It isn't just an integral part of American history—it is, in many ways, the story of this country, and it never went away and may never go away. And, inevitably, Theo will learn that the hard way, and I dread it. But we have to talk to him about it, preferably before that happens. We've started to, in a way.

My concern is that I don't want to braid racism so tightly with racial identity the way my mother proudly did anti-Semitic persecution and Judaism—but I worry that that's my white privilege talking. So Meredith and I are working on figuring out how to strike that balance. We adopted Theo when he was a newborn, five months before Trayvon Martin was murdered. I was forty and she was forty-one and we had spent years thinking about what kind of parents we wanted to be—call it one of the rare lesbian privileges, planning when and how to have a child, with no risk of accidentally being thrust into parenthood too soon. But you can only plan so much before you know who your child will be.

I will never forget the first question his birth mother asked me when we spoke two months before he was born: "Are you sure you want a black, African-American boy?" At the time I took her question at face value, vigorously assuring her that we absolutely did, that we would love him like crazy and give him the best possible life. Still, we had to reckon with the reality that he would be living in a white household—living with two white women, with two sets of white grandparents, but thankfully a racially and culturally diverse chosen family of friends, in Brooklyn. Would we be able to make him feel like he's not always the only brown face in the room? We would have to make sure of it.

After Trayvon was murdered, I started to think about Theo's birth mother's question, wondering if I'd misinterpreted it: Was she really asking if we knew what it meant to raise a black son? I ask myself this question every day—wondering about both the meaning behind her question and whether Meredith and I have the answer, whether we're doing right by our son.

Last year, we recognized in Theo's "bad guys" conversation—and Trump, for that matter—an opportunity to introduce a conversation about racism with Theo. He was four—a young four—but he had opened the door to it because of those new games of tag at the playground: everyone divided into good guys (cops), and bad guys (criminals) who, when tagged, were sidelined in some sort of make-shift jail. Theo, who loves to run, liked tag, but he wasn't much interested in cops or guns—he still isn't—in part because unlike a lot of white parents of white children, we have never told him to seek the help of a police officer if he's in trouble. *What is a bad guy? What is jail?* he wanted to know. Now we were able to broach the topic of police brutality and race, a conversation we will be revisiting time and again—and the difference between making bad choices and being an actual bad guy, which is rarer. And that, too, was our first acknowledgment of Trump in our household.

At the time, despite the warnings from black friends and pundits, we really believed Trump was more of a fluke than a threat to our government—though the hate he dredged up at his rallies was another matter—so I felt comfortable telling Theo that the man we've come to call the Orange Menace was a bad guy. Meredith and I explained that not all bad guys go to prison, even when they do bad things, even though they should—like Trump. And that there are good guys who make bad choices, and good guys who get blamed for bad things they didn't do, and these good guys *do* go to prison. And sometimes they even get shot by cops. And none of this is fair. "Fair" and "unfair" were words he understood, though I'm not sure what else he took away from the conversation—but it was a good start. We followed it up by taking him to his first rally, for Black Lives Matter, following the murders of Philando Castile and Alton Sterling.

Now Theo attends a public elementary school where white kids are in the minority in his classroom—his classmates are black, mixed race, Latinx, and more than a few are first-generation Americans. One of the first lessons they learn—and revisit throughout their years at the elementary and middle school—is how to be an ally to one another. The election results were treated like a terrorist bombing by the administrators, who sent several emails throughout the day to parents about how they would discuss the results with the students, a follow-up about how they responded, and another to invite parents to come in and unload.

In our household, as the election drew closer and the race grew tighter, Meredith and I had an understanding that we would not talk about Trump—we found it more exciting to focus Theo's attention on the possibility of having our first female president. I remember telling him, "One day you'll grow up and be like, 'Whoa, the first two presidents I ever knew were our first black president and our first female president!' How lucky, cuz Mommy and me, our first president was a guy named Nixon, who was a crook." I should have taken it as a sign.

The conversation we began over a year ago continues—we've been reading together about the civil rights movement of the 1960s and are working our way backward in history—and I'm grateful that his school engages in these discussions with the students and their parents. There will come a time, very soon, when he's going to learn about slavery—as with delving more deeply into racism, I hope we can broach the topic first. Because we dread the day he first hears the N-word and other epithets. Will we have prepared adequately when he's bullied by other kids, by authority figures, by people in power? Will he be ready? Can we protect him, or will he be able to protect himself?

Since the election, we've taken him to a couple of rallies around the city—for, among other things, racial justice, and against the Muslim ban. We taught Theo to throw his fist straight up and say, "Black lives matter!" "Resist!" and "No ban, no Wall!" In doing so, I realized what it was that my mother forgot to instill in me, what I thankfully discovered on my own, and what Meredith and I may be correcting, what we *can* correct: that we can pair difficult, vicious truths with action and community, and that lends a genuine sense of hope. It's imperative to confront the brutal reality of racism—and anti-Semitism, Islamophobia, xenophobia, misogyny, homophobia—that toxic blend of hate and fear. And it is unbearable to consider that an embittered, incompetent failed businessman, a grifter, a fascist, and a traitor, holds the most powerful job in the country and one of the most powerful in the world—in the ultimate display of white male supremacy and insecurity. But confronting these bitter truths doesn't need to wholly define us—because it's too easy to succumb to despair. We can't let that happen to Theo's beautiful soul.

My son has dreams of growing up to be a parent—he's talked about it since he was old enough to articulate it, and we want more than anything for him, and his generation, to have that and more. To have a glorious future. We are eager to impress upon him, especially now, that when there is injustice (and when isn't there?), he has a voice, that he can rise up. That protest is powerful, that resistance is powerful, that when people join together to fight for justice, it is not only effective but can restore hope for the future and faith in humanity. I've not seen him feel discouraged (except by his math lessons) or genuinely terrified—not yet—but we have seen him feel buoyed, positively energized by being in the company of passionate activists at actions he refers to as "parades." And boy, does our kid love a parade.

COUNTRY CROCK

Samantha Irby

BEFORE OUR WEDDING, I thought that my soon-to-be wife and I could pioneer a new type of marriage that some "relationship expert" would eventually dissect in *The New Yorker*. It would be the kind of marriage where she could continue to hang laundry on a line and churn her own butter (probably?) in rural Michigan while I spent the days counting down to my early death in my small, refrigerated apartment in Chicago. She could keep withering under the blazing sun while picking her own blueberries to make jam and knitting socks to sell at the Christmas bazaar while I ordered $17 cocktails at rooftop bars and waited four hours for a brunch table downtown. We'd meet up occasionally to talk about married shit (um, property taxes? which big box retailer has the best deal on economy-size containers of powdered soup?) and pretend we're still interested in having sex. Sounds like a dream, right? But oh no, fam, apparently marriage involves a little thing called compromise, a concept of which I'd been previously unaware, which for her meant having to wake up to a framed photo of Jheri curl–era Ice Cube on her bedroom wall but for me meant giving up everything I ever loved.

Last July I packed a suitcase full of clothes you have to dry clean and my wilted houseplants into a mid-size SUV with four-wheel drive and drove through Indiana's industrial ghost towns to the sticky-sweet southwest Michigan fruit belt, immediately regretting my decision to move in with my wife as I drove past billboard after billboard advertising AM Christian radio stations. I grew up in a Very Liberal Suburb of Chicago. My family definitely did not have any money for frivolous things that might make childhood worth surviving (LOL, what is a lunchbox?) and qualified for every government assistance program in existence, but my parents had the foresight to live in Section 8 housing in a Chicago-adjacent city where there were music and art classes available to me. And sure, I might have gone to school wearing some classmate's dad's old work shirt because it had been in a donation bin at the Salvation Army, but at least when I started wearing all black and got really into Ani DiFranco junior year not a single one of my progressive classmates was like *HA-HA LESBIAN, GO KILL YOUR-SELF*. I was lucky enough to grow up in a Super-Nice Town where it was okay if you dyed your hair purple and wrote mopey song lyrics on the white parts of your knockoff Chuck Taylors; a Culturally Accepting Haven where (Jewish or not) we learned about the Holocaust and got Rosh Hashanah and Yom Kippur off from school; a Promiscuity Province in which part of my sex education included the coach of the golf team sternly watching my fingers as I carefully rolled a lubricated spermicidal condom down the rigid shaft of a lunchroom banana.

I can give a rudimentary explanation of how evolution works and sing a nursery rhyme in Swahili, but I didn't learn any useful small-town shit while I was busy trying to look smart reading Vonnegut and pretending I was interested in skateboards. I didn't take home ec in high school; I took gender studies and shaved my head and started spelling "women" with a *y*. All these things are well and good for someone nestled safely between high-rise buildings. But how are any of the limited number of skills I've acquired—like hailing cabs at

midnight and having artisanal cupcakes delivered to my apartment—
going to translate to living in a place that has roving deer brazen
enough to just walk up onto your porch and sort through your junk
mail while waiting for you to toss the compost out, but doesn't have
streetlights lining the sidewalk to warn you of their impending ar-
rival!? I get nervous living in places that get too dark at night and
where you can't get a pizza after 9 p.m. I do not possess the handi-
ness to make myself useful around a toilet I'm responsible for fixing
if it breaks, which was number one on the list of reasons why I thought
leaving the cozy confines of a place with on-site maintenance was a
terrible idea. And okay, sure, the country has its perks. Gas is approxi-
mately thirty-seven cents a gallon. You can buy shoes at the grocery
store. You're never going to stand shivering outside in the cold trying
to get in the club after 10 p.m. The farmers market is full of actual
farmers instead of bearded hipsters in distressed flannel bloviating at
you about peak asparagus season while criminally overcharging you
for Pink Lady apples.

It sounds cute but I am living in an actual nightmare. I hate nature! Birds are terrifying flying rats and the sun will fry you and give
you cancer and large bodies of water are made up of mostly garbage
and liquefied human waste. I am a blue-state city slicker to my very
core, perfectly happy to ignore the outside world in favor of convenience apps and cable television. Everything here is dangerous and/or
irritating: mosquitos the size of a fist biting me through my practical
long sleeves and leaving itchy, egg-size welts in their wake; loud-ass frogs
in our backyard pond (why do we even have that?) with their deafen-
ing croaks all goddamned night; bats hysterically flapping their leath-
ery wings while trapped in the woodstove; the maniacal squirrels
aloft in the branches over the deck hurling walnuts at our heads as
we mind our human business grilling farm-stand corn for lunch.
Sick raccoons falling out of our trees, fat groundhogs busting through
the fence to eat the okra and tomatoes I refuse to help harvest but

am happy to eat, field mice scurrying around the basement that the cats disembowel in the middle of the dining room at dawn. Americana Horror Story.

Since I moved I have had very few encounters with humans who live here because too many of these yards have Trump signs and I'm terrified they'll smell the pro-choice on me and start lecturing me about embryonic stem cells. The first time I met one of my neighbors it was a man out walking his golden retriever by our house as I was dragging the garbage can up the driveway from the curb. He stopped and said, "You must be new here." How did he know I was new? Could he smell the lingering stench of unreliable public transportation on me? Could he see in my eyes that I couldn't really tell the difference between a cucumber and a zucchini without cutting it open? Did he register my smooth, uncallused hands and instinctively know I had never driven a tractor!? What kind of sorcery is this? How did this retired middle school principal know my secrets? Trying not to judge a Republican by his sensible dog-walking cardigan, I said, "I don't speak English!" and then I ran away and left the recycling bin in the street before he could say "emails" or "Benghazi." Although in hindsight I'm surprised there wasn't an ICE raid at our crib later that afternoon.

It's one thing to deal with the casual, everyday racism of progressive cities and the suburbs immediately surrounding them, right? I can deal with the Whole Foods cashier's visible shock as my card goes through for three hundred dollars' worth of spirulina or whatever because honestly: I'm kind of surprised, too. But she's probably not going to punch me in the stomach because I'm bringing that reusable canvas shopping bag home to my wife. And I'm not so naive that I don't understand that one can be hate-crimed practically anywhere, it just seems much more likely to happen in a place where I've had to pull over to make room for a tractor.

I've never paid much attention to politics and I don't really care about voting. Until this year I lived in a blue state and was always scheduled to work a twelve-hour shift on Tuesdays, plus I'm not really sure if this is real or not but I don't want to be stuck trying to think up ways to paint myself as an undesirable juror to overworked Cook County public defenders ever again so I'm like, "HARD PASS," when optimistic young people approach me on the street about registering to vote. Also, maybe this is the wrong place to admit it, but I am never going to care about who is running for circuit court judge. How does a statute work? What does "adjudication" mean? You're kidding yourself if you think a person who couldn't remember how the number of electors for each state is decided on the eighth-grade Constitution test is the same person who should be deciding who's the best candidate to interpret the law. Can you turn in a ballot if only one-third of it is filled in? Seriously, does your vote actually count if you don't take the time to fill in every single school-board bubble!? But since I had to move to a little blue dot in what turned out to be a big red state to participate in this cross-cultural experiment in cohabitating, when the post office clerk asked if I'd like to register to vote as I filled out my change-of-address form I sighed and said, "Girl, I guess."

I voted for Barack Obama one time, in 1998. Not that I wouldn't have voted for him again, but I didn't think I could get my boss to buy the "new black holiday" line two elections in a row. I had already gotten a pay raise out of him by citing reparations and I am definitely not clever enough to pull off that kind of magic twice in a row. I'll never forget all of the winks and nods and knowing looks exchanged with every brown face in line as one by one we cast our votes for our boy Barry, and I will also never forget walking what felt like 137 miles through downtown Chicago and Grant Park to watch the election results roll in with thousands of my new best friends and, once he won and delivered that super-inspiring speech as African Americans' first president-elect, getting pushed and shoved and stampeded as we fought to get a spot on the northbound el train as everyone realized it was two in the damn morning and we all had to be at work the next day.

The most exhilarating part of Obama's Post-Racial America for me was when, in lieu of the Newly United States of America's Yes We Can Parade the day after his inauguration, salty white people taped Lipton tea bags to all of the fedoras and straw hats gathering dust in their closets and started saying "nigger" with abandon in the middle of the grocery store. Remember when liberal white people tried to trick us into thinking racism was over while every night their uncles were on the news, their DON'T TREAD ON ME and GO BACK TO KENYA signs on proud display? I was too preoccupied sitting at home waiting for the mailman to deliver my reparations check Obama was surely going to sign himself, but I heard that some of you post-racial idealists had your hearts broken when the lady who called the police on your dreadlocked cousin that one time didn't start leaving her front door unlocked and inviting you over for a cold glass of milk and a warm slice of the American dream.

I can't reliably find West Virginia on a map, but I knew that eight years of the Socialist in Chief, or whatever people who watched Bill O'Reilly called him, was going to break bad as soon as Volvo-purchasing, college-educated white (and self-hating black? and super-Catholic Latino?) America saw its opportunity. I thought for sure it was gonna be Ted Cruz, but when Donald Trump won the nomination I was like, *Oh shit, these dudes ain't playing. And now I live across the yard from them.* My wife and I went out to eat the other night at the kind of place where you slop a pile of room-temperature food out of a chafing dish onto your plate while fogging up the sneeze guard keeping it free of everyone's germs. As I was raising an egg roll stuffed with pale mystery meat to my mouth, in walked a group of rowdy dudes in un-ironic MAKE AMERICA GREAT AGAIN apparel looking to shovel ambiguously Chinese food you pay for by the pound into their freedom-loving mouths and I braced myself for a conflict: I am a black lady with a white wife in a red state and I can't be sure that bro with the backward visor (LOL, WHY?) isn't about to start some shit with me just because I have the nerve to show my face in public.

This new political edgelord kind of bro is usually pretty easy to spot. He is wearing a North Face fleece and mirrored sunglasses made of neon-pink plastic, possibly shorts, and definitely shower shoes. He's probably not saying any real English words, just grunting and whooping at varying volumes. He looks you right in the eye for an uncomfortably long time, and if you challenge him he'll throw an unlandable punch in the direction of your face and grumble unintelligibly about you going back to Africa, a continent that you have never visited. His friends are all named Brody and Kevin and Kyle and they punch each other a lot and call things they don't like "gay." These are dudes who know what $37 worth of Taco Bell tastes like and nothing will get in the way of their path toward total domination, not the opposition-party media propagating their fake news, nor the shrill feminazis stepping on the white man's dick with their unsexy man-shoes. On a typical weekend he's kicking over Planned Parenthood barricades defending "life," he's shitting his cargo shorts in the back of an Uber on his way home from the college bar he's definitely too old to still party in, he's railing at anyone who will listen about exorbitant taxes he has never actually paid, he's saying "state's rights" so you won't think he's racist, he's grabbing women by the pussy, and he's back in the office bright and early on Monday denying you a lower rate on your mortgage.

I'm pretty well versed in unintentional racism, or latent racism, or hipster racism, or whatever you'd call "Wow, I can't believe someone like you really read that new Ann Patchett novel" racism, but it's one thing when a lady in overpriced exercise clothes starts overenunciating her order to the young immigrant man working at the coffee shop and quite another when a person dressed in the American flag on any day other than the Fourth of July loudly reminds your queer ass that you currently reside in an open-carry state. Which, until recently,

I thought was just a hilarious punchline to the joke of my new life. But then last week in a movie theater, a guy with a salt-and-pepper 1970s mustache wearing an inside vest and sitting behind me told me with a laugh that he might shoot me if I took my phone out to text during the movie. And not that context matters—should I actually be shot for ruining a climactic scene with my tiny glowing rectangle of doom? Well, probably?—but it was half an hour before the movie even started. Like, the lights were fully illuminated and that *Entertainment Tonight* movie trivia that plays before the previews hadn't even started yet. My stomach fell out of my butt as I contemplated being murdered while Maria Menounos patiently waited for my answer to "What is the name of the kleptomaniac monkey in Disney's animated film *Aladdin*?"

You just scoff at the latte lady and roll your eyes behind her back as you mumble shit about "microaggressions" under your breath and hope that the Land Rover she left idling in the middle of the street has a ticket on it when she goes back out there. But I'm not used to this other kind of bold racism just yet, the kind that screams THE PERSON WEARING THIS RED HAT MIGHT ACTUALLY HURT YOU. I don't have a plan ready if he spray-paints a swastika on my car or loses his shit on the Mexican woman at the apple orchard while I'm paying the real price for a half peck of freshly picked Honeycrisps. I know in my soul that I can't fight but would I try? If a "fiscal conservative" asked me what my hair feels like in downtown Chicago I could recite some Ta-Nehisi Coates at him or whatever but I'm not 100 percent confident what I should do if an American Worker Who Loves Winning decides to fuck with me for fun. Maybe I can just watch reality TV in my house and avoid eye contact at the co-op for the next few years. I mean, I talk a lot of shit and everything but I'm a doughy creative and I live with a lady who cans her own pickles and doesn't know how to box, so I'll watch my back when I drag my uninsured gay recycling out to the curb.

REFUSING TO NUMB THE PAIN

Sarah Hepola

ON THE NIGHT Obama was elected, I was in a crowded Brooklyn bar called Commonwealth holding hands with my friend Amy and openly weeping, which tells you how happy we were, and also how drunk. Much of that night is a blur to me now, but at some point, the entire bar poured into the street and danced in a circle—strangers laughing, holding hands, singing. We stopped traffic, but the cars didn't honk or yell or throw things. They pulled over to the side of the road and joined us. This was our America: the first black president and $6 pints and anyone on any street corner having sex with whomever they liked. Don't you see? *Everything had changed.*

I woke up at 5 a.m. with a hangover. I could never sleep when I drank so much. That morning, unlike most, I felt no shame for the previous night. I scrolled through ecstatic headlines telling the same story with different adjectives. Dance circles had erupted all over the country, it turned out. The videos were on YouTube. It was hard to tell them apart—which group of young, drunk Brooklynites was *our* group of young, drunk Brooklynites. But I smiled knowing I'd been a witness to history, even if I couldn't remember how I got home.

Of course, what soon became clear was that everything had *not* changed. The world continued to be full of cruelty and danger and people with plates much emptier than others. The machinery of Washington remained intractable. Sometimes, I would think back on that night at Commonwealth, twinkly with hope and love freely given, and feel a stab of despair. Why did we think it would be so easy? An election does not mean the fight has been won. An election means the fight is beginning.

But I also looked back on that night with tremendous nostalgia, because two years later, at the age of thirty-five, I quit drinking. I had passed the crucial tipping point where alcohol takes more than it gives you. During those first shaky months, my mind would travel back to the magic of that crowded bar: all of us snuggled up safely in the open palm of patriotism, sucking down fellowship from a foamy pint glass. I would think: What if a night like Obama's election came along again, and I couldn't drink? What would I do? How would I celebrate? This may sound ridiculous, but it gave me real panic. What if history cracked open again—*and I couldn't drink a beer*?

My first year without alcohol was like being stranded in a strange and unwelcome land. Nothing had changed, and yet my perspective had. I would meet a friend at a bar and be struck by the loudness of the music, the stench of puke and sticky hops. Had it always been like this—and I was just noticing? For so long, I believed in the warm, trickle-down theory of booze as holy communion. I believed alcohol bonded me to strangers and made all of us stronger and more powerful. Now I sipped my seltzer as drunk people walked into walls, and repeated what they just said, and spoke so close to my face it's like they were leaning in to kiss me.

I envied them anyway. Recovery was a turtle crawl, the opposite of alcohol's instant delivery service. But I was starting to understand that no matter how good the alcohol had felt, it didn't *change* anything. Alcohol was a numbing agent that never addressed the original wound. In fact, it usually created new wounds. It could be fun, and it could be freeing, but it did not *fix* anything. Booze only allowed me to forget things were broken.

Obama ran on a platform of change, which is a pretty foolproof plan, because change is the only constant. It's like promising sunshine, eventually. But sometimes the change that arrives is different from the change requested. The way it works in recovery rooms is that people will come in desperate to give up alcohol, but they don't want anything else in their lives to shift. They want to keep their job, and their bar buddies, and their questionable boyfriend—but it doesn't work like that. Booze is an attempt at equilibrium, and if you subtract the alcohol, you will force a new equation. I had to downshift my job. I had to move from New York to Dallas, a city I could actually afford. Change is scary, because it creates more change—in our own lives as well as the political landscape. The first black president might make history, but he may also rewrite the future in ways no one can predict.

In the year leading up to the 2016 election, I thought Hillary had it. I could not help noting, by the way, that the other guy was a teetotaler like me. Alcohol had destroyed his older brother, and he'd stayed away from the stuff, preferring the dopamine bump of cresting financial markets and golden toilets. Meanwhile, the Clinton camp had once passed around pictures of their candidate knocking back drinks with heads of state. One of Hillary's ongoing battles was the perception that she was aloof and perfectionistic, a scolding grandma, and the pictures of her hoisting a shot glass in that sharp pantsuit made her look loose and fun-loving, they made her look— let's admit it—*cool.*

By then, drinking had become a lifestyle brand for women, an emblem of our liberation. Hillary was exactly the kind of woman who might enjoy knocking back a glass or five—the smartest woman in the room, dinged from all sides about how she behaved, the size of her ambition, the size of body parts that had nothing whatsoever to do with her ambition. There are many reasons drinking rose over recent decades among women, particularly successful and affluent ones. But a big reason might be that during an era when many of us felt like we were failing—as a mom, as a sex kitten, as a bad-ass heroine—alcohol became a stout glass of the world as we wanted it to be.

And yet, the world continued in its own direction. In the final days of Trump's campaign, his team circulated rumors of "drunk Hillary." She clearly had a problem, this riff went: *Look at those pictures.* I doubt this smear moved the needle much, but it still made me mad. You send out pictures to prove you can hang, and they ding you for being a lush.

I spent the 2016 election in my bed, watching all the air deflate from my Twitter feed. Around 9 p.m., the grim jokes started: *I need a drink. Pass the whiskey. I'm not drunk enough for this.* My friends couldn't check out fast enough, and I didn't blame them. If I hadn't quit six years before, I would have been right there with them, unscrewing the bottle caps.

But I worried about people like me, who can't afford that easy escape anymore because it turns into more of a trap. Giving up alcohol is challenging on a good day, but in the weeks after the election, the country felt catastrophic. ("What if the world ended—*and I couldn't drink a beer?*") I tried to remind the folks who were struggling that alcohol wouldn't *do* anything. I tried to remind myself. But dread had become something of a national anthem. A popular piece from *New York* magazine was titled "See You in Four Years When I Wake from My Medically-Induced Coma." The curious thing about this sudden doom was that the world was technically the same world it had been before November 8. But millions of us felt stranded in a strange and unwelcome land. Nothing had changed, and yet our perspectives had.

There is a saying you hear a lot in recovery: "One day at a time." The first and fiftieth time someone told me to take it "one day at a time," I wanted to throw a chair across the room. "One day at a time," though, turns out to be less like wisdom and more like acknowledgment of fact. It is the only way life *can* be lived. Time refuses to fast-forward for us, no matter how often we fiddle with the remote. What I have found is that as I trudge along, mastering one small plot of land as it arrives under my feet, the five hundred thousand problems that faced me back at the starting line will begin to resolve themselves, or fade into the background, or they will wait patiently until I get to them. This is not how I used to do business. I would freak out in times of crisis and drink a bunch of wine to make all my problems go away, which is a perfectly understandable behavior as long as we can all admit *the problems don't go anywhere.* They lurk. They wait for morning. This is a different path I'm on now, and it demands I move slowly, and pay attention: one crisis today, and tomorrow, another. There is really only one way we figure out how to get through this time—by living it.

Lately I find myself caught between two warring impulses: calls to get angry and reminders to stay sane. On Twitter and Facebook, I see my feminist friends whipping others into action: *Get out. Get mad. Refuse to stay silent.* In recovery rooms, I watch old-timers calming people down. *Take a breath. Slow down. Stop yelling for a while.* Both of these instincts are correct, and though they feel incompatible, I don't think they are. One of the many challenges of the next few years will be finding balance between necessary rage and some slice of inner peace. Between speaking your mind and listening to another person's perspective. This is tricky business, and I don't know about you, but I can't imagine threading this needle with a three-martini buzz. I need my full faculties about me. An election does not mean the fight is over. An election means the fight is beginning.

Part of my own resistance is refusing to dehumanize people who voted differently than I did. If you don't like this plan, fair enough. You don't have to share it. But experience has taught me that calling people names and cutting them out because I don't approve of their beliefs only diminishes my worldview. Maybe this has been informed by living in Texas, where you can't create your own bespoke echo chamber. I also think it's informed by sitting in recovery rooms, because I can't tell you the number of people who opened their mouths and said something I couldn't stand, only to follow up with something that revealed me to myself, or rendered human behavior in a new light. Part of my education has been discovering how much I have in common with people I don't like, and how much another side can teach me. These are uncomfortable truths, but discomfort can also be a sign you are growing.

I wouldn't blame anyone for drinking through the Trump years. I drank through the Clinton years, and I *liked* that guy. But there is something to be said for refusing to numb the pain. There is something to be said for opening your eyes to the world as it is, and not as we want it to be. I spent the first weeks of this administration watching documentaries on social movements, reading Gail Collins's book on feminism in the twentieth century, and listening to a podcast on fascism. In contrast, I spent the first weeks of Obama's administration sitting in dive bars breaking into chants of "Yes, we can!" as I lit another Parliament Light off the cherry of my last one.

I still think back to that bar in Brooklyn sometimes. What an epic night. But when I look closer, the stardust begins to scatter. Those people in the bar—I didn't know them. I wouldn't recognize any of them on the street. They were nameless and faceless and voiceless to me, which made them exceedingly easy to love, because they were extensions of my own fantasy—that everything had changed now, and we would all get along. This is drunk logic, the entire world seen through beer goggles, and it feels incredibly good, but it is another one of the comforting myths I have been forced to discard. Life is full of them. But as those illusions drop away, the gift is that our vision sharpens, our depth of field grows deeper. Mine is no longer the hazy motion blur of a seven-beer buzz; it is the quiet focus of a soldier in the trenches. If we ever want to change the world—first we must see it.

DISPATCHES FROM A TEXAS MILITARIZED ZONE

Melissa Arjona

SOUTH TEXAS IS A RAPIDLY growing area with a vibrant culture. It's an area that has continued to thrive in spite of constant government oversight: the thrum of border patrol helicopters flying overhead and the sight of various law enforcement agencies' vehicles stationed along quiet rural roads are all facts of life from which there is no escape.

Some of the more egregious tools of government surveillance are interior border patrol checkpoints. Over one hundred such checkpoints exist around the U.S., and six of them are located along the Texas–Mexico border.[1] People who do not have the required documentation cannot cross these checkpoints without risking deportation. Almost 7.5 million people live in American communities along this perimeter, and for those who live south of the checkpoints, there's no other way to access the rest of the United States.[2]

I've been through the Falfurrias, Texas, checkpoint—one of two in south Texas—hundreds of times. Growing up, I crossed with my family on countless road trips. Later, I attended a university in central Texas, and would make the five-hour drive home at least once a month. The process is always the same. Outside, signs proudly display year-to-date statistics regarding the number of "undocumented aliens" apprehended, alongside the stats for the pounds of drugs seized. Cars driving through are funneled past an alarming array of cameras that line both sides of each lane. Travelers wait their turn, and when they reach the front of the line, a dog sniffs their vehicle for drugs. A border patrol agent will speak to the passengers before determining whether they can proceed north. People traveling by bus have it harder: a border patrol agent will climb on board and walk row by row to look at everyone's documentation. *That* takes a long time.

After finishing my master's degree, I moved back home to south Texas and found part-time work as an adjunct. By that point, my vehicle and I had traversed both of the United States borders and a whole bunch of the states in between, well over 100,000 miles. The car was looking rough, but with student loan repayment in full swing and nary a full-time job offer in sight, I was determined to hold on to it for as long as possible.

It was at this point, when I wasn't just a dark-skinned Mexican but a dark-skinned Mexican in a busted-ass car, that crossing those checkpoints became a hassle. I'd have my phone at the ready as I waited in line. Tweeting variations of "crossing checkpoint . . . about to be racially profiled!" became a new habit. A border patrol agent would question me, confer with fellow agents in hushed tones while giving me suspicious glances, and reluctantly let me drive on.

Checkpoint crossing continued this way until my mother and I decided to go to Austin for a quick weekend getaway. This time, instead of the usual line of questioning, they had me pull my car off to the side because "the dog" had picked up on something, an excuse that gave the officers probable cause to conduct a search. My mom and I were instructed to get out of the vehicle. I was prevented from sending the obligatory "I'm being more racially profiled than usual" tweet because an agent yelled at me to put my phone away.

As I watched my car get torn apart, several male agents surrounded my mother and me and asked the same questions over and over: Where were we *really* going? Did we do drugs? One young, smug officer kept trying to get me to admit that I smoked weed since I was in college. I pointed out that I was an instructor and not a student. "But when you get home you smoke out, right?" Wink, nudge. By this point, my mother—who does not so much as drink and gets scandalized over the slightest hint of illicit behavior—was panicked. I was furious.

When everyone came up empty-handed, I was instructed to drive to the end of the checkpoint. There, they made us stand aside yet again while a truck equipped with a huge X-ray machine drove in circles around my vehicle ("standard procedure"). Only when their search proved fruitless yet again were we allowed to leave.

I've since bought a new car, a 2016 model that you don't see too often on the road. The officers no longer ask me where I'm going and if I'm a United States citizen. Instead, they smile and ask if I get good mileage.

I don't smile back.

The Rio Grande Valley, where I live, doesn't usually register on people's mental cartography; for many, "south Texas" seems to stop at San Antonio or perhaps Corpus Christi. But farther south, in a different reality, immigration is the dark cloud hanging over everyone, and no one living on the border, not even the most privileged, can remain unaffected by it. As a reproductive-justice activist in south Texas, my feminism intersects with immigration by necessity. Local activists cannot afford to focus on a single issue at the risk of ignoring other injustices that affect our community. It's all tied together.

The feminist movement has long since ceased to be a monolith that moves toward a couple of central goals, and to many, I'm sure its parameters seem blurrier with each passing year. Feminism is no longer coming in solid waves that last decades at a time; the waves roll in faster now, sometimes crashing into each other as they try to keep pace with an ever-changing cultural landscape.

This is troubling to some who consider themselves feminists but have no idea what to make of the contemporary feminist lexicon. *Intersectionality. QUILTBAG. Latinx* (a gender-neutral alternative to "Latina" or "Latino"). These terms signal the broader shift toward social justice that feminism is embracing, but some fear that this shift will water down the meaning of feminism and wash away feminists' identity as women. Throw your feminist hat in the ring for Marissa Alexander or try to bring up Rekia Boyd—heck, even try to break down pay inequity by race—and you might experience some pushback. *Is this feminism or egalitarianism?* some harrumph. *We need to be unified and focus on women's issues now more than ever.* In reality, it's neither possible nor desirable to compartmentalize the different aspects of one's identity, and bringing more issues under the feminist tent does not mean pushing other issues out.

Two of the poorest counties in the United States are located in "the Valley," as it is called by locals. Rural roads there are dotted with colonias, neighborhoods that are often comprised of substandard housing and sometimes even lack basic infrastructure such as clean water and paved roads. A lot of undocumented immigrants live in these communities, and it was these impoverished areas that were most targeted by Operation Strong Safety.

That was what the Texas Department of Public Safety called it when, in 2013, they began setting up mobile checkpoints around the Rio Grande Valley. This temporary "surge" of state troopers into the Valley was publicized as a way to improve public safety along the border. While the state focused on rounding up the bad guys, it was argued, local law enforcement would have time to get their jobs done. A win-win, right?

Operation Strong Safety was put into effect for a three-week period. Temporary checkpoints sprung up along rural roads for a few hours at a time. Law enforcement officers imported from around the state checked all who crossed through for driver's licenses, vehicle registration, and outstanding arrest warrants.

Although the DPS asserted that officers were not checking immigration status, panic quickly spread. People began staying home. Undocumented parents stopped taking their children to school regardless of whether their children were United States citizens. My sister, who worked at a school in an impoverished area at the time, noted that both directions of the road leading to her campus were often blocked by checkpoints; a rise in student absences was reported. The risk—the terror—of being questioned and possibly detained out on the road was too high.

In response to the checkpoints, a grassroots resistance swiftly took shape. Using text messages, walkie-talkies, and various social networks, the very people who were targeted started to take back some control. Facebook pages and dedicated Twitter accounts warned followers whenever a new checkpoint sprang up. People could now go out feeling at least slightly more confident that they would be able to plan alternate routes around a pop-up checkpoint, should the need arise.

A few weeks after Operation Strong Safety was over, the Texas Department of Public Safety released statistics proclaiming the program a success despite a lack of any discernible long-term drop in criminal activity. Local law enforcement gave their support of the initiative, and a year later, the Rio Grande Valley received two hundred new permanent state officers as well as hundreds of millions of dollars earmarked for border security. More officers and federal money are on the way.[3]

In the Valley, immigration is a reproductive-justice issue, and reproductive justice is an immigration issue. Reproductive justice, which
merges social justice with reproductive rights, puts a heavy focus on
the ways that people and their families are impacted by laws restrict-
ing bodily autonomy and their very right to exist in a society that de-
monizes anyone living on the margins. In this light, raising your
children free from the threat of police brutality is a reproductive-
justice issue. Being able to take your child to school without being
deported—and being able to focus on your classwork instead of
worrying about your parent being deported—is a reproductive issue.
And, of course, accessing necessary reproductive health care is a
reproductive-justice issue.

Defunding Planned Parenthood may now be in vogue with a certain segment of the politicians in Washington, but Texas has long
been controlled by Republicans who are hell-bent on disenfranchis-
ing minorities and regulating reproductive health. In 2012, the state
voted to exclude Planned Parenthood from the Texas Women's Health
Program. It was a hard blow to Planned Parenthood clinics around
the state, which served almost half of the low-income women enrolled
on Medicaid.

In the Valley, clinics were forced to close or sever their affiliation
with Planned Parenthood in order to keep their state funding and stay
open. Planned Parenthood clinics had never offered abortion services
in the Valley; those services had always been provided by independent clinics. In Brownsville, Texas, the closing of the local Planned
Parenthood, which provided some of the only medical care that
residents had access to—particularly those residents who lived in
colonias—have had a catastrophic impact on people's health.[4]

In 2015, the National Latina Institute for Reproductive Health
gathered twenty Valley residents to testify before a global human
rights panel about the dire state of women's health in south Texas.
Latinxs, who face some of the highest rates of cervical cancer, were

left even more vulnerable to serious ailments.[5] Women gave testimony about themselves or close family members who had tumors but had no way to receive medical attention; they simply went unchecked. Others relayed their fears about not being able to get regular checkups.

By this time, Texas's HB 2—an anti-abortion omnibus bill that, among other things, required providers to have hospital admitting privileges and clinics to meet the strict building specifications required of major surgical units—was also in full effect. One of the two abortion clinics serving the Valley was closed, a casualty of a law that was ultimately ruled unconstitutional by the United States Supreme Court in *Whole Woman's Health v. Hellerstedt.* Unconstitutional or not, the damage had been done. Texas lost roughly half of its abortion clinics when HB 2 first went into effect. Although one new clinic has opened since, none of the original clinics that closed has reopened.

Whole Woman's Health in McAllen, Texas, bore the brunt of the public's scrutiny in the months leading up to the Supreme Court ruling. Undocumented immigrants completely lost their access to a safe and legal abortion when the McAllen clinic closed for a six-month period in 2014. McAllen is in the south of the state; because of the interior border patrol checkpoints, anyone who did not have the required documentation could not travel north to the next closest clinic in San Antonio. People who could not afford to travel out of the Valley for the procedure also lost their access. When Whole Woman's Health reopened later that fall, a game of legal Ping-Pong ensued; the clinic was forced to close again for a two-week period until the Supreme Court intervened and issued a stay, allowing it to reopen. Meanwhile, women and their health were at the mercy of court proceedings.

It is in times like these that the Valley's isolation becomes its saving grace. The nearest big city is San Antonio, a four-hour drive through mostly undeveloped open land. Had the clinic been located near a metropolis, there's no doubt that protesters from out of town would have descended in droves because of Whole Woman's Health's central role in the court case.

Instead, the McAllen clinic is targeted by a small but dedicated group of local protesters. Outsiders who witness patient-protester interactions firsthand are often surprised by the way patients demur from standing up to protesters. In any big city, rosary-wielding little old ladies, cultish men oozing old-school machismo, and hyped-up Jesus freaks shouting graphic "truths" about abortion might elicit derision from patients. But in the Valley, the accusations cut deep, and protesters know it.

Much of this is cultural; some patients do stand up for themselves, but Latinx culture demands deference to one's elders. The Catholic traditions that permeate Valley life add another layer of deference as well as shame. The Valley's isolation may help shield it from becoming a target of large anti-abortion organizations, but that isolation also makes its cultural influence that much more insidious.

For a couple of weeks, I noticed the white blimp floating in the sky and paid it no heed. From far away it looked like a publicity gimmick meant to draw attention to a business. A car dealership, perhaps? In the fall of 2016, I'd been assigned to teach one class at a campus in a more rural part of south Texas, and on the thirty-minute drive to work, along a road that had been a popular target for mobile checkpoints a few years before, the sight of the tethered blimp would immediately register in my mind and then fade as more pressing concerns of the day popped into my head.

But finally it hit me: that blimp. *Wasn't it here yesterday? Where is the car dealership? And isn't it kind of high for a publicity thing?*

I looked at how high it was and where it was tethered just off the main road. I'd heard about these things before, but having never actually seen one, the sudden realization that my biweekly commute involved driving under a floating border wall sent chills down my spine.

Since 2015, five of these aerostats, which originally offered high-tech surveillance to the military in Iraq and Afghanistan, have been repurposed for use along the Texas–Mexico border. Soaring at an altitude of up to five thousand feet, they can zoom in on license plates or use night-vision capabilities to spot people crossing into the United States from up to twelve miles away. Stationed along the border, they can easily peer into Mexico. The border patrol loves them. They're buying more.

What exactly do these blimps see?

If an aerostat can zoom in on a license plate from thousands of feet away, does it also peer into the windows of the homes it flies over? Does it observe the everyday lives of unwitting Mexican citizens across the river?

If an aerostat can help the border patrol pinpoint and intercept people in the dark, does it also witness women being raped on their journey across the border, the violent and common price of admission into the United States that so many are forced to pay to their smugglers?

Does it look away?

There is something distinctly ominous about these eyes in the sky. Once I knew what the blimp was, I was constantly scanning the horizon for it. "My" aerostat usually flew above a doctor's office and a bunch of neighborhoods, but sometimes it was brought low to the ground, presumably to be moved to a different location. Some days, it would be positioned a little farther north. On clear days, I could sometimes spot a second aerostat floating in the distance farther west. Seeing more than one aerostat always brought to mind old World War II photos of barrage balloons flying over London.

When did south Texas become a war zone?

All of these things happened under previous presidential administrations. It was President Obama who approved the purchase of the aerostats and deported more undocumented immigrants than any other president in history, and the border wall has been a political hot issue for decades now. Things were already bad in south Texas, and local activists lamented that no matter who moved into the White House in 2017, things were going to stay bad.

Donald Trump ascended to the presidency on a ghastly platform of racism, sexism, and bigotry with an intensity that has brought all the trolls out from under their bridges. "Build the Wall!"—a wall on the southern, browner border of the United States—became a rallying cry concomitant with the rise of xenophobia, despite the infeasibility of such a structure.

A wall already exists along many parts of the southern border, and there's always local pushback whenever new sections of the wall are proposed. Building a wall allows the government to claim people's land through eminent domain. It's devastating to the native and migratory animals who rely on open access to the Rio Grande for survival. It's visually heartbreaking: on holidays such as Mother's Day, separated families sometimes meet on opposite sides, sharing tearful exchanges through the steel slats in the fence. And it's expensive: the MIT Technology Review estimates that the real cost of the Wall will be almost $40 billion, plus millions of dollars a year for upkeep. That's a grotesque waste of money considering how many families, including United States citizens, still reside along unpaved roads within a few miles of the border.

The president and his supporters want a wall. They might get a few more sections up—they might even manage to get the whole thing erected—and border wall proponents will pat themselves on the back for protecting America from foreign invaders. But the human, environmental, and financial toll is incalculable. More than likely, the real wall that goes up will be invisible. It will be a high-tech web of cameras, sensors, and aerial surveillance facilitated by the use of aerostats and drones. Impoverished areas along the border will become even more vulnerable, and those in power will have even more gadgets to play—and abuse people—with.

If the future is feminist—and it is—it is also intersectional. It has to be. When Immigration and Customs Enforcement (ICE) raids happen, families are torn apart. Individuals, including children, might be held in ICE detention centers for an indeterminate amount of time with little to no legal recourse. Detained undocumented parents of children who are U.S. citizens should not have to worry about being separated from their children, who could be forced into an overburdened foster care system that is plagued by abuse. These are all feminist issues.

On the border, feminism means fighting so that everyone—U.S. citizen or not—can live free from the threat of a militarized state.

It means standing in solidarity with Muslims targeted by the unlawful ban that Trump implemented in the early days of his presidency, particularly since many marginalized Texans have themselves had negative experiences at checkpoints.

It means acknowledging that people who are trying to access reproductive-health care might have more to worry about than just the "right" to an abortion: numerous socioeconomic, religious, cultural, and legal factors are often at play, as is the widespread lack of basic reproductive-health education.

The need for an intersectional approach to justice is something that border feminists know all too well, and will continue to insist upon in the age of Trump—because it works. Isolated from the rest of the state, small Valley activist groups have learned to work together and pool resources; their issues are intertwined. Farmworker activists show up to defend Whole Woman's Health during mass protests, and pro-choice chants will gleefully morph into queer-positive slogans at the sight of anti–marriage equality banners. Colonia activists will show up for Black Lives Matter, which in turn shows up for immigrant rights marches. Every organization has its own mission, but we also know that helping each other move forward benefits the entire community. It's a unique thing to be a part of. And against all odds, this burgeoning alliance of intersectional activists is paving the way for effective resistance.

1. "The Constitution in the 100-Mile Border Zone," American Civil Liberties Union. Accessed on June 13, 2017, at https://www.aclu.org/other/constitution-100-mile-border-zone.

2. "United States–Mexico Border Area," *Health in the Americas, 2012*, Pan American Health Organization. Retrieved at http://www.paho.org/salud-en-las-americas-2012/index.php?option%3Dcom_docman%26task%3Ddoc_view%26 gid%3 D153% 26Itemid%3 D&sa=D&ust=1496208754440000& usg=AFQjCNHXqZuXsrRkDBfm-WqqhljFxZ2RkQ.

3. "DPS Is Hiring More Hispanic State Troopers, and Texas' Border Surge Is a Big Reason Why," *Dallas News*, June 28, 2016. Accessed on June 13, 2017, at https://www.dallasnews.com/news/texas-politics/2016/06/28/dps-hiring-hispanic-state-troopers-texas-border-surge-big-reason.

4. "Nuestra Voz, Nuestra Salud, Nuestra Texas: The Fight for Women's Reproductive Health in the Rio Grande Valley," Center for Reproductive Rights, 2013. Accessed at https://www.reproductiverights.org/document/nuestro-texas-the-fight-for-reproductive-health-in-the-rio-grande-valley.

5. "Latinas and Cervical Cancer in Texas: A Public Health Crisis," National Latina Institute for Reproductive Health, January 2013. Accessed at http://latinainstitute.org/sites/default/files/Latinas-and-Cervical-Cancer-inTexas-NLIRH-Fact-Sheet-January-2013.pdf.

PULLING THE WOOL OVER THEIR EYES
The Blindness of White Feminists

Collier Meyerson

"This is our march," my friend Shirley quipped as she sipped her champagne flute cartoonishly, her pinky finger pointed out, her lips puckered and her eyes rolled sassily to the side. While tons of my white friends descended upon the nation's capital or into their city streets for the Women's March the day after Trump was inaugurated, I sat drinking mimosas with two girlfriends in my friend's apartment. Over plates piled high with roasted potatoes and cheesy eggs, we looked out through the balcony's sliding doors onto the sea of pink protesters in Oakland. Shirley said she couldn't relate to the march's unifying language; that being inside, close to other black women whom she loved, was what felt radical to her.

But outside our tiny cocoon, something seismic was happening. Nearly every white woman I knew was out in the streets, making her voice heard in opposition to our new president. My Instagram feed was mobbed with photos from my white women friends at the march, and excited and encouraging messages filled the comments section below their photos. "Great sign" and "Fuck this guy" were refrains.

The optics of the march reveal much about who this fledgling

anti-Trump movement is speaking to and how it's being characterized. In images and videos from the march, white women had smiles
on their faces, they shook hands with law enforcement who lined the
streets, sometimes they danced. Much of the day is remembered for
its witty signs, knitted pink "pussy hats," and good humor. There
were no arrests. There was, instead, palatability. In her speech, actress
Scarlett Johansson addressed Trump: "I want to be able to support
you," she bellowed to the crowd, "but first I ask that you support
me." Despite all of Trump's unrelenting provocations and incendi-
ary attacks on women, Muslims, and Latin American immigrants,
Johansson expressed a desire to support him, if he supports her.
Johansson's wasn't a demand for unilateral justice, but a quid pro
quo. From all that I read and watched, the march looked like a cele-
bration, and also like boilerplate and mainstream feminism. A universal angry and hostile rejection of Donald Trump's misogyny or of
women's inequality writ large, it did not appear to be.

The march's diluted message was reflected most sharply in the experiences of many women of color. A Native woman documented
her experience on Twitter. "We started a prayer circle in the morning
in front of the American Indian Smithsonian Museum, next to all
those ancestors. It was powerful," wrote the Twitter user @Hokte. "Multiple [white women] scolded us for being 'too loud.' Multiple [white
women] mocked me for lulu'ing (war cry, of sorts) alongside [my
friend] Ashley while she chanted."

The response to @Hokte's Twitter thread lays bare the problem of
feminism in the age of Trump. While many supported her, there
were just as many who were offended by her lamenting the gaze of
white women. "I'm sorry you had a bad march experience, but we are
ALL women and therefore ALL sisters. Let's focus on unity instead
of intersectionalism! [*sic*: intersectionality]" wrote the Twitter user

@sydnerain. Intersectionality, a core third-wave-feminist concept, coined by Kimberlé Crenshaw, recognizes that race, gender, sexuality, ethnicity, and class shape one another. Intersectionality is hardly anathema to unity, and instead a building block toward achieving it.

Some black women expressed similar grievances with the protests. "White women were not called to action by the voice of intersectional resistance," wrote Aurielle Marie Lucier for *Essence*. "They weren't hoping to lift the burden of resistance that Black women have been carrying in concentration for the past three years. No, they were simply mobilized by the fear that something had gone awry in their lily-white world of privilege." It's true that the march certainly didn't resemble the Black Lives Matter movement I covered for the last three years as a journalist. In contrast, those gatherings were filled with people whose anger was palpable, whose opposition to the hegemon was clearly expressed, through civil unrest and what always felt like an insurmountable tension.

Resistance won't and shouldn't be uniform, but the optics of the Women's March has a lot of critics and writers wondering what feminism under Trump will look like. Black Lives Matter founder Alicia Garza wrote in *Mic* a compelling argument for why it's important to embrace the newfound feminism of white women. "If our movement is not serious about building power, then we are just engaged in a futile exercise of who can be the most radical," she wrote. And it is true; a movement cannot be built on cynicism alone.

Yet, as the excitement of white feminists at the Women's March extends into a new political mobilization, what I'll call the "All Women Matter" sector of feminists is becoming louder and louder. Take, for example, the feminism embodied by Taylor Swift, who famously said, "As a teenager, I didn't understand that saying you're a feminist is just saying that you hope women and men will have equal rights and equal opportunities." It's pop-feminism, as Amanda Hess writes in *The New York Times Magazine,* a brand of feminism that favors uncontroversial platitudes over nuance and intersectionality. That is, feminism you can wear, feminism that is benign. It's feminism like this that ignores issues for women at the margins, women who have already been, as my friend and writer Doreen St. Felix said in an Instagram post, "marching every day."

The shape of this newest iteration of the women's movement isn't what the march's organizers, three out of four of whom are of color, might have had in mind. "We believe Gender Justice is Racial Justice is Economic Justice," the group declared on its website as a core principle. "We must create a society in which women—in particular Black women, Native women, poor women, immigrant women, Muslim women, and queer and trans women—are free and able to care for and nurture their families, however they are formed, in safe and healthy environments free from structural impediments." But there is a disconnect between the beliefs espoused by the group's platform and how those tenets are being played out publicly.

Tamika Mallory, one of the march's organizers, who is black, talked about how she deals with white liberal people who are shocked by the new presidency. "I tell people, 'Welcome to my world,'" she said. "To be a black woman or a woman of color carrying the weight on her back of the entire community. Welcome to what it feels like to be a Mexican-American, a Latino person in this country. We've been here. We've been dealing with the Trumpisms." In this interview, Mallory also addressed the tensions in the emerging movement. "We want people to have difficult, challenging, and courageous conversations with one another," she said.

But even with women of color at the helm encouraging uncomfortable and robust dialogue, a conventional and uncomplicated feminism still emerges, and it's one that builds on tensions from past feminist movements that the privileged white middle-class voices. In her book

Feminism Is for Everybody, bell hooks writes of second-wave feminism, "Given the reality of racism, it made sense that white men were more willing to consider women's rights when the granting of those rights could serve the interests of maintaining white supremacy." Straight, white, middle-class women have long dominated feminism's main stage, and so have their issues.

This phenomenon, what hooks calls "lifestyle feminism," was present during Hillary's bid, too. Though her staff and campaign message was inclusive of black and brown women, the social and economic power white women maintain in American culture led Clinton's messaging into that familiar garden-variety "lifestyle feminist" zone.

During the 2016 primaries, and in the general election campaign, black feminists and organizers were not quiet about being critical of Clinton's record. Writing for *The Nation,* writer and professor Michelle Alexander outlined why she, a black woman, believed Clinton did not deserve the black vote. Alexander cited Bill Clinton's expansion of the prison system: the 1994 crime bill, the "three strikes" rule, expanded police forces, and life sentences for three-time offenders. "Some might argue that it's unfair to judge Hillary Clinton for the policies her husband championed years ago," Alexander wrote. "But Hillary wasn't picking out china while she was first lady."

Black Lives Matter activists echoed Alexander's words with protests, interrupting Clinton at campaign stops. In August 2015, activists implored the former senator to "say her name," that is, acknowledge all the black women, like twenty-nine-year-old Sandra Bland, who have been affected or lost their lives due to police violence. At a private event in February 2016, two Black Lives Matter activists confronted Clinton about racially inflammatory comments she made as First Lady about bringing "[at-risk youth] to heel." One of the two protesters, Ashley Williams, told Clinton "I am not a superpredator," a term Clinton used to describe inner-city black youth.

Williams then asked Clinton, "Will you apologize to black people for mass incarceration?"

Clinton not only apologized, but promised to roll back some of her husband's policies in a criminal justice platform she released in October 2015. In addition to pressures from her Democratic-socialist opponent, Bernie Sanders, there is no doubt that Clinton moved further to the left due to pressure from Black Lives Matter, a distinctly intersectional feminist movement.

Clinton's commitment to righting some of the wrongs committed by her husband did shore up votes. Ninety-four percent of black women came out and voted for Clinton in the general election. But we never got to see if she'd make good on those promises, because she failed to capture the majority of white women's support, let alone white men's.

During the third presidential debate, Donald Trump interrupted Hillary Clinton and called her a "nasty woman." It was a particularly shocking moment during a campaign full of them and it was one that lent itself well to jokes, memes, and fund-raising campaigns. Within a day or two NASTY WOMEN VOTE and NASTY WOMAN T-shirts were being sold online. Certain T-shirt makers donated their proceeds to Planned Parenthood, but not all. Also commodified were Clinton's love of pantsuits and being a grandmother. "Marketplace Feminism," as writer and Bitch Media cofounder Andi Zeisler called it.

In an interview one of the manufacturers who sold NASTY WOMEN VOTE T-shirts said, "Well shoot, if she's a nasty woman, then so am I. Then so is every woman I think is cool." The manufacturer, who identified as a Bernie supporter, said that the shirts were a much-needed bridge for the gap, unifying women under Hillary.

Now, I'm not a killjoy, or an ideologue, and I think memes and T-shirts are great, but when they become the dominating cultural touchstone or clarion call for all feminists, they obscure the more substantive aspects of the movement. In other words, there was no

"Nasty Women Vote" or pink pussy hat equivalent to the work of Black Lives Matter activists. Is this why their message and activism did not catch on broadly among white feminists? Did the issues and problems facing black women need cuter packaging to translate for white women?

And many women of color are feeling the sting. Ninety-four percent of black women who voted for Hillary Clinton are paying for 53 percent of white women's failure of empathy. A few photos featuring women of color from the Women's March made their way around the Internet. In one Amir Talai, a Persian-American actor, held up a sign that read, I'LL SEE YOU NICE WHITE LADIES AT THE NEXT BLACK LIVES MATTER MARCH, RIGHT? Another sign that garnered lots of attention was held by Angela Peoples, a black LGBTQ organizer: DON'T FORGET: WHITE WOMEN VOTED FOR TRUMP. In the background three white women in pink pussy hats took selfies and fiddled on their cell phones. In her column for *The New York Times Magazine,* Jenna Wortham writes, "That photo cuts to a truth of the election: While black women show up for white women to advance causes that benefit entire movements, the reciprocity is rarely shown."

What Wortham, and others, points to is not a new tension within feminism, but a very, very old one. Hess writes, "A vision of whiteness was ingrained in the leaders and the arguments of the mainstream [suffrage] movement. Even the suffragists' signature white clothes were deliberately chosen to signal purity. This ideal of feminine virtue did not extend to black women, or working-class ones." This was true in the 1970s women's liberation movement. "Even though individual black women were active in the contemporary feminist movement from its inception, they were not the individuals who became the 'stars' of the movement, who attracted the attention of mass media," bell hooks wrote in 2000.

It doesn't appear as though President Trump intends to soften his tone or curb his fascistic political agenda. Every day since his inauguration, Trump has unleashed some new assault against marginalized people in America. If women continue to show up in large numbers over the next four years, then it is imperative that white women embrace more than pussy hats and "nasty" proclivities. If not, the women's movement could go the way of Hillary Clinton's campaign—with the majority of white women sitting out on justice and black and brown women, like Shirley and me, staying at home.

A NATION GROOMED AND BATTERED

Rebecca Solnit

WOMEN TOLD ME they had flashbacks to hideous episodes in their past after the second presidential debate on October 9, or couldn't sleep, or had nightmares. The words in that debate mattered, as did their delivery. Donald Trump interrupted Hillary Clinton eighteen times (compared to fifty-one interruptions in the first debate). His reply to moderator Anderson Cooper's question about his videotaped boasts of grabbing women by the pussy, which had been released a few days earlier, was "But it's locker room talk, and it's one of those things. I will knock the hell out of ISIS . . . And we should get on to much more important things and much bigger things." Then he promised to "make America safe again"—but not from him. That week, women and ISIS were informally paired as things Trump promised to assault.

But words were secondary to actions. Trump roamed, loomed, glowered, snarled, and appeared to copulate with his podium, grasping it with both hands and swaying his hips, seeming briefly lost in reverie. The menace was so dramatic, so Hitchcockian, that the Hollywood composer Danny Elfman wrote a soundtrack for a video edit

playing up all the most ominous moments. "Watching Trump lurch-
ing behind Hillary during the debate felt a bit like a zombie movie,"
Elfman said. "Like at any moment he was going to attack her, rip off
her head, and eat her brains." Friends told me they thought he might
assault her; I thought it possible myself as I watched him roam and
rage. He was, as we sometimes say, in her space, and her ability to
remain calm and on message seemed heroic. Like many men throughout the election, he appeared to be outraged that she was in it. The
election, that is. And her space.

In the ninety-minute debate, Trump lurched around the stage gaslighting, discrediting, constantly interrupting, often to insist that
Clinton was lying or just to drown out her words and her voice, sexually shaming (this was the debate in which he tried to find room in
his family box for three women who had accused Bill Clinton of
sexual harassment or assault), and threatening to throw her in prison.
Earlier in the campaign he'd urged his supporters to shoot her.
"Hillary wants to abolish, essentially abolish the Second Amendment,"
he rumbled at one of his rage-inciting rallies, following a patent untruth
with a casual threat: "By the way, if she gets to pick her judges, nothing
you can do, folks. Although the Second Amendment people, maybe
there is, I don't know." At the Republican National Convention, Chris
Christie led chants of "Lock her up!" In the spring, Trump retweeted
a supporter who asked: "If Hillary Clinton can't satisfy her husband
what makes her think she can satisfy America?" Perhaps the president
is married to the nation in some mystical way; if so America is about to
become a battered woman—badgered, lied to, threatened, gaslighted,
betrayed, and robbed by a grifter with attention-deficit disorder.

Trump is patriarchy unbuttoned, paunchy, in a baggy suit, with
his hair oozing and his lips flapping and his face squinching into
clownish expressions of mockery and rage and self-congratulation.
He picked as a running mate buttoned-up patriarchy, the lean, crop-
haired, perpetually tense Mike Pence, who actually has experience in

government, signing eight anti-abortion bills in his four years as governor of Indiana, and going after Planned Parenthood the way Trump went after hapless beauty queens. The Republican platform was, as usual, keen to gut reproductive rights and pretty much any rights that appertained to people who weren't straight, or male, or white.

Misogyny was everywhere. It came from the right and the left, and Clinton was its bull's-eye, but it spilled over to women across the political spectrum. Early on some of Trump's fury focused on the Fox presenter Megyn Kelly, who had questioned him about his derogatory comments about other women's appearance. He made the bizarre statement on CNN that "you could see there was blood coming out of her eyes. Blood coming out of her wherever." He also denigrated his opponents' wives and the businesswoman Carly Fiorina's face; he obligingly attacked Alicia Machado, the former Miss Universe, in a flurry of middle-of-the-night tweets after Clinton baited him about his treatment of her; he attacked the women who accused him of assaulting them after the grab-them-by-the-pussy tape was released.

Trump's surrogates and key supporters constituted a sort of misogyny army—or as Star Jones, the former host of the talk show *The View,* put it, "Newt Gingrich, Giuliani and Chris Christie: they've got like the trifecta of misogyny." The army included Steve Bannon, who as head of the alt-right site Breitbart News hired Milo Yiannopoulos and helped merge the misogynistic fury of the men's rights movement with white supremacy and anti-Semitism to form a new cabal of far-right fury. After being dismissed from Fox News in July, when more than two dozen women testified about his decades-long sexual harassment, degradation, and exploitation of his female employees, Roger Ailes became Trump's debate coach, though they soon fell out—according to *New York* magazine's Gabriel Sherman, Ailes was frustrated by Trump's inability to focus.[1] The Fox anchor Andrea Tantaros claimed that under Ailes, Fox was "a sex-fueled, Playboy Mansion–like cult, steeped in intimidation, indecency and misogyny." It seems telling that the rise of the far right and the fall of truthful news were to a meaningful extent engineered by a television network that was also a miserable one-man brothel. But that old right-wing men are misogynists is about as surprising as the fact that alligators bite.

Clinton was constantly berated for qualities rarely mentioned in male politicians, including ambition—something, it's safe to assume, she has in common with everyone who has ever run for elected office. *Psychology Today* called her, in a headline, "pathologically ambitious." She was criticized for having a voice. While Bernie Sanders railed and Trump screamed and snickered, the Fox commentator Brit Hume complained about Clinton's "sharp, lecturing tone," which, he said, was "not so attractive." And while MSNBC's Lawrence O'Donnell gave her public instructions on how to use a microphone, Bob Woodward bitched that she was "screaming" and Bob Cusack, the editor of the political newspaper *The Hill*, said, "When Hillary Clinton raises her voice, she loses." One could get the impression that a woman should campaign in a sultry whisper, but of course if she did that she would not project power. But if she did project power she would fail as a woman, since power, in this framework, is a male prerogative, which is to say that the setup was not intended to include women.

As Sady Doyle noted, "She can't be sad or angry, but she *also* can't be happy or amused, and she also *can't refrain from expressing any of those emotions.* There is literally no way out of this one. Anything she does is wrong." One merely had to imagine a woman candidate doing what Trump did, from lying to leering, to understand what latitude masculinity possesses. "No advanced step taken by women has been so bitterly contested as that of speaking in public," Susan B. Anthony said in 1900. "For nothing which they have attempted, not even to secure the suffrage, have they been so abused, condemned and antagonized." Or as Mary Beard put it last year, "We have never escaped a certain male cultural desire for women's silence."

Trump harped on the theme that Clinton had been in power for thirty years, seeming to equate her with feminism or liberalism or some other inchoate force that he intended to defeat, and in these narratives her power seemed huge and transcendent, looming over the nation the way he'd loomed over her in the second debate. By figures on both the right and the left, Clinton was held to be more responsible for her husband's policies than he was, more responsible for the war in Iraq than the rarely mentioned Bush administration, responsible for Obama's policies as though he had carried out her agenda rather than his own. The narratives cast her as a demoness with unlimited powers, or as a wicked woman, because she had had power and aspired to have power again. One got the impression that any power a woman had was too much, and that a lot of men found women very scary.

The very existence of Clinton seemed to infuriate a lot of people, as it has since at least 1992. It's complicated to talk about misogyny and Clinton, because she is a complex figure who has been many things over the decades. There are certainly reasons to disagree with and dislike things she has said and done, but that doesn't explain the overwrought emotionality that swirls around her. Raised as a conservative (and hated on the left during this campaign for having been a "Goldwater Girl," though she stumped for him as a nonvoting high school student), she soon became a radical who campaigned for the most left-leaning Democratic candidates in 1968 and 1972; registered Latino voters in Texas in the latter election; wrote a thesis on Saul Alinsky, who afterward offered her a job; advocated for rights for women and children; and shifted right in the 1980s, perhaps to adapt to her husband's home state of Arkansas or to the Reagan era.

You could pick out a lot of feminist high points and corporate and neoliberal low points in her career, but for anyone more interested in the future of the U.S. and the world her 2016 platform seemed most relevant, though no one seemed to know anything about it. The main networks devoted thirty-two minutes to the candidates' platforms in their hundreds of hours of election coverage.[2] Lots of politicians have been disliked for their policies and positions, but Clinton's were often close to Sanders's, and similar to or to the left of those of every high-profile male Democrat in recent years, including her husband, Obama, Biden, Kerry, and Dean. But what was accepted or disliked in them was an outrage in her, and whatever resentment they elicited was faint compared to the hysterical rage that confronted her as, miraculously, she continued to march forward.

Trump's slogan "Make America great again" seemed to invoke a return to a never-never land of white male supremacy where coal was an awesome fuel, blue-collar manufacturing jobs were what they had been in 1956, women belonged in the home, and the needs of white men were paramount. After the election, many on the left joined in the chorus, assuring us that Clinton lost because she hadn't paid enough attention to the so-called white working class, which, given that she wasn't being berated for ignoring women, seemed to be a euphemism for "white men." These men were more responsible than any group for Trump's victory (63 percent of them voted for him, 31 percent for Clinton).

One might argue she lost because of the disenfranchisement of millions of people of color through long-plotted Republican strategies: cutting the number of polling stations; limiting voting hours; harassing and threatening would-be voters; introducing voter-ID laws such as the Crosscheck Program, which made it a lot harder for people of color to register to vote. Or because of the FBI's intervention in the election; or because of years of negative media coverage; or because of foreign inter-vention designed to sabotage her chances; or because of misogyny. But instead we heard two stories about why she lost (and almost none about why, despite everything, she won the popular vote by a margin that kept growing until by year's end it reached almost three million).

The We Must Pay More Attention to the White Working Class analysis said that Clinton lost because she did not pay enough atten-tion to white men, since the revived term "white working class" seemed to be a nostalgic reference to industrial workers as they once existed. Those wielding it weren't interested in the 37 percent of Americans who aren't white, or the 51 percent who are women. I've always had the impression—from TV, movies, newspapers, sport, books, my education, my personal life, and my knowledge of who owns most things and holds government office at every level in my country—that white men get a lot of attention already.

The other story was about white women, who voted 43 percent for Clinton to 53 percent for Trump. The general idea was that white men deserved sympathy but white women deserved scorn for voting for Trump, on the grounds that all women, but only women, should be feminists. That there are a lot of women in the United States who are not feminists is not surprising. To be a feminist you have to believe in your equality and rights, which can make your life unpleasant and dangerous if you live in a marriage, a family, a community, a church, a state, that does not agree with you about this. For many women it's safer not to have those thoughts in this country, where the National Coalition Against Domestic Violence reports that a woman is beaten or assaulted every nine seconds. And those thoughts are not so available in a country where feminism is forever being demonized and distorted. It seems it's also worse to vote for a racist if you're a woman, because while white women were excoriated, white men were let off the hook (across every racial category, more men than women voted for Trump; overall 54 percent of women supported Clinton; 53 percent of men voted for Trump).

So women were hated for not having gender loyalty. But here's the fun thing about being a woman: we were also hated for having gender loyalty. Women were accused of voting with their reproductive parts if they favored the main female candidate, though most men throughout American history have favored male candidates without being

accused of voting with their penises. Penises were only discussed during a Republican primary debate, when Marco Rubio suggested
Trump's was small and Trump boasted that it wasn't. "I don't vote with
my vagina," the actress Susan Sarandon announced, and voted for
the Green Party candidate, Jill Stein, who one might think was just
as vagina-y a candidate as Clinton but apparently wasn't.

"One of the many lessons of the recent presidential election campaign and its repugnant outcome," Mark Lilla wrote in *The New York
Times,* "is that the age of identity liberalism must be brought to an
end," and he condemned Clinton for calling out explicitly to African-
American, Latino, LGBTQ, and women voters at every stop. "This,"
he said, "was a strategic mistake. If you are going to mention groups
in America, you had better mention all of them." Who's not on that
list, though it's one that actually covers the majority of Americans?
Heterosexual white men, notably, since it's hard to imagine Lilla was
put out that Clinton neglected Asians and Native Americans.

"Identity politics" is a disparaging term for talking about race or
gender or sexual orientation, which is very much the way we've talked
about liberation over the last 160 years in the U.S. By that measure
Frederick Douglass, Harriet Tubman, Elizabeth Cady Stanton, Susan
B. Anthony, Ida B. Wells, Rosa Parks, Bella Abzug, Ella Baker, Bayard
Rustin, Malcolm X, Del Martin, and Harvey Milk were just lowly
practitioners of identity politics, which we've been told to get
over. Shortly after the election Sanders, who'd got on the no-identity-
politics bandwagon, explained: "It is not good enough to say, 'Hey,
I'm a Latina, vote for me.' That is not good enough. I have to know
whether that Latina is going to stand up with the working class of
this country . . . It is not good enough for someone to say: 'I'm a
woman, vote for me.' No, that's not good enough."

In fact, Clinton never said this, though one could argue that
Trump had said, incessantly, aggressively, *I'm a white man, vote for me,*
and even that Sanders implicitly conveyed that message. *Vox* journalist

David Roberts did a word-frequency analysis on Clinton's campaign speeches and concluded that she mostly talked about workers, jobs, education, and the economy, exactly the things she was berated for neglecting. She mentioned jobs almost six hundred times, and racism, women's rights, and abortion a few dozen times each. But she was assumed to be talking about her gender all the time, though it was everyone else who couldn't shut up about it.

How the utopian idealism roused by Sanders's promises last winter morphed so quickly into a Manichean hatred of Clinton as the anti-Bernie is one of the mysteries of this mysteriously horrific election, but it was so compelling that many people seemed to wake up from the Democratic primary only when Trump won; they had until then believed Clinton was still running against Sanders. Or they believed that she was an inevitable presence, like Mom, and so they could hate her with confidence, and she would win anyway. Many around me loved Sanders with what came to seem an unquestioning religious devotion and hated Clinton even more fervently. The hatred on the right spilled over into actual violence over and over again at Trump rallies, but the left had its share of vitriol.

I had seen all around me a mob mentality, an irrational groupthink that fed on itself, confirmed itself, and punished doubt, opposition, or complexity. I thought of the two-minute group hate sessions in *1984*:

> *The horrible thing about the Two Minutes Hate was not that one was obliged to act a part, but, on the contrary, that it was impossible to avoid joining in. Within thirty seconds any pretence was always unnecessary. A hideous ecstasy of fear and vindictiveness, a desire to kill, to torture, to smash faces in with a sledgehammer, seemed to flow through the whole group of people like an electric current, turning one even against one's will into a grimacing, screaming lunatic. And yet the rage that one felt was an abstract,*

undirected emotion which could be switched from one object to another like the flame of a blowlamp.

That emotion was directed at Clinton, and was ready to swerve toward anyone who supported her, accompanied by accusations of treason and other kinds of invective. When *Harper's Magazine* posted its election-aftermath cover with a picture of Trump behind bars (and my name on it) on Facebook, an angry Sanders devotee jumped in right away: "I am tired of being reminded of how people like Rebecca Solnit gave us a Donald Trump presidency and now have the gall to talk about 'stopping him.' " And then she addressed me directly: "You supported Hillary with your silence. You supported Hillary by never calling her out for what she is. You may not have said it out loud, but it was clear. . . . You supported Hillary. [By the way], the Hillary campaign [*sic*] use of her sex as a selling point made me sick." The writer evidently believed, as many did, that since (of course) Sanders would have defeated Trump, supporting Clinton even by not loudly supporting Sanders was criminal. (She didn't explain how the criminality continued when Sanders was no longer a candidate.) The fury from the Sanders camp came from plenty of women, including this one, though most of the personal venom directed at me came from men.

Many supporters fell silent or took to supporting her in secret, which is not the kind of support a candidate needs. San Franciscan Jacqueline Smay wrote to me in December:

Every woman I know and almost every journalist or opinion writer who planned to vote for her included in every single positive statement about her—everything from Facebook posts to lengthy major media articles—something to the effect of "She is of course not a perfect candidate, but . . ." or "I of course have serious problems with some aspects of her record, but . . ." It became the boilerplate you had to include to forestall the worst of the rage-trolls (inevitably eventually someone would pop up anyway to accuse you of trying to shove your queen's coronation down everyone's throat, but at least the boilerplate delayed it).

"I've come to believe," Sady Doyle wrote, "that, in some ways, saying nice things about Hillary Clinton is a subversive act."

Mentioning that she'd won the popular vote upset many of the men I am in contact with, though they would not or could not conceive it that way. I wrote this at the time: "With their deep belief in their own special monopoly on objectivity, slightly too many men assure me that there is no misogyny in their subjective assessments or even no subjectivity and no emotion driving them, and there are no grounds for other opinions since theirs is not an opinion." Then these men went back to talking about what a loser Clinton was. There was considerable evidence that we had not had a free and fair election, evidence that might have allowed us to contest it and to stop Trump. But these men of the left were so dedicated to Clinton's status as a loser that they apparently wanted Trump to win, because it vindicated something that went deeper than their commitment to almost anything else.

If you did not think Trump was good for life on earth, addressing the delegitimizing influence of Russian intervention in the election and collusion on the part of Trump and his henchmen seemed like a useful thing to do. But, curiously, many on what was supposed to be the left were furious to deny it and smack down those of us who tried. From autumn of 2016 into the spring of 2017, they went hard after the very idea that there was evidence of Russian intervention or that Julian Assange and Wikileaks had anything to do with Russia. Some put forth a strangely antique notion that not thinking nice thoughts about Russia was McCarthyism or red scare or a revival of the Cold War. Many insisted on simplistic frameworks: If the United States was a bad country, then countries opposing it were not bad, or if U.S. intelligence had lied to the public in the past, it always lied (though the case, as *Washington Post* journalist Anne Applebaum pointed out early on, could stand without the intelligence agencies' input), or that if you hated Trump or thought the election was messed up, you loved not truth, nor consequences, but Clinton.

The highly gendered term "hysteria" was used over and over, and indeed many of the people who spoke up most powerfully about it early on—journalists Sarah Kendzior, Summer Brennan, Anne Applebaum, Democratic Party activists Andrea and Alexandra Chalupa, among others—were women, and the most furious merchants of doubt were prominent left-wing male media stars. Even six months later, men were reciting to me the tautological argument that Clinton lost because she was a loser, with almost erotic or religious fervor. They objected to any other interpretation, though by that time the Russian role was undeniable and seemed to be, as I had thought in the fall, the best lever for undermining the new administration.

Trump was a candidate so weak that his victory needed the disenfranchisement of millions of voters of color, the end of the Voting Rights Act, a long-running right-wing campaign to make Clinton's use of a private email server—surely the dullest and most uneventful scandal in history—an epic crime, the late intervention, with apparent intent to sabotage, of the FBI director James Comey, as well as aggressive intervention from and, most likely, Trump-team collusion with Russia. We found out via Comey's outrageous gambit that it is more damaging to be a woman who has an aide who has an estranged husband who is a creep than actually to be a predator who has been charged by more than a dozen women with groping and sexual assault.

Hillary Clinton was all that stood between us and a reckless, unstable, ignorant, inane, infinitely vulgar, climate-change-denying white-nationalist misogynist with authoritarian ambitions and kleptocratic plans. A lot of people, particularly white men, could not bear her, and that is as good a reason as any for Trump's victory. Over and over again, I heard men declare that she had failed to make them vote for her. They saw the loss as hers rather than ours, and they blamed her for it, as though election was a gift they withheld from her because she did not deserve it or did not attract them, rather than that voting was a decision we each made about the fate of the world. They did not blame themselves or the electorate or the system for failing to stop Trump.

1. Emily Jane Fox, "Bad Blood? Donald Trump and Roger Ailes Reportedly No Longer Speak," *The Hive*, May 25, 2017. Accessed on June 6, 2017, at http://www.vanityfair.com/news/2016/10/roger-ailes-donald-trump-no-longer-speak?mbid=social_twitter.

2. Andrew Tyndall, *Tyndall Report*, October 25, 2016. Accessed on June 6, 2017, at http://tyndallreport.com/comment/20/5778/.

THE PATHOLOGY OF DONALD TRUMP

Sady Doyle

THERE HAS PROBABLY never been a more frightening president than Donald Trump. Above and beyond his terrible politics, there's a visceral sense of something *off* about the guy, some uncanny-valley quality to how he moves. You fear Trump with your gut, on instinct, before you can put the threat into words.

It hit me in the second presidential debate, when Trump, evidently peeved by the fact that his opponent, Hillary Clinton, was allowed any speaking time whatsoever, left his corner of the stage and began stomping toward Clinton while her back was turned, face visibly contorted with anger. *Oh my God,* I thought, bracing myself against my chair. *He's going to do it. He's actually going to hit her.*

He didn't. But the fact that I thought he would—that I had fully expected a U.S. presidential debate to devolve into a fistfight, for even one split second—crystallized my reaction to Trump, and shed some light on the air of threat that surrounds him. It lies in the sense that anything is possible; there are no norms tempering his cruelty. There is nothing to stop him from going too far.

No presidential candidate would ever think of posting a picture of his opponent's wife on Twitter and encouraging his supporters to mock her looks—but Trump did just that to Heidi Cruz. No decent human would ever boast about sexually assaulting women—but Trump was caught on tape giggling about it with Billy Bush. And no one who genuinely repented committing or joking about sexual assault would then dismiss women who'd come forward to accuse him of sexual assault by claiming they were too ugly for him—but Trump did exactly that to a *People* reporter who accused him of backing her against the wall and kissing her by force during an assignment. ("She said I made *inappropriate advances* to her . . . You take a look, take a look at her, look at her words. I don't *think* so.")[1] And who would self-derail in the middle of a serious political campaign to re-litigate decades-old celebrity feuds with Rosie O'Donnell or Alicia Machado? Who would repeat bizarre conspiracy theories about his opponents— Ted Cruz's father killed JFK, Barack Obama "is the founder of ISIS"[2]—on a national stage, in full seriousness? Who is that dishonest, that thin-skinned, that ruthlessly, personally cruel; who could be so clearly and entirely driven by a desire to humiliate and dominate anyone who so much as questioned him? Leaving politics out of the equation as far as possible, focusing solely on how this one man treats the other human beings in his life: What kind of guy *does* this shit?

As it turned out, many women knew exactly what kind of guy would do this shit. They'd met that guy, at least once, sometimes many times over; they'd seen what he was capable of, and how he got away with it. That giddy, sickening, snapped-elevator-cable feeling that Trump gave off—the sense that there were no rules anymore, that anything could happen at any time—was one they were familiar with, one they'd felt when other angry men came toward them in other rooms.

Yet, by the end of his first two weeks in office, the media and the Democrats had produced a new official explanation for who Trump was, and why, and it had very little to do with the testimony of those women. Donald Trump, they proclaimed, was crazy.

"Then there is the obvious question of the president's mental and psychological health. I know we're not supposed to bring this up—but it is staring us brutally in the face,"[3] wrote Andrew Sullivan on February 10. "This man is off his rocker. He's deranged; he's bizarrely living in an alternative universe; he's delusional . . . At the core of the administration of the most powerful country on earth, there is, instead, madness."

Sullivan, as it turns out, has never graduated medical school, or received any kind of certification as a mental health professional. But this did not stop his diagnosis from ricocheting across the blogosphere, or meaningfully distinguishing him from the hordes of other journalists coming to the same conclusions. *Mother Jones* blogger Kevin Drum approvingly quoted Sullivan in a piece entitled "Will the White House Send Donald Trump over the Edge Into Madness?" ("[Before] this year he was mainly in the entertainment industry, where his delusions were more or less harmless . . . We don't know how Trump's fragile psyche will respond to continuous rolling disasters[.]"[4]) Investigative reporter Kurt Eichenwald tweeted that "I believe Trump was institutionalized in a mental hospital for a nervous breakdown in 1990,"[5] before retracting the tweet and admitting that he had no evidence of such a hospital stay. Sometimes Trump's mental illness was so severe that it was said to afflict his entire administration: "Are Donald Trump and his acolytes sinister or just crazy?"[6] *Maclean's* magazine wondered.

This quickly became the most widely accepted way for critics to speak about the Trump administration and its terrors: as a medical catastrophe, a case of pathology becoming policy. This line was not just mean gossip or blog fodder; it informed real political action. Democrats openly aspired to use the Twenty-Fifth Amendment to declare Trump mentally unfit and thus remove him from office—seemingly ignoring that the Constitution required the co-operation of "the Vice President and a majority of either the principal officers of the executive departments or of such other body as Congress,"[7] meaning that both Pence and Trump's own cabinet would have to turn on him for this play to work. Representative Ted Lieu (D-CA) introduced a bill that would require Trump to work under the supervision of a White House psychiatrist ("we're now in the 21st century. Mental health is just as important as physical health," Lieu said, before proclaiming that "it is very clear [Trump] has a disconnection from the truth" and that he was "a danger to the republic").[8] Representative Jason Chaffetz (R-UT) announced he would support legislation forcing Trump to undergo psychiatric evaluation ("if you're going to have your hands on the nuclear codes, you should probably know what kind of mental state you're in").[9]

There was just one problem with this: no one had any proof that Trump was ill. There were no medical records to examine; none of his doctors had given testimony on his mental status. So not only did Trump not know what "mental state" he was in, neither did Jason Chaffetz, or Andrew Sullivan, or anyone else. Nor would any credible doctors have provided such proof, even if they had it. Since 1973, the American Psychiatric Association's code of ethics has forbidden its members to give "professional opinions" on celebrities they have not personally treated: "In such circumstances, a psychiatrist may share with the public his or her expertise about psychiatric issues in general. However, it is unethical for a psychiatrist to offer a professional opinion unless he or she has conducted an examination and has been granted proper authorization for such a statement."[10] Even if the psychiatrist has treated the public figure in question, the patient would need to give consent for his or her diagnosis to be shared with the media.

Yet not all the medical ethics in the world could dissuade the mounting army of journalists producing Trump mental-health clickbait, who were increasingly certain not only that the president was insane, but that they knew precisely which kind of insane he was. The diagnosis most often given from afar was Narcissistic Personality Disorder, a disease characterized by grandiosity, hypersensitivity to criticism, and a lack of empathy. NPD, as a medical diagnosis, was so controversial that it was nearly removed from the *Diagnostic and Statistical Manual of Mental Disorders.* But "narcissist," as an epithet, is so trendy that it had been applied to nearly every polarizing public figure of recent years. As Kristin Dombek wrote in *The Selfishness of Others,* her book on the narcissism craze: "Narcissism is the favorite diagnosis for political leaders in whatever party opposes one's own— either Paul Ryan is a narcissist, or Nancy Pelosi is—and for policies: either the Affordable Care Act is narcissistic, or the privatization of Medicare is. Among the many presidential narcissism memes in circulation is one that superimposes over President Obama's face the DSM's entire, lengthy definition of NPD."[11]

No one could deny that Trump was, indeed, grandiose and hostile to criticism. But the press corps's attempts to find diagnostic evidence verged on cringe comedy. "Trump's shortage of empathy can be seen clearly by his stances on topics like immigration," *Raw Story* noted, adding that "[when] he thought he had been treated unfairly by Fox News host and Republican debate moderator Megyn Kelly, he responded by calling her a 'bimbo' and later saying that she had 'blood coming out of her eyes, blood coming out of her wherever.' . . . If the news host would have pegged him as a bona fide narcissist from the beginning she might have expected such shamelessly flagrant behavior."[12] Of course, Trump's immigration policies and sexist comments were also evidence of, well, racism and sexism, both of which are common traits in conservative politicians; if anti-immigrant rhetoric is a sign of NPD, then the disease has afflicted every Republican politician since 1994.

Meanwhile, over at *Vanity Fair,* psychotherapist Charlotte Prozan insisted that Trump was "easy to diagnose": "'You're fired!' would certainly come under lack of empathy,"[13] she noted. And it might, if it were not also a catchphrase on a reality-competition show, a genre where it is traditional for contestants to be eliminated via kicky catchphrase at least once per episode; as it stands, Prozan leaves the reader to wonder whether she also believes Ted Allen's frequent repetitions of "You've been *Chopped*" are a sign of his unchecked homicidal tendencies.

Perhaps the most bizarre example came when *Mic* sought out "body language experts" to analyze Trump's handshake with Japanese prime minister Shinzō Abe. "The extra pat Trump does with his left hand is actually a narcissistic tendency," *Mic* reported, quoting "political psychologist" Bart Rossi as saying that "[Trump] is making more of the handshake to enhance himself and make himself look extra good."[14]

Of course, in the midst of all this, there was the still, small voice of one Dr. Allen Frances. "I wrote DSM criteria for Narcissistic Personality Disorder," he tweeted. "Trump doesn't meet them. He's [a] terrible person & classic schmuck—not mentally ill."[15] And: "Somehow comforting to see all bad behavior as mental illness. Trump gets mislabeled this way as do mass murderers & terrorists. Bad, not mad."[16] And: "Psychiatric name calling will never stop Trump & distracts from what will—concerted political action."[17]

On the other hand, did you see that handshake? Patting with the left hand! While shaking with the right! *Insanity!!!!*

Rules against armchair-diagnosing politicians exist for good, solid reasons, none of which are about defending the honor of Donald J. Trump. The most famous precedent, and the case the APA rule is named after, is that of Republican presidential candidate Barry Goldwater. In 1963, a magazine called *Fact* sent out a survey to over 12,300 psychiatrists, asking whether they believed Goldwater was psychologically fit to be president—then ran a full-page headline on its cover, proclaiming that "1,189 Psychiatrists Say Goldwater Is Psychologically Unfit to Be President!"[18] This number represented less than one in ten of the psychiatrists surveyed, but that didn't matter to people who saw the *Fact* cover at a newsstand. Nor did it matter to Barry Goldwater, who lost the election and successfully sued *Fact* for libel.

This isn't just a problem for right-wing candidates. A similar fate befell Democratic candidate Michael Dukakis in his 1988 presidential campaign. When news broke that his brother Stelian had been hospitalized following a suicide attempt, Dukakis was hounded with questions about his own "mental stability" and fitness for office. This was spectacularly cruel, especially since the most damning rumor was that Dukakis had seen a therapist to cope with Stelian's unexpected death in a hit-and-run. Ultimately, he was forced to release a letter from his doctor, stating that "he has had no psychological symptoms, complaints or treatment."[19]

The breaking point was a nasty joke from sitting president Ronald Reagan; when asked if he thought Dukakis should release medical records, Reagan simply smiled and said, "Look, I'm not going to pick on an invalid."[20] Reagan likely had early Alzheimer's at the time, and his own aides had discussed removing him from office under the Twenty-Fifth Amendment during the Iran-Contra scandal—but no one knew that, and so he was able to play the part of a sane man dunking on a lunatic. Dukakis lost the election to George Bush, and now works with his wife, Kitty, as an advocate against mental health stigma.

Which is all to say: people very rarely raise questions about a politician's mental health out of genuine concern for that politician. These accusations are made to destroy, discredit, and degrade the targets; they undermine credibility by invoking our cultural stereotypes of the mentally ill as inherently immoral, or evil, or violent, or untrustworthy, or stupid, or just plain weak. That damage can never be confined to "deserving" politicians, because everyone has a different idea of who is "deserving." For every Goldwater, there is a Dukakis; for every meme about Trump's NPD, there is a meme about Obama's—or, for that matter, a meme about Hillary Clinton, whose own apocryphal "brain injury" or "seizure disorder" was frequently invoked by Republicans when she ran against Trump.

Some of the people who invoke these stereotypes may even believe that their targets are ill, but that does not change the fact that this is essentially a political tactic, and that the accused seem "crazy" primarily because they have different politics than their accusers. Call it the *Psycho* effect: when pop culture spends decades portraying mentally ill people as killers, monsters, and villains, every real-life villain starts to look mentally ill.

The effect is exaggerated when it comes to Trump, because he does fit many aspects of the stereotype. He genuinely is untrustworthy, for example: he lies constantly, about everything from the size of his inauguration crowd to the prevalence of voter fraud in U.S. elections to a series of imaginary terrorist attacks that the news media supposedly "refuses" to report. He frequently does seem stupid: when asked about his favorite books, Trump assured his interviewer that "I like a lot of books. I like reading books,"[21] but was unable to name one. *The New York Times* reported that Trump had requested that his standard three-to-six-page policy option papers be shrunk down to single-page documents that were primarily composed of graphics. Most important, Trump is immoral, and he is—by many accounts, including his own—violent. If you define "evil" as intentionally, needlessly, and remorselessly causing pain, then Trump is an evil man.

But that's exactly why Donald Trump should not become any kind of mascot for mental illness. He fits the "crazy villain" stereotype so well that he winds up resembling very few crazy people in real life. He does, however, resemble many other evil men—not anomalously, spectacularly evil men, but a banal variety that many of us encounter in our daily lives. Trump is less an outlier than he is a rational outcome of the society that made him, an exceptionally skilled practitioner of the villainy practiced by sane men every day.

He is also exceptionally successful. Those diagnosing Trump from afar, Allen Frances wrote, "ignore the further requirement that is crucial in defining all mental disorders—the behaviors also must cause clinically significant distress or impairment. Trump is clearly a man singularly without distress and his behaviors consistently reap him fame, fortune, women, and now political power. He has been generously rewarded, not at all impaired by it."[22]

This is the possibility that may be hardest to accept: that Donald J. Trump is fully, hideously sane, and the scope of his wrongdoing is grim proof of exactly how sane he is. It's not a comforting idea. But it is backed up by at least as much evidence as the tale of Trump's top-secret NPD. So try to entertain the possibility, if only for as long as it takes to read one essay, that Trump is not crazy. And, if you want to know what "mental illness" looks like, start by looking to the women at the end of his fist.

One of the most significant stories of the Trump campaign was also one of the earliest. In July 2015, before voting began in the Republican primaries, *The Daily Beast* wrote that Ivana Trump had accused her ex-husband of raping her. According to the story, Trump was recovering from scalp-reduction surgery to minimize a bald spot. He'd gotten the procedure from Ivana's surgeon. Apparently, Trump was so furious about the results that he pinned his wife by the arms and "began to pull out fistfuls of hair from her scalp, as if to mirror the pain he felt from his own operation."[23] He then took her clothes off and penetrated her, while continuing to rip out her hair.

Ivana used the word "rape" to describe the encounter to friends and in her divorce deposition, though she backpedaled after the divorce, saying simply that "as a woman, I felt violated" and that "I do not want my words to be interpreted in a literal or criminal sense."[24] It could be that Ivana genuinely felt she had exaggerated. Then again, her caution could also be the predictable after-effect of an encounter with Trump's legal team. Not only did Trump's attorney Michael Cohen inform *The Daily Beast* that "by the very definition, you can't rape your spouse" (spoiler: you can), he added that "[you] write a story that has Mr. Trump's name in it, with the word 'rape,' and I'm going to mess your life up . . . for as long as you're on this frickin' planet . . . you're going to have judgments against you, so much money, you'll never know how to get out from underneath it."[25]

More stories piled up over the course of the election: There was the infamous *Access Hollywood* tape, where Trump claimed that "when you're famous, they let you do it. Grab [women] by the pussy, you can do anything."[26] There was the *People* reporter's account of being cornered and kissed against her will in his home; there was the British businesswoman who claimed he'd grabbed her breasts and tried to force his hand up her skirt while she sat next to him on a plane. There was Alicia Machado, who testified that, during her term as Miss Universe, he'd taunted her about her race and weight until she developed an eating disorder. By the end of his campaign, twenty-four women had come forward to accuse him of some degree of sexual harassment or assault. But all those stories, no matter how grotesque they were, did nothing more than to confirm what many women had already learned from Ivana Trump.

Even as the "Trump is mentally ill" narrative was gaining steam, many women were beginning to process Trump through a different frame entirely: as *abusive*. "Donald Trump Is a Textbook Abuser, and Women Everywhere Know It,"[27] ran one article in *The Nation*. *Vox* ran a video analysis, listing all the emotionally abusive tactics Trump had used (humiliation, deflection, threats, intimidation, etc.) in the second presidential debate alone.[28] "Donald Trump Is Triggering,"[29] *Cosmopolitan* reported; *Slate* ran a piece on "The Triggered Electorate,"[30] and specifically on sexual-assault survivors who were reliving their trauma as the result of witnessing his campaign.

As it turned out, nearly everything strange and disquieting about Trump—his punitive response to even mild criticism, his viscerally personal insults disguised as "jokes," his willingness to spread wild rumors about his targets in order to discredit or shame them, his inability to stop lashing out or degrading certain women years after they'd left his life—was also a commonly reported behavior of domestic abusers. Even Trump's famed dishonesty, the most frequently cited proof of his detachment from reality, made more sense when viewed as "gaslighting," the abusive tactic of controlling the victim's perception of reality in order to escape accountability. The only clear difference between Trump and an emotionally abusive partner was that, instead of using these tactics to accumulate power and dominance in a relationship, Trump was using them to accumulate power on the world stage.

Here's the problem: the vast majority of abusers are not mentally ill; they just try to look that way. Lundy Bancroft, a behavioral counselor for abusive men, writes that many victims initially believe their partners are "crazy"; it seems like the only explanation for what looks like paranoia, mood swings, and a tendency to violently "lose control" for no reason. In fact, the myth of "losing it," the belief that the abusers didn't mean to do any harm and sincerely regret it, is exactly what leads most victims to forgive and stay with their abusers after the initial assault.

Yet, Bancroft writes, most abusers only "lose control" when they choose to: not with their bosses, or their friends, but only with their chosen victims. They also "lose control" repeatedly without being caught, divorced, dumped, or jailed. That requires a complex, logical thought process; even as the abuser is screaming his head off or ripping out fistfuls of hair, Bancroft writes, "his mind maintains awareness of a number of questions: 'Am I doing something other people could find out about, so it could make me look bad? Am I doing anything that could get me in legal trouble? Could I get hurt myself? Am I doing anything that I myself consider too gross, cruel, or violent?' "[31] One case study in Bancroft's book would beat his wife until the moment the police arrived, then immediately switch on a calm, cheerful demeanor when speaking to them. His wife, meanwhile, couldn't switch off her tears or anger; her obvious distress would make her seem crazy, and the cops would leave without making an arrest.

Abusers are not crazed, irrational fonts of random violence. They are almost always rational people who make a game of figuring out exactly where the boundaries are—how far they can go, and how much harm they can inflict, without getting caught or facing consequences—and then seeing how far they can bend those rules without breaking them. Go back to that moment in the second debate, Trump careening toward Clinton with rage written all over his face. In retrospect, the single most important thing about that moment may have been the fact that Trump *didn't* hit Clinton. He simply conveyed that he could hit her, and even that he wanted to hit her, with such force that it landed like a real blow—without breaking any rules, or engaging in any violence that would have gotten him arrested or removed from the stage.

A man in the throes of uncontrollable emotion, let alone psychosis, would not or could not pull off such a finely calibrated threat. But a clear-headed abuser, invoking his alpha-male status to shut down and belittle a female opponent, could and did.

This is not to say that mental illness and abuse are unrelated. They have a very clear relationship: abuse causes mental illness all the time.

As per Bancroft, "the emotional effects of partner violence are a factor in more than one-fourth of female suicide attempts and are a leading cause of substance abuse in adult women."[32] Between 54 to 84 percent of domestic violence survivors have post-traumatic stress disorder; 38 percent to 75 percent develop anxiety symptoms, and 63 percent to 77 percent develop depression.[33]

Sexual violence carries much the same toll. The average rape survivor has somewhere between a 50 and 95 percent chance of developing

PTSD.[34] Women who are raped or sexually assaulted while underage are "about three times more likely to suffer from psychological disorders and over four times more likely to suffer from drug and alcohol abuse in adulthood," as per the Medical School of Virginia; Commonwealth University,[35] RAINN, the Rape, Abuse & Incest National Network, lists the after-effects of sexual abuse as including "flashbacks," "dissociation," "depression," "substance abuse," "eating disorders," and "suicide."[36]

Think back to Alicia Machado, berated and ritually humiliated by her boss until she began throwing up her food. This isn't the story of a sick man picking on a sane woman; it's a story about a sane man picking on a woman until he made her sick. In fact, Machado had experienced symptoms of anorexia and bulimia before she met Trump—he didn't create her illness from scratch, but he did take advantage of her vulnerability to aggravate her symptoms.

This is important, because, as women's mental illnesses escalate in severity—leaving the relatively well-understood realms of depression and anxiety, and entering the deeper waters of schizophrenia and bipolar disorder—women don't become any more likely to abuse, or to commit violent crimes. But they do become more likely to *experience* violence. One 2014 study by University College and Kings College, London, determined that 21 percent of neurotypical women surveyed had been sexually assaulted as adults—a number that's more or less consistent with the commonly cited statistic of one in four or one in five. But for women with severe mental illness, the rate of adulthood sexual assault nearly tripled, standing at 61 percent. Not only were the assaults more common, they were more severe: 40 percent of mentally ill women, versus 7 percent of non–mentally ill women, reported experiencing rape or attempted rape.[37]

If abusive and sexually violent men make a game of finding and bending the rules, then it should be no surprise that they are also canny enough to target women with preexisting vulnerabilities. One illustrative case comes from a sixty-three-year-old woman in Maryland. She had schizoaffective disorder, and experienced levels of anxiety so high that she had severe trouble leaving the house. In order to improve, she practiced going for short walks. But, on those walks, she was unfortunate enough to meet Myles Bowersox, who spoke to her for long enough that he was able to figure out where she lived. Following a fight with his girlfriend, Bowersox drove back to the woman's apartment, broke in, and raped her. The woman's symptoms returned with such severity that, by the time of her trial, she was not only terrified of the outdoors, she could not speak to testify. She'd managed to make a 911 call before she shut down, and that was all that saved her.

Once again, no matter how "crazy" Bowersox's violence looked, it followed a logical pattern. He didn't rape his girlfriend, for one thing. She knew more about him; she had been seen with him; she would find it easier to report him, and even within a rape culture that automatically doubts women's testimony, she had a better chance of being believed. Instead, when Bowersox was angry at one woman, he took out that anger by raping someone else—the most helpless woman he knew, the woman who would be the most easily intimidated and have the most trouble seeming credible, a woman that he likely thought would be unable to dial 911.

When we talk about prejudice against the mentally ill, we usually do so in highly sanitized terms. "Stigma," we say, or "representation." It can seem needlessly PC, or church-lady patronizing, a way of "being kind to the less fortunate." What we don't talk about is this: the nightmare of being targeted for violence, over and over, and of being told—every time you try to speak about it, and no matter what has happened—that *you* are the violent one. You are evil, you are a liar, you are unlovable, you are scary. There is something wrong with you, and no matter how hard you try, you will always be a monster. You should be put away, locked up. Nothing you say can be trusted. And even while people are recoiling from you in fear, more bad men come and go, hurting you with impunity and secure in the knowledge that you will never be believed.

That isn't "stigma." That's torture. So I ask you to imagine this, no less than I ask you to imagine the horror of Donald Trump's sanity: Imagine seeing your rapist, or your abuser, on television every day. Watching him get away with it, over and over, and becoming almost unimaginably powerful. Imagine being horrified by him in a new way every day, sometimes every hour. Now imagine everyone you know turning to you, tsk-tsking, and saying, *See? He's just like you.*

In the end, the discussion of Trump's craziness—like all such discussions—comes back to the question of *why*. If Trump is fully in touch with reality, then why is his behavior so continually out of line? If an abuser hasn't lost control, then why does he hit someone he claims to love? If evil people know that what they are doing is wrong, then why do it at all?

It's a disturbing question to contemplate, precisely because it does open up the possibility that evil is a rational choice for some people; that doing evil has real practical benefits, and that people can make a reasoned analysis of their situation and still decide to do terrible things. It also forces us to consider that we might be less innocent than we think. If Trump isn't crazy, then evil is less a medical condition than it is a series of decisions—and there is no test we can take, or pill we can swallow, or doctor's note we can provide, that prevents us from being evil ourselves. We all could be; if evil is a choice, we all *can* be, every day of our lives, just as Trump chooses every day to be who he is.

Bancroft and Frances, the domestic-abuse expert and the narcissism expert, seem to agree on one core insight—it's not crazy if it's working. No matter how shocking or out of control an abuser's behavior seems, it usually gets him what he wants: a one-sided relationship in which he holds all the power, and his partner has been fully intimidated into submission. No matter how horrifying Trump's abusive behavior might be, it also got him what he wanted: the presidency.

Progressives call Trump "crazy" for the same reason that we mistook him for a "weak candidate"—his values are so alien that it's impossible to imagine anyone sharing them. Left-wing publications have manufactured countless think pieces on the "economic anxiety" of the Trump voter, and how it led the white working class to excuse or ignore his racism, simply because we cannot imagine that anyone would see Trump's explicit racism as a positive quality. And yet, millions of people did. We cannot imagine that Trump physically intimidated his female opponent on a debate stage purposefully, because we assume it would backfire, or make people dislike him. But here's the thing: it didn't. In a nation where one in three women has experienced physical violence in a relationship,[38] it only stands to reason that there are millions of physically abusive men who saw that moment and were proud of Trump for handling an unruly woman. Those men vote, just like everyone else. Hillary Clinton got some sympathy, but Donald Trump got the job.

The politics of abuse are effective—effective enough that Trump's violence will now be played out structurally, as well as interpersonally. His flippant attitude toward sexual assault will be reflected not only in individual cases of abuse, but in how Title IX is construed to handle college rape cases. Mentally ill women will once again be targeted more intensively than neurotypical women, not just with "stigma" or by individual abusers, but by having their health care and access to medication ripped away with the repeal of the ACA, or by giving the entirely unqualified Ben Carson control of HUD, which provides disability housing for people like that Maryland woman.

These are genuinely violent acts, which result in real injury; without housing, up to 63 percent of mentally ill women are raped.[39] But they will never be seen as such as long as we use the term "mentally ill" as a convenient synonym for "violent" or "evil." If we keep conflating the mentally ill with their abusers, the American public will be too frightened or disdainful to help them, and their nightmare will never end.

As for Donald Trump: his values are more widely shared than most of us would ever want to believe, and his behavior is more common than it will ever feel safe to admit. As long as we keep insisting that Donald Trump is "other" or inhuman—not like us, not healthy, not normal—then we're blinding ourselves to the everyday evil of our neighbors, our coworkers, our family members, and all the countless anonymous men and women who think like Trump, behave like Trump, and gave Trump power as a means of giving it to themselves. We can keep calling him "crazy," but we shouldn't be surprised when that "craziness" turns out to be his safest option—nor can we claim innocence, when we turn out to have provided him with the excuse he'll use to get away with it once again.

----

1. Justin Baragona, " 'Look at Her!' Trump Dismisses *People* Reporter's Claims He Forcibly Kissed Her," *Mediaite*, October 13, 2016. Accessed at http://www .mediaite.com/election-2016/look-at-her-trump-dismisses-people-reporters -claims-he-forcibly-kissed-her/.

2. "Donald Trump: 'President Obama Is the Founder of Isis,'" *The Guardian*, August 11, 2016. Accessed at https://www.theguardian.com/us-news/video/2016 /aug/11/donald-trump-president-obama-is-the-founder-of-isis-video.

3. Andrew Sullivan, "The Madness of King Donald," *New York*, February 10, 2017. Accessed at http://nymag.com/daily/intelligencer/2017/02/andrew-sullivan-the -madness-of-king-donald.html.

4. Kevin Drum, "Will the White House Send Donald Trump over the Edge into Madness?" *Mother Jones*, February 10, 2017. Accessed at http://www.motherjones .com/kevin-drum/2017/02/will-white-house-send-donald-trump-over-edge -madness.

5. Paul Farhi, "A Reporter Tweets His Way into Trouble with a Claim About Trump That Lacked Evidence," *Washington Post*, September 14, 2016. Accessed

at https://www.washingtonpost.com/lifestyle/style/a-reporter-tweets-his-way-into
-trouble-with-a-claim-about-trump-that-lacked-evidence/2016/09/14/f8bd2a54
-7a95-11e6-beac-57a4a412e93a_story.html?utm_term=.f17fcbfd7353.

6. Terry Glavin, "Are Donald Trump and His Acolytes Sinister or Just Crazy?" *Maclean's,* February 10, 2017. Accessed at http://www.macleans.ca/politics
/washington/how-to-make-sense-of-trumpism.

7. U.S. Constitution: Twenty-Fifth Amendment, as archived at http://www.law
.cornell.edu/constitution/amendmentxxv.

8. Jennifer Bendery, "Congressman to File Bill Requiring a Psychiatrist at the White House," *Huffington Post,* February 8, 2017. Accessed at http://www
.huffingtonpost.com/entry/donald-trump-mental-health-ted-lieu_us
_589a4b70e4b0c1284f2930cd.

9. Ibid.

10. Maria A. Oquendo, M.D., "The Goldwater Rule: Why Breaking It Is Unethical and Irresponsible," American Psychiatric Association, August 3, 2016. Accessed at https://www.psychiatry.org/news-room/apa-blogs/apa-blog/2016/08
/the-goldwater-rule.

11. Kristin Dombek, *The Selfishness of Others: An Essay on the Fear of Narcissism* (New York: Farrar, Straus & Giroux, 2016), chapter 1.

12. Bobby Azarian, "A Neuroscientist Explains: Trump Has a Mental Disorder That Makes Him a Dangerous World Leader," *Raw Story,* January 18, 2017. Accessed at http://www.rawstory.com/2016/01/a-neuroscientist-explains-trump
-has-a-mental-disorder-that-makes-him-a-dangerous-world-leader.

13. Henry Alford, "Is Donald Trump Actually a Narcissist? Therapists Weigh In!" *Vanity Fair,* November 11, 2015. Accessed at http://www.vanityfair.com/news
/2015/11/donald-trump-narcissism-therapists.

14. Brianna Provenzano, "Donald Trump's Weird Handshake, Explained by Body Language Experts," Mic.com, February 10, 2017. Accessed at https://mic.com
/articles/168322/donald-trump-s-weird-handshake-explained-by-body
-language-experts#.SNKVeaxO6.

15. Allen Frances Twitter account, December 19, 2016. https://twitter.com
    /AllenFrancesMD/status/811038227595280384.

16. Allen Frances Twitter account, February 3, 2017: https://twitter.com/Allen
    FrancesMD/status/827653433381433344.

17. Allen Frances Twitter account, February 2, 2017: https://twitter.com/Allen
    FrancesMD/status/826940300266393600.

18. John D. Mayer, Ph.D., "Libel, in Fact . . . the 1189 Psychiatrists," *Psychology
    Today,* August 9, 2009. Accessed at https://www.psychologytoday.com/blog
    /the-personality-analyst/200908/libel-in-factthe-1189-psychiatrists.

19. Andrew Rosenthal, "Dukakis Releases Medical Details to Stop Rumors on
    Mental Health," *New York Times,* August 4, 1988. Accessed at http://www
    .nytimes.com/1988/08/04/us/dukakis-releases-medical-details-to-stop-rumors
    -on-mental-health.html.

20. Ibid.

21. Paul Constant, "I Like Reading Books," *Seattle Review of Books,* January 18,
    2017. Accessed at http://www.seattlereviewofbooks.com/notes/2017/01/18/i
    -like-reading-books/.

22. Allen J. Frances, M.D., "Trump Isn't Crazy," *Psychology Today,* January 31,
    2017. Accessed at https://www.psychologytoday.com/blog/saving-normal
    /201701/trump-isnt-crazy.

23. Tim Mark and Brandy Zadrozny, "Ex-Wife: Donald Trump Made Me Feel
    'Violated' During Sex," *Daily Beast,* July 27, 2015. Accessed at http://www
    .thedailybeast.com/articles/2015/07/27/ex-wife-donald-trump-made-feel
    -violated-during-sex.html.

24. Ibid.

25. Ibid.

26. Ben Mathis-Lilley, "Trump Was Recorded in 2005 Bragging About Grab-
    bing Women 'by the Pussy,'" *Slate,* October 7, 2016. Accessed at http://www

.slate.com/blogs/the_slatest/2016/10/07/donald_trump_2005_tape_i_grab
_women_by_the_pussy.html.

27. Ann Jones, "Donald Trump Is a Textbook Abuser, and Women Everywhere
Know It," *The Nation,* June 14, 2016. Accessed at https://www.thenation.com
/article/donald-trump-is-a-textbook-abuser-and-women-everywhere-know-it.

28. Liz Plank, "Donald Trump's Behavior Is Textbook Emotional Abuse, and Hillary Clinton Isn't His Only Victim," *Vox,* October 11, 2016. Accessed at http://
www.vox.com/2016/10/11/13234010/donald-trump-textbook-emotional
-abuse-debate.

29. Hannah Smothers, "Donald Trump Is Triggering," *Cosmopolitan,* October 18, 2016. Accessed at http://www.cosmopolitan.com/sex-love/a6105688
/donald-trump-triggering-misogyny.

30. Michelle Goldberg, "The Triggered Electorate," *Slate,* October 18, 2016. Accessed at http://www.slate.com/articles/double_x/doublex/2016/10/donald
_trump_is_a_human_trigger.html.

31. Lundy Bancroft, *Why Does He Do That?: Inside the Minds of Angry and Controlling Men* (New York: Berkeley Books, 2003), chapter 2.

32. Ibid., chapter 1.

33. National Institute for Mental Health data, 2009, as quoted by the Florida
Coalition Against Domestic Violence. Accessed at https://www.fcadv.org
/projects-programs/trauma-mental-health-and-domestic-violence.

34. Population Reports: Ending Violence Against Women, 2000.

35. School of Medicine Virginia Commonwealth University, 2000.

36. "Effects of Sexual Violence," RAINN, see https://www.rainn.org/effects-sexual
-violence.

37. H. Khalifeh, P. Moran, et al., "Domestic and Sexual Violence Against Patients with
Severe Mental Illness," *Psychological Medicine,* 45, no. 4 (March 2015): 875–86.

38. National Coalition Against Domestic Violence, http://ncadv.org/learn-more
/statistics.

39. L. Roy, A. G. Crocker, et al., "Criminal Behavior and Victimization Among Homeless Individuals with Severe Mental Illness: A Systematic Review," *Psychiatric Services,* 65, no. 6 (June 2014): 734–50, as quoted by the Treatment Advocacy Center: http://www.treatmentadvocacycenter.org/storage/documents /backgrounders/how%20often%20are%20individuals%20with%20serious%20mental%20illness%20victimized%20final.pdf.

NASTY NATIVE WOMEN

Mary Kathryn Nagle

IN RESPONSE TO President Trump's election, many Americans are discussing polarization. Many say this time is one of the most polarized in our history. Many feel despair, or fear for the first time that our country is so deeply divided, we will never reconcile our deep-seated differences and work together for the democracy that this nation was founded upon.

And yet, for Native women, President Trump's election is no different than the election of the forty-four presidents who have led the United States since it first came into existence. From General Washington to Thomas Jefferson to General Jackson to Abraham Lincoln to Barack Obama to Donald Trump, Native women have always worked to ensure the elected president of the United States upholds the sovereign-to-sovereign relationship between the United States and Tribal Nations. No matter who lives in the White House, since the dawn of the United States, our survival—as Native women—has depended on our ability to counter the dehumanization of our people and re-humanize ourselves in a United States that says we should no longer exist.

———

I am a citizen of the United States and of the Cherokee Nation—a nation that as a result of forced removal is now located in present-day Oklahoma, the home of thirty-nine Tribal Nations. And so it is as a survivor of one of the worst times of presidential polarization in the history of the United States that I reflect on the challenges we face today.

One hundred eighty years ago, my great-great-great-great-grandfather served as Speaker of the Cherokee Nation Council, which established the Cherokee Nation Supreme Court. We opened our supreme court in 1825, twenty years before the state of Georgia opened its own.

At that time, like today, our Cherokee women were raped and assaulted by non-Natives who visited, and lived on, Cherokee lands. At that time, like today, Cherokee Nation passed a law criminalizing the rape of women on Cherokee lands. And Cherokee Nation prosecuted perpetrators regardless of whether they were Indian or not. If you raped a woman on Cherokee lands, you would be prosecuted by Cherokee Nation.

In the 1830s, Andrew Jackson rose to the pinnacle of power based on a platform that included the eradication of my people and my nation. Some of the people who voted for him were mean-spirited. Some were bigoted. Some just wanted a better of life for their children, and Andrew Jackson promised it. But his promise—a promise of better economic times for white Americans—was premised on the destruction of my people.

Today, in the United States, we hear a lot about "us" and "them." In the 1830s, my grandfathers were the "them." In response to this dehumanization, my grandfathers Major Ridge (*Ka-Nun-Tla-Cla-Geh*, "he who walks along the ridge") and his son, John Ridge, fought to save an entire nation—not with a gun on a battlefield, but with a petition in a court of law. In 1832, my grandfathers—along with Principal Chief

John Ross—took our people's case, *Worcester v. Georgia,* to the Supreme Court of the United States. The state of Georgia had arrested a non-Indian living on Cherokee lands, Christian missionary Samuel Worcester, and my grandfathers vigorously argued that Georgia could exercise *no* jurisdiction on Cherokee lands. In response, Georgia asserted that because Worcester was an American citizen and not Cherokee, Cherokee Nation had no jurisdiction over him on Cherokee lands. The Supreme Court disagreed and ruled that Cherokee Nation—and Cherokee Nation *alone*—could exercise jurisdiction on Cherokee lands.

In an unprecedented decision, Chief Justice John Marshall issued a ruling declaring Cherokee Nation to be a sovereign, "distinct community," with the inherent right to exist and the exclusive right to exercise jurisdiction within borders that predated the borders of Georgia. The court upheld the inherent right of Indian nations to protect their citizens. Of course, the court's decision called into question the legitimacy, and constitutionality, of President Jackson's Indian Removal Act. If Tribal Nations truly held exclusive jurisdiction over their lands, how could the United States take them?

Following this victory, my grandfather John Ridge visited President Jackson in the White House to ask how the federal government would enforce the court's decision. Andrew Jackson told him: "John Marshall has issued his decision. Let him enforce it."[1]

President Jackson defied the U.S. Supreme Court and refused to free Samuel Worcester.

Recognizing that neither the federal government nor the state of Georgia would abide by our right to remain in our sovereign territory, my grandfathers signed the Treaty of New Echota, agreeing to relinquish our cherished homeland in exchange for land in what is now Oklahoma. Following the signing of the treaty, President Van Buren forcibly placed sixteen thousand Cherokee in concentration camps for holding until they were "sent" to what is today Oklahoma. Thousands died on the journey, now known as the Trail of Tears.

For signing the Treaty of New Echota and acquiescing to the removal, my grandfathers (both Major Ridge and John Ridge) were considered traitors. Not long after they arrived in Indian Territory, they were brutally assassinated by their fellow Cherokee.

Andrew Jackson is the only president, so far, in the history of the United States to openly defy an order from the Supreme Court. But he is not the only president to disrespect, undermine, or discard the inherent jurisdiction of Tribal Nations to protect their citizens from violent, dangerous assaults.

In 1978, the Supreme Court decided *Oliphant v. Suquamish Indian Tribe,* wherein the court declared that Tribal Nations could no longer exercise criminal jurisdiction over non-Indians who commit crimes on tribal lands.[2] To circumvent the controlling precedent articulated in *Worcester,* the Supreme Court reached back to an 1823 decision—*Johnson v. M'Intosh*—that preceded (and arguably was overruled by)[3] *Worcester.*[4] According to the court in *Johnson,* Tribal Nations could not claim legal title to their own lands because they were uncivilized "heathens" and "fierce savages,"[5] and thus pursuant to the "doctrine of discovery." Once a white Christian *discovers* tribal lands, those lands no longer belong to the Tribal Nation that has lived on them since time immemorial and, instead, suddenly belong to the white Christian who "discovered" them.[6] In 1978, the *Oliphant* court relied on this jurisprudence embedded in *Johnson* to conclude that if Tribes could not claim legal title to their land, they could not exercise criminal jurisdiction over the non-Indians who come onto it.[7]

For the first time in United States history, in 1978, the Supreme Court stripped Tribal Nations of their inherent right to exercise jurisdiction over anyone and everyone who resides on or enters their lands. And the president at the time, Jimmy Carter—a Democrat who is now widely regarded as a human rights advocate—took no action to restore the inherent jurisdiction of Tribal Nations that the Supreme Court wrongfully took.

Because of *Oliphant,* today Tribal Nations have no jurisdiction to prosecute non-Indian perpetrators who rape, abuse, and/or murder Native women and children on tribal lands. It took 140 years to fully come into effect, but Andrew Jackson's campaign to eliminate tribal jurisdiction has reaped devastating, life-and-death consequences for Native women.

Because of *Oliphant,* non-Indian-perpetrated violence against Native women and children has become a crime that, for the most part, goes unprosecuted.[8] Many perpetrators have learned they can abuse and harm Native women and children with impunity—and so they take advantage of the shield *Oliphant* provides them.[9] As a result, Native women and children are more likely to be raped, murdered, and/or abused than any other population in the United States.[10]

In 2013, Congress sought to address the black hole created by *Oliphant,* passing a reauthorization of the Violence Against Women Act (VAWA 2013), which included what is referred to as an "*Oliphant* fix" for cases of domestic violence.[11] Tribal Nations that comply with the requirements of the law are now permitted to exercise inherent criminal jurisdiction over non-Indians.

However, the scope of the fix is extremely narrow—applying only to crimes of domestic violence, dating violence, and violation of protection orders. VAWA 2013, therefore, does not restore Tribal Nations' criminal jurisdiction over non-Indians who commit sexual assault, child abuse, murder, or any other crime that non-Indians continue to commit on tribal lands.

Those who witness the polarization of America today have asked, will President Trump attempt to repeal VAWA 2013? Will the polarizing rhetoric of his campaign be used to declare Tribal Nations, Tribal Courts, and all of tribal law inferior to the laws and courts of the United States? Would such a prejudicial view of Tribal Nations and their institutions be used to declare tribal jurisdiction over non-Indian American citizens unconstitutional?

My answer: perhaps. But as Native women living in a country built on the foundations of Tribal Nations that predate colonial conquest, our response will be the same as it has always been:

Nothing about us, or our governments, is inferior. The argument that Indian Nations cannot exercise jurisdiction over non-Indians finds no support in the Constitution.

Tribal jurisdiction over non-Indians predates the United States Constitution. So tribal jurisdiction isn't unconstitutional. It's pre-constitutional.

And no sovereign, not even the United States, can strip my nation of its inherent right to protect me and my fellow Cherokee women.

It is true that, in response to my grandfathers' attempt to maintain Cherokee Nation's sovereign right to remain within its territory, Jackson famously stated in his fifth annual message: "They [the Cherokee] have neither the intelligence, the industry, the moral habits, nor the desire of improvement which are essential to any favorable change in their condition. Established in the midst of a superior race, and without appreciating the causes of their inferiority or seeking to control them, they must necessarily yield to the force of circumstances and ere long disappear."

And it is true that President Trump has placed a portrait of Andrew Jackson in the Oval Office. But Andrew Jackson is not alone in his historic dehumanization of American Indians, or his opposition to tribal sovereignty and/or jurisdiction.

In drafting the Declaration of Independence, Thomas Jefferson referred to us as "merciless savages." President Jefferson initiated the Corps of Discovery expedition of Lewis and Clark up the Missouri and Columbia rivers—an expedition that resulted in numerous rapes and assaults committed against Native women by non-Indians.

President Jackson himself did not oversee the Trail of Tears. President Martin Van Buren ordered the forced removal of my people, and under *his* leadership, United States soldiers assaulted and raped

Cherokee women, as noted by the missionaries who accompanied the Cherokee on the Trail.[12] President Van Buren took no action to protect our women.

President Roosevelt ordered the creation of Japanese-American internment camps during World War II and placed them on the reservation lands of many Tribal Nations—despite the objections and refusals of those sovereign tribal governments where the internment camps were placed.

And under President Barack Obama's administration, the United States Army Corps of Engineers (on July 25, 2016) granted Dakota Access Pipeline, LLC several federal permits without considering the public interest implications of the proposed pipeline on the health, safety, and welfare of Native women. Tribal, federal, and state officials have all publicly documented the clear link between an earlier increase in extractive industries in the Bakken region of North Dakota—the point of origin for the proposed Dakota Access Pipeline—and a corresponding increase in violence against Native women and children in North Dakota. Dakota Access's stated goal is to increase capacity for the transportation of up to 570,000 barrels per day ("bpd") of oil from the Bakken to Illinois, and the company has stated its pipeline has "an expected day-one volume of 450,000 barrels per day."[13] Thus, working at capacity, the Dakota Access Pipeline could increase oil extraction in the Bakken by as much as 60 percent. An increase in oil extraction near tribal communities, without the consent of tribal governments or consideration of the health and safety of tribal communities, creates a significant risk of increased violence in the Bakken—and in particular, against Native women and children.

And now, in the present climate of polarization, President Trump continues to refer to Senator Elizabeth Warren as "Pocahontas." President Trump's inability to discern the difference between Senator Warren and Pocahontas is not surprising: his attack on Senator

Warren's Native identity reflects a dominant American culture that has made every effort to diminish Native women to nothing other than a fantastical, oversexualized Disney character.

Think about it. Did you ever wonder why an Indian princess should be used as the symbol to sell butter? Have you skied on Squaw Mountain? Were you told your grandmother was a Cherokee Indian princess? Have you seen the Pocahottie costumes being worn at frat parties or on Halloween? Have you worn one?

Today, Native women are more likely to be murdered, raped, and abused than any other American population.[14] Until *all* individuals—not just President Trump—are held accountable for their trivialization of Native women's identity and bodies, we will continue to be murdered and abused at rates that originated at the time of colonization. Such trivialization, in my view, isn't "making America great"; it is extremely polarizing.

It is not without irony that 2016 brought us these two things: the removal of Andrew Jackson from the front of the twenty-dollar bill and the election of Donald Trump as president.

But despite the comparisons, Donald Trump is not Andrew Jackson. He is Donald Trump. And no president can polarize a nation without our consent.

So let us make a conscious decision to not repeat the past. Let us create our own future. Let us come together.

Please stand with Native women as you work to end violence in America and be sure to advocate for the full restoration of tribal jurisdiction and sovereignty.

As the inevitable constitutional challenge against the partial restoration of tribal jurisdiction in the 2013 reauthorization of VAWA makes its way up to the Supreme Court, stand with us. Advocate for the restoration of Justice Marshall's judicial understanding in *Worcester* that tribal jurisdiction over non-Indians is not *given* by Congress or even the United States—but rather, tribal jurisdiction constitutes an inherent attribute of sovereignty that the Supreme Court never had the constitutional power to *take.*

My nation, Cherokee Nation, has the inherent right to protect me on Cherokee Nation lands and no president—not Andrew Jackson, Franklin Roosevelt, Barack Obama, or Donald Trump, no one—can take that from us.

---

1. According to my grandmother, Frances Polson Nagle, John Ridge's great-granddaughter.

2. *Oliphant v. Suquamish Indian Tribe,* 435 U.S. 191 (1978).

3. Lindsay G. Robertson, *Conquest by Law: How the Discovery of America Dispossessed Indigenous Peoples of Their Lands* (New York: Oxford University Press, 2005) 133 (asserting that in *Worcester v. State of Georgia,* Chief Justice Marshall intended to overrule *Johnson v. M'Intosh*).

4. See *Oliphant v. Suquamish Indian Tribe,* 435 U.S. 191, 209 (quoting *Johnson v. M'Intosh,* 21 U.S. [8 Wheat.] 543, 574 [1823]).

5. *Johnson v. M'Intosh,* 21 U.S. (8 Wheat.) 543, 590 (1823).

6. Ibid., 543, 576–77 (1823).

7. See *Oliphant* (quoting *Johnson v. M'Intosh,* 21 U.S. [8 Wheat.] 543, 574 [1823]).

8. See Angela R Riley, "Crime and Governance in Indian Country," 63 *UCLA L. Rev.* 1564, 1568 (2016) ("But the federal government's limited resources combined with an array of disincentives to investigate and prosecute Indian country crimes means that remarkably few are ever even superficially pursued."); see also Dewi Ioan Ball, *The Erosion of Tribal Power: The Supreme Court's Silent Revolution* 197–198 (2016) [OCLC # 948427430] (noting that "[f]ederal authorities were neglecting to investigate thousands of cases—94 percent of reported crimes").

9. See Heidi Heitkamp, "Jurisdictional No-Man's Land: Explaining to FBI Director Comey Why Our Tribes Need a Cop on the Beat," *Medium,* June 6,

2016. Accessed at https://medium.com/@SenatorHeitkamp/jurisdictional-no
-mans-land-explaining-to-fbi-director-comey-why-our-tribes-need-a-cop-on
-the-e960be5578f1 (last visited January 15, 2017). "Because major crimes on
tribal lands fall under the jurisdiction of federal law enforcement—criminals
believe that there is a good chance their crimes will go uninvestigated and
unprosecuted—and they're right. In Indian Country, such jurisdictional issues
leave no cop on the beat to stop them. . . . Criminals seeking refuge on tribal
land ha[ve] been ravaging Native communities."

10. Steven W. Perry, Bureau of Justice Statistics, "American Indians and Crime: A
    BJS Statistical Profile," 1992–2002 (December 2004). Accessed at https://www
    .ncjrs.gov/App/Publications/abstract.aspx?ID=203097.

11. Violence Against Women Reauthorization Act of 2013, Pub. L. No. 113–4, tit.
    IX, 127 Stat. 54, 118–26.

12. John Demos, *The Tried and the True: Native American Women Confronting
    Colonization* (New York: Oxford University Press, 1995).

13. Final Environmental Assessment 9 (August 2016). Accessed at https://assets
    .documentcloud.org/documents/3036302/DAPLSTLFINALEAandSIGNED
    FONSI-3Aug2016.pdf.

14. 151 Cong. Rec. S4873 (daily ed., May 10, 2005) (statement of Sen. John
    McCain).

FAREWELL TO MERITOCRACY

Jamia Wilson

"THE SYSTEM IS RIGGED." But not in the way Donald Trump described it in his rant a month before election day, when he tweeted that "the election is absolutely rigged by the dishonest and distorted media pushing Crooked Hillary—but also at many polling places—SAD."[1]

President Donald Trump is right about one thing: the system is rigged, but not against him, rather *for* him. But like many other maxims that have taken on new meaning with the rise of Trumpism, the concept of a rigged system, in which the underdog loses, is now meaningless. As democracy erodes into autocracy and we enter a "post-truth" landscape, the ideals that informed principled populist movements, like Occupy Wall Street and Black Lives Matter, are now being manipulated to justify tyranny, to eliminate accountability, and to scapegoat marginalized groups.

This election showed me that the meritocracy we have been taught to believe in is a farce—the first woman presidential candidate from a major party lost to an unqualified and boastful misogynist. Although I'm not surprised that some folks who feel entitled to the promise of meritocracy—the idea that people are given fair access to resources based on their level of hard work and ability—feel cheated when it evades them, it still irks me that this emotion can drive votes.

Using the language of Franklin Delano Roosevelt's famous New Deal–era call to "build from the bottom up and not from the top down," and "put faith once more in the forgotten man at the bottom of the economic pyramid," the newly sworn-in President Trump distorted these populist messages to advance an agenda that will undoubtedly reward the rich and reinforce white and male privilege.

Polls conducted by Reuters/Ipsos before the election revealed that a significant number of Trump's supporters hold racial animus about the intelligence level, work ethic, and lawfulness of people of color, immigrants, and Muslims. Although the same research shows that while Hillary Clinton and Bernie Sanders supporters hold "racial resentments" of their own, Trump supporters ranked disturbingly higher.

Keeping up with his pattern of appropriating populist ideology to advance demagoguery, Trump declared that "every single American will have the opportunity to realize his or her fullest potential" on the inaugural stage. Veiling the ideals that fueled his emergence into the presidency with inclusive language, he sounded off a dog whistle to a swath of his base that perceives the rise of so-called politically correct progressive values and diversity as a threat to their entitlement to the American Dream.

"Meritocracy," as defined by the Merriam-Webster dictionary, is "a system in which the talented are chosen and moved ahead on the basis of their achievement." At some point, the non-billionaires among Trump's supporters, and especially the 53 percent of white women who voted for him, will eventually be hit by the reality that their whiteness will not protect them from the loss of Social Security, or the pain of policies that will impact their communities negatively, like lost or limited health and elder-care access, which are truths many marginalized communities know too well.

If nothing else, the 2016 election confirmed for those who weren't already in the know: our nation's promise of meritocracy is an "alternative fact." From our first preschool utterances of the Pledge of Allegiance onward, the "big M" taunts us with its uncertain promises, until the tragically inevitable rites of passage I grew up referring to as "black girl lessons" inform us that "liberty and justice for all" holds no guarantees.

While some of his disciples tout the former reality-TV star and real estate mogul as a so-called working-class millionaire who exemplifies meritocracy, they conveniently omit the fact that he's a prime example of how inherited privilege functions in our society.

Deemed credible because he was born into wealth, Trump celebrated his wealthy white masculinity, and thereby made up for his bankruptcies, sexual assault allegations, and cases of bilking contractors in the eyes of many of his supporters. Although his opponent outmatched him on political and foreign policy experience, Trump's education at some of the nation's finest institutions and status as a celebrity business owner mattered more than his competence.

Trump managed to win the electoral college despite well-documented conflicts of interest, his loss of the popular vote, protests from the Congressional Black Caucus regarding voter suppression, and ties to a foreign government that the CIA reports interfered with our electoral process. These are just a few examples of how our system is hardwired to ensure that legacy privilege trumps justice most of the time (pun intended).

It's more important than ever to expose meritocracy as a political fiction disguised as an aspirational truth that distracts from the real casualties of a broken economic and political system. This reality looms especially large in the aftermath of the loss of Hillary Clinton, a former secretary of state and senator, and undeniably the most qualified presidential candidate in history. She lost to a man who is the first commander in chief with no political, military, or foreign policy experience.

But if I'm going to ask others to get real about a meritorious system that shrouds its underpinnings of racialized, gendered, and ableist oppression, while gift-wrapping itself as a cherished American virtue, I have to take responsibility for perpetuating meritocracy's poison myself.

After "playing by the rules" and still getting passed over repeatedly for opportunities, promotions, raises, etc., for those who were less qualified on paper but traded credentials of whiteness, maleness, and/or wealth for competence, I've long understood that meritocracy and "self-made" people are about as real as unicorns.

Despite the fact that I've been able to build a career that aligns with my passion and interests, I've had to jump over the fiery hurdles of everything from daily microaggressions, nepotism, workplace bullying, and "glass cliffs" to get here—even in some self-described progressive spaces.

Although I learned early on that ideological individualism mostly benefits people who closely resemble Trump and his monochromatic cabinet, its allure still appealed to me. While I've always known deep down that people can't prove themselves into liberation, overstriving provided me with a sense of control and energy that distracted me from feeling helpless against the clutches of institutional obstacles.

Despite my lived experiences with the limits of "upward mobility," I became aware of the bitter truth. Although I went to a prestigious college-prep school and earned the scores I needed to be admitted into highly selective universities, I still encountered some peers, bosses, and teachers who explained my positioning as being a result of quotas and affirmative action instead of my hard work.

Part of me still bought into the idea that overworking my way to freedom was a viable survival mechanism within the trappings of a social structure driven by competition and greed.

Now, the day I memorialize as 11/9 marks the moment when my relationship to meritocracy changed dramatically. When an ill-equipped bully took the helm over a seasoned, proven, and tenacious stateswoman—I realized that pursuit of the so-called American Dream was futile for those of us for whom it was not designed to serve.

I lost what faith I had in the system and decided to trade in my ballot-box pantsuit for the armor of a resistance warrior. Clinton's loss led me to actively reject social conditioning and internalized oppression, by focusing less on how to be included in systems with ever-moving goalposts, and more on paving insurgent ground by building new structures and more inclusive movements within my own community.

The crushing loss of the nation's most qualified candidate, who happened to be a woman, brought back visceral memories of having my ideas credited and rewarded to men, boys, and/or white people at school and at work. Hillary Clinton's defeat was also reminiscent of other haunting moments when I was pressured into shrinking myself and my accomplishments to preserve the imbalanced social order. It brought back irksome memories of being attacked for getting media exposure and/or public recognition by either white or male colleagues, or being retaliated against by a former boss who reprimanded me for reporting and speaking out against workplace diversity and inclusion issues during a formal evaluation process.

In the midnight cab ride home from Hillary Clinton's election night party at the Javits Center, a montage of discussions with classmates, friends, family, teachers, mentors, and colleagues became one unified monologue. The internal din was so loud that I covered my ears until I remembered no one else could hear:

I read that you said it was racist and sexist that your white male journalism professor told you to straighten your natural hair in order to move forward in this field, but honestly it's the cost of entry. I would have told you the same thing if you worked for my TV network. It's the same thing I had to deal with as a white woman who is not naturally blond. I dyed my hair. You need to change your attitude.

I didn't get into that honor society and you did. I can't believe it! It must have been affirmative action.

Did you know you're making twenty thousand dollars less than white people here with similar experience, and in some cases less?

You're dealing with workplace bullying and harassment? I mean, given the realities of your positioning in your career and your job it's a luxury problem compared to what even some blue-collar white dudes have to experience. If you get to interact with a board of directors at your age, you've got it pretty good.

Well, you shouldn't be upset that you were passed over for that job even though you were the most qualified person and possess the most years of experience. You know these things are political, right? It's best not to make a fuss. So what if they're paying him way more than they offered you? Find comfort in the fact that you've still done so much.

It doesn't comfort me when you tell me that you didn't get into some of the programs you applied to as well. Don't you get it? Don't tell me about the system. The system is supposed to work for me and people like me, and that's why I'm upset.

You didn't have to get HR involved to get me to bring you in for this interview. Yes, I know you were working on this project for a while, too, but I didn't realize that you were so qualified. Let me see your résumé again?

As your supervisor, I'm not surprised you're leaving. I had a chance to promote you twice and I know you noticed that I promoted him first. You're smart, and capable. I expected this.

Well, baby, you're smart, you're a woman, you're black. It's going to be hard, you've got to work twice as hard to get half as much.

Did your parents do that science project for you? I know you won the science fair, but there's still time to admit that you didn't do it. I just can't believe you could achieve that yourself.

In these memories, I was reminded about the indignities and

underestimation, hyper-invisibility and -visibility, women of color and black women, specifically, endure daily.

I continued to question my inclination to "work harder, learn more, or behave better" to counter Trump and his supporters' narratives about me and my community. Deep down, I knew that no amount of proving myself or my competence would result in their respect for my humanity.

Although there's a great many differences between my life and Hillary Clinton's, the similarities between our experiences as women are a testament to the power of systemic challenges. She played the game and followed the rules. She did everything our society told her was right, and was a shining example of American exceptionalism as a hardworking leader with Midwestern middle-class roots turned world-renowned millionaire and political powerhouse.

In spite of this, even she couldn't escape the consequences of being born a woman in a patriarchal society, which led to her competence and worth being challenged in regards to her marriage, attractiveness, age, and even the tone of her voice.

To be sure, Secretary Clinton benefited from an abundance of privileges. It is also true that there were times when she, as many others have in her social, political, and economic position, unacceptably leveraged this power in ways that undermined more marginalized communities. But despite her whiteness, wealth, and conformity to mainstream standards for able-bodied cisgender professional women, misogyny outpaced her hard-earned accomplishments.

The reality is that a historic win for Secretary Clinton wouldn't have guaranteed a change in the way sexism operates and functions. Even if Clinton had been elected president, she would still, like all other women in the United States, live in a country where she is technically not guaranteed equal rights under the Constitution in the absence of an equal rights amendment. Her victory would be a step toward progress, but would not have resulted in immediate parity in a nation that ranks seventy-second in women's political participation, and comes in last on maternal and family leave.

Although her victory wouldn't have ensured that what she defined as the "highest, hardest glass ceiling" would have been shattered for me and other women of color, she had the potential to open up avenues of possibility for our future first woman of color president due to her trailblazing, and her track record of hiring, mentoring, and promoting women of color.

Implicit bias informed the lens with which my aptitude was regarded in each of the conversations above, and often without regard for my real capabilities, past track record, stamina, or skill level. Although I've known this for years, my experience in the cab after the world's most depressing party in history solidified for me that I needed to stop pushing for affirmation in a system that has its mind made up about who I am and where I'm going.

Black feminist foremother Audre Lorde warned us that "the master's tools will never dismantle the master's house." It's more important than ever for women to create and sustain our own networks, and make our own rules. Since we've learned that playing by the rules won't guarantee a roadmap to our success or liberation, it's high time that we pour our energy into lifting each other up instead of supporting systems that harm us. That's why I've decided to spend more of my energy, time, and influence on moving from a baseline of consciousness raising to more actively and transparently fighting for a new solidarity-driven paradigm at every level of my life and work.

My mantra moving forward is "Instead of asking what I need to do to be included, I wonder what I can build to pave new ground." Instead of putting my focus on moving up meritocracy's broken ladder, I'm committing myself to showing up and speaking up more loudly for myself and for my community. In lieu of attempting to gain recognition in spaces that inherently exclude me, I'll work with like-minded change makers to build and sustain our own spaces.

My aim is to help build power and resources for the next generation by disrupting dysfunctional institutions and developing healthier movements. By supporting and mobilizing the next generation of feminist leaders, I hope to advance a more inclusive society and culture, fueled by fierce solidarity as an alternative to toxic masculinity and white supremacy.

1. Donald J. Trump's Twitter page, accessed July 20, 2017, https://twitter.com /realDonaldTrump/status/787699930718695425?ref_src=twsrc%5Etfw&ref _url=https%3A%2F%2Fwww.vice.com%2Fen_us%2Farticle%2Fdonald -trump-rigged-election-timeline.

PERMISSION TO VOTE FOR A MONSTER
Ivanka Trump and Faux Feminism

Jessica Valenti

FOR SO MANY WOMEN, the 2016 presidential election wasn't just a loss—it was a death. An evisceration.

When I stepped out of the privacy booth in the school auditorium, I waited for the tears of happiness to come. Nearly every woman I knew told me about weeping with joy at the ability to cast a vote for the first female president. I have worked my entire life for feminist causes; it seemed inevitable that I would react similarly.

But in that moment—even with my daughter and me wearing matching gray shirts with FEMINIST emblazoned across the front, even after watching her fill out the circle next to Hillary Clinton's name—my eyes were dry.

At the time, I thought it was the excitement of the day that kept me steely, but now I believe something different: somewhere in my bones I knew she wouldn't win.

Americans were so caught up in the celebratory feminist moment of Hillary's eventual victory that we ignored our instincts and experiences. The lead-up to this election day had been as full of ugly sexist rhetoric as any public campaign ever: a Republican candidate accused of sexual assault by a dozen women, caught on tape bragging about "grabbing pussy," with an army of misogynist and racist supporters targeting journalists and Clinton supporters.

And yet at the same time it felt like the country was closing in on the feminist moment we had been waiting for. Nearly every mainstream publication was promoting stories by women about their lives and concerns, while books with "feminist" in the title were climbing the bestseller lists. Beyoncé was declaring herself a feminist in forty-foot lights, and the media were covering sexism with the seriousness it warranted. Feminism was no longer misunderstood or maligned—it was, of all things, cool.

So that morning in November, women across the country went with their mothers and daughters to the voting booth. They wore NASTY WOMAN T-shirts and left I VOTED stickers on Susan B. Anthony's gravestone. They readied the champagne and prepared to watch the final glass ceiling shatter. Instead, they were met with a slap in the face.

The historic gender gap that pollsters predicted didn't materialize, and while 94 percent of black women voted for Clinton, the majority of white women voted for Trump. That so many would vote against their own gender and self-interest is, in part, thanks to the lie that feminism is simply anything a woman does rather than a well-defined movement for justice. Perhaps no one embodies this dangerous perversion of feminism more than Ivanka Trump—a woman who epitomizes what happens when the movement turns into something so nebulous and broadly defined that women could help elect a monster and call themselves "empowered" because of it.

For years I've watched conservative women's organizations, anti-choice leaders, and Republican pundits as they went from deriding feminism at every turn to desperately trying to paint themselves as the "real" feminists once the movement gained cultural cachet. I've seen these conservative women try to defund the Violence Against

Women Act while claiming to care about victims of domestic violence, or argue that the wage gap doesn't really exist because women choose to work at less demanding jobs.

These conservative female leaders—mostly white, skinny, and telegenic—smile behind podiums while arguing that everything is just fine for women. To Republican men, they're shining examples of true womanhood: poised, smart, and satisfied with whatever rights men choose to bestow them with. Even better, their presence in the conservative movement serves as a shield against accusations of sexism. How could the GOP be misogynist and promote misogynistic policies when they have the staunch support of such remarkable women?

Ivanka Trump—dutiful daughter, loving wife and mother, smart and polished businesswoman—embodies this brand of palatable white femininity so venerated by the conservative movement. Throughout Trump's presidential campaign, Ivanka functioned as a beautiful and articulate buffer between her father and the many, many accusations of misogyny leveled against him. She touted Trump's female-friendly bona fides by talking about all the women he had hired over the years, lovingly mentioned the way he supported her career—she even called him a feminist.

When *The New York Times* ran a story about Trump's sketchy history with women,[1] Ivanka insisted her father was "not a groper."[2] When a video was released of her father bragging about being a groper, Ivanka had his back. She released a statement calling his comments "inappropriate and offensive," but said she was glad he apologized. In a later interview, she dismissed the tape as "crude language"[3] and claimed his words didn't match up with the man she knew.

Ivanka's continued support, combined with her Teflon-like public image—*The New Yorker*'s Emily Nussbaum called it "weaponized graciousness"[4]–convinced many women who may have been otherwise turned off by Trump that he must be a good person despite all evidence to the contrary. Anne Helen Petersen at *BuzzFeed* dubbed them the "Ivanka voters": "If Trump produced someone that classy, that's a testament to something," one woman told her.[5]

And so for some women on the right, Ivanka was more than a symbol of conservative femininity—she was permission to vote for a monster: the face of a distorted "feminism" that helped to usher in 53 percent of white women's votes. Now, with a powerful role in her father's presidential administration, Ivanka will continue to be used as a salve for Trump's overt sexism and racism.

As feminism gained cultural cachet over the last decade, women on the right saw an opportunity to use that power to their advantage. Anti-abortion groups stopped calling women murderers and instead held signs that said women "deserved better" than abortion. Conservatives—once horrified by all things women's rights—embraced feminist rhetoric, calling themselves "independent women." In the 2008 presidential campaign, Sarah Palin, the Republican vice presidential nominee, called herself a feminist, sparking a national debate on who can and can't identify with the term. Feminism, in the mind of those who would co-opt it, became simply anything a woman does rather than a specific movement for justice. The shiny veneer of empowerment, without any substance, was enough.

And in that way, Ivanka is a perfect fit for this kind of faux feminism. She's branded herself as a sort of Sheryl Sandberg Lite: Ivanka's website hosts a "Women Who Work" campaign; she reportedly pushed her father to adopt a maternity leave policy; and at the Republican National Convention her widely lauded speech called for equal pay and focused on Trump's supposed support of women in the workplace.

But look beyond the surface and there's not much there.

"Women Who Work" is a series of photos and a hashtag, not a campaign that actually does anything for working mothers. The parental leave policy Trump suggested and Ivanka counseled him on doesn't cover fathers, same-sex couples, single moms, or adoptive parents. As for her RNC speech, "You felt like she was introducing Betty Friedan or Gloria Steinem, not Donald Trump," Debbie Walsh, director of the Center for American Women and Politics at Rutgers University, told me at the time. And for all the lip service Ivanka gives her father for hiring and promoting women, not discriminating against employees because of gender is a legal requirement, not a brave feminist stand.

In the end, no matter what hashtag she uses or speech she gives, Ivanka is still supporting a bigot and misogynist. As Nussbaum put it, "Ivanka has made a conscious choice to deodorize the stink of her father's misogyny, to suggest that because he loves her that means he loves women—to erase the actual policies he supports."

And that's the most important thing to understand about the trend that Ivanka represents: It's not just about any one woman who chooses to present herself as a feminist while supporting policies that oppress others. It's about the way these women and their appropriation of feminism are used to enable misogyny as a tangible force in people's lives.

We're already seeing it in action: Reproductive rights are being rolled back, shrouded in the language of "helping women." Trump is planning on making massive cuts to the Violence Against Women office and legislation, yet cites fear of rape to justify his discriminatory immigration ban. Republicans and the Trump administration will continue to use their nonexistent regard for women to push through a regressive, sexist agenda for America.

Now is the time for us to clearly define what feminism is about and reject the attempts by the right to co-opt the movement when it is at its strongest. Because we truly are at an incredible moment. Millions of women marched around the globe on inauguration weekend—some veteran feminists, some who had never been to a protest in their life. We have an opportunity, and an obligation, to ensure that the next wave of feminist activism is so clearly defined that it will be impossible for conservative women to claim it.

1. Michael Barbaro and Megan Twohey, "Crossing the Line: How Donald Trump Behaved with Women in Private," *New York Times,* May 14, 2016. Accessed at http://www.nytimes.com/2016/05/15/us/politics/donald-trump-women.html?_r=0.

2. Anna Brand, "Ivanka Trump: My Father Is 'Not a Groper,'" NBC News, May 18, 2016. Accessed at http://www.nbcnews.com/card/ivanka-trump-my-father-not-groper-n576026.

3. Eugene Scott, "Ivanka Trump: Dad's Remarks Were 'Crude Language,'" CNN, October 19, 2016. Accessed at http://www.cnn.com/2016/10/19/politics/ivanka-trump-donald-trump-crude.

4. Emily Nussbaum, "The R.N.C. on TV: Ivanka's Weaponized Graciousness," *The New Yorker,* July 22, 2016. Accessed at http://www.newyorker.com/culture/culture-desk/the-r-n-c-on-tv-ivankas-weaponized-graciousness.

5. Anne Helen Petersen, "Meet the Ivanka Voter," *BuzzFeed*, November 2, 2016. Accessed at https://www.buzzfeed.com/annehelenpetersen/meet-the-ivanka-voter?utm_term=.pqPRpK4eo%22%20%5Cl%20%22 .qhAzm3Ogl.

DONALD TRUMP'S WAR ON THE WORKING CLASS

Sarah Jaffe

ON MARCH 8, dozens of red-clad women marching to the tune of "Bread and Roses," the hundred-year-old labor song associated with women's workplace struggles, converged on downtown Lafayette, Indiana, bearing signs that read I STRIKE FOR LABOR RIGHTS, I STRIKE FOR FULL SOCIAL PROVISIONING, and I STRIKE FOR ANTI-RACIST AND ANTI-IMPERIALIST FEMINISM. They spoke into a megaphone, declaring their intentions to the city, a part of an international action that in the United States largely took aim at the administration of Donald J. Trump.

The Trump administration has done its best to prove the age-old labor adage that "the boss is the best organizer." Its attacks on multiple vulnerable populations right at the outset drove millions into the streets, pushed thousands into joining or creating new political organizations, and turned many occasional voters into die-hard activists declaring themselves part of the resistance.

Since Trump resembles nothing so much as a tyrannical boss (after all, his signature line, before "Make America Great Again," was "You're fired"), it shouldn't be surprising that labor terminology and tactics have similarly seen a revival. When the executive order banning immigrants, travelers, and refugees from seven Muslim-majority nations was released, thousands rushed to their local airports to demand that detained travelers caught in transit be allowed entry. But one group of people went further. Taxi drivers, who usually line up at cab stands at New York City's major airports waiting for fares, went on strike, refusing to take fares from John F. Kennedy Airport.

Members of the Taxi Workers Alliance, which called the strike, are overwhelmingly Muslim and Sikh and often face violent attacks at times of increased Islamophobia, according to the alliance's executive director, Bhairavi Desai. "Already, drivers are twenty times more likely to be killed on the job than other workers," she said. "We are one of the most visible immigrant and Muslim workforces. Our members tend to be on the frontlines of that hate and violence." Such workforces as the taxi drivers, made up of people of color, immigrants, and women, live at the intersections of the violence of Trump's proposals.

The drivers' strike was greeted with an emotional outpouring of support across the country—a nation that is largely disconnected from workers' struggles, as both union membership and the frequency of such strikes have plummeted over the past few decades in the face of right-wing attacks on workers' rights. Despite that disconnect, Americans were outraged when Uber, the so-called sharing economy ride-hailing app, announced it was turning off its infamous "surge pricing," dropping rates in what protesters perceived as an attempt to break the strike. #DeleteUber trended; *The New York Times* reported that 200,000 people did so in response to Uber's scabbing. Solidarity, that age-old labor movement value, was alive and well.[1]

The enthusiasm for the taxi drivers' strike helped to amplify the calls for another, bigger strike that had been building since before Trump was sworn into office. The general strike is labor's sharpest and strongest weapon, an attempt to shut down an entire city by having all workers refuse to work. It can be the ultimate act of solidarity, and it can be—as it has been framed in Trumplandia—a way of making demands on the state. As Rosa Luxemburg wrote in *The Mass Strike*, such a strike is spurred by historical conditions, becoming possible when it seemed impossible, reversing the power dynamics of society, combining economic and political struggle.

The term was brought back to public consciousness in the Obama era, first during the Wisconsin (and then Ohio and Indiana) labor uprisings of early 2011. In those moments, the idea of workers refusing to work was in response specifically to an attack on union rights, on the women and people of color who make up the majority of the public-sector workforce nationwide, the teachers and social workers and nurses who lost their collective bargaining rights under Governor Scott Walker's Act 10. The massive protests in Madison, Wisconsin, brought hundreds of thousands to the "People's House," their term for the capitol, in what might have tipped over the edge into a general strike. The Occupy movement seized on the idea of a general strike next, first in Oakland, California, when longshore workers and others acted in solidarity with the Occupiers who had been evicted from their camp and shut the port and a variety of other businesses, and then nationwide for actions on May Day, the holiday celebrated as International Workers' Day in most countries outside of the U.S. (despite the day's roots in a massive general strike for the eight-hour workday in Chicago, in 1886).

The Chicago Teachers Union called something akin to a general strike on April 1, 2016, bringing the low-wage workers of Fight for $15, organizations aligned with the Movement for Black Lives, and community organizations across Chicago out with them in a massive day of action for public schools and public services, demanding the city and the state pass a budget that funded education, raised wages, and shifted spending away from prisons and police.

But many of the calls for a general strike against Trump came from those more disconnected from the struggles of the working class. Famed novelist and scholar Francine Prose wrote in *The Guardian* in praise of disruptive protest, noting, "The struggles for civil rights and Indian independence, against apartheid and the Vietnam war—it's hard to think of a nonviolent movement that has succeeded without causing its opponents a certain amount of trouble, discomfort and inconvenience."[2]

Prose was correct that power, to steal a frame from Frederick Douglass, concedes nothing without disruption. But when she called for a "general strike" she showed a lack of understanding of just what a general strike actually is. "Let's designate a day on which no one (that is, anyone who can do so without being fired) goes to work," she wrote. Such a framing has been echoed elsewhere, as people call for a strike-that-isn't-a-strike. After all, if the boss gives you permission to stay home, you're no longer on strike.

That's not to take away from the importance of business owners who shuttered their shops in solidarity with strikes like February 16's Day Without an Immigrant or the Yemeni business owners who closed their stores on February 3 to protest the Muslim ban. But it *is* to say that a strike without risk is not much of a strike. And a strike of those who can strike without risking being fired is likely to leave out the very people who will suffer the most from Trump's regime. As Luxemburg argued, "If the mass strike, or rather, mass strikes, and the mass struggle are to be successful they must become a real people's movement."[3]

This very disconnect among liberals from the struggles of working people was evident from the beginning of Hillary Clinton's campaign for the presidency, and was a key reason why Donald Trump was able to beat her. The Democratic Party's decision to turn to Wall Street and the wealthy for funding decades ago mirrored a corresponding policy shift toward "free trade" deals that ship jobs to wherever the wages are lowest and the regulations fewest, crunching both

working people in the U.S. and abroad, and helping to spike xenophobic beliefs about foreign-born workers. The disappearance of the
wages and benefits that generations of workers had struck and struggled for fueled a deep-seated rage that Washington political insiders
were totally unprepared to deal with. A protest movement that rein-
scribes those same mistakes rather than learning from them is one
that is doomed to come up short again.

Prose and many others who deleted Uber simply switched to Lyft,
a company that may not have publicly scabbed on a strike and that
quickly moved to donate to the ACLU to burnish its image, but which
relies on the same business model as Uber—one that requires its workers to bear all the costs of their job while controlling their movements and setting their fares. A job action might have incited the
#DeleteUber move, but the indifference of so many to previous criti-
cisms of Uber and Lyft underlines the class split within the anti-Trump
movement.

Clinton's refusal on the campaign trail to endorse a $15-an-hour
minimum wage—even while courting the fast-food workers' movement, a movement made up primarily of black and Latinx workers,
a majority of them women—continues to rankle. The unexpected
challenge of Bernie Sanders to Clinton's left heightened the focus on
her past support for welfare "reform" and NAFTA, her proposals to
potentially reduce Social Security benefits, her hedging on wages and
college debt, and her outright refusal to consider single-payer health
care. And since the election, prominent Clinton aides like Jennifer
Palmieri, who told MSNBC's Chuck Todd that "you are wrong to
look at these crowds and think that means everyone wants $15 an
hour," have continued to sound that sour note. Palmieri's defense of
"identity" politics continued: "I support you, refugee. I support you,
immigrant in my neighborhood. I want to defend you. Women who
are rejecting Nordstrom and Neiman Marcus are saying—they're
saying this is power for them."

Thankfully, the protests are not simply made up of the Nordstrom class, and the biggest wins for the disparate movement known simply, most of the time, as the Resistance came largely from the people for whom avoiding Neiman Marcus is not a choice. (Lest we forget, some 42 percent of the country would get a raise if the minimum wage was raised to $15 an hour; the top 1 percent, meanwhile, owns about 40 percent of the nation's wealth.[4])

The workers of the Fight for $15 brought down Andrew Puzder, CEO of the company that owns Hardee's and Carl's Jr. and accused spousal abuser. The nomination of Puzder to run the labor department seemed like the punchline on the string of bad jokes that were Trump's cabinet nominations. In the wake of a massive movement around the country demanding higher wages and union rights, kicked off in 2012 by fast-food workers in New York City, putting a fast-food CEO in charge of the department that regulates labor practices was nothing less than a giant "fuck you" to American workers. And Puzder's withdrawal from the process—because, according to an anonymous source, "he's very tired of the abuse"[5]—was a victory for those same workers, who went on strike and rallied around the country against his confirmation. Worker organizations maintained that Puzder's restaurants had sexual harassment rates 1.5 times higher than the already-sky-high 40 percent rate of harassment in the fast-food industry as a whole, and made the connection to the company's sexually suggestive ads.[6] "Customers have asked why I don't dress like the women in the commercials," one Hardee's employee told researchers. Puzder's response to criticisms of the ads was that "We believe in putting hot models in our commercials, because ugly ones don't sell burgers."

While sexual harassment is often painted in the media and in fiction as a barrier that women face on their way to shattering glass ceilings, the fact is that the people more likely to endure it are working-class service employees, who also struggle with wage theft, forced overtime, and lack of paid sick time. Service industry jobs are dominated by women, people of color, and immigrants—those facing multiple attacks from Trump's proposed policies, from crackdowns on abortion rights to deportation to violence from emboldened police forces that mostly endorsed the president.

But as political scientist Corey Robin notes, the location where most people face routine oppression and denial of their rights is the workplace. Puzder's labor record is just another stark reminder of that fact—as is the tendency for Immigration and Customs Enforcement to raid workplaces to round up undocumented workers, sometimes with the collusion of employers who want to get rid of pesky employees who might have tried to organize a union or make some demands. This is why so many of the protests against inequality and austerity during the Obama era kicked off with demands for union rights or against the denial of those rights, and why the idea of a general strike against Trump hovers in the collective consciousness.

It might seem ironic that a perceived attention to workers' needs is what put Trump in the White House, yet on the campaign trail he continually slammed Clinton for her ties to Wall Street and her support for trade deals, while promising to bring back manufacturing jobs to the U.S. Reporters continue to assert that Trump's base is the "white working class," and though the truth is far more complicated than that simple narrative, it is telling that the "white working class," to most people who discuss it, is little more than another identity box: white men who work in manufacturing and wear baseball caps like the one Trump ostentatiously paraded around in on the campaign trail (and continues to sell to supporters).

But class is not, as I have written elsewhere, a baseball cap. It is a relation of power; it is one's position in the economy and the world. It is shaped by one's gender and race and immigration status; one's sexuality, gender expression, and ability, and many other things besides. To understand this, think about the fact that transgender

DONALD TRUMP'S WAR ON THE WORKING CLASS

women of color face the highest unemployment rates in the country and are regularly criminalized for simply existing in public, making it even harder for them to find legal work and creating a vicious cycle of poverty and prison.[7] Caring about class, then, means understanding that bills to deny trans people access to restrooms will affect their economic conditions, throwing them out of work and impacting the economic and political power that they have.

That Trump's lip service to class concerns was something that some working people wanted to hear desperately enough to believe a billionaire shows how bad things have gotten. In Wisconsin, where labor battles have been central, Hillary Clinton's inattention amounted to campaign malpractice. The swing toward Trump in locations like Waterford, New York, where a hundred-day strike at the Momentive chemical plant saw workers huddled over burn barrels to stay warm on the picket line most of the winter, was not complete, but it was enough to flip a district that had voted for Obama into the Trump column. Lip service, or as Indiana organizer Tom Lewandowski told me, "emotional representation" was better than the tone-deaf "America is already great!" messaging that offered the status quo with a couple of tweaks around the edges.[8] Trump echoed back at them the anger of working-class men who felt their purpose dwindling with their paychecks, that anger twisted to blame the less powerful rather than the boss—who might, as had been the case at Momentive, be one of Trump's buddies, after all. Economic concerns shaded all too easily into xenophobia and racism, as Mexican workers took the blame for jobs departing or being filled by more exploitable immigrants. And the willingness of some Democrats to use Islamophobic rhetoric against Muslim-American congressman Keith Ellison when he challenged for the Democratic National Committee chair position should remind us all that Democrats have not been blameless when it comes to race baiting.

But Trump's promise to shred trade deals that have contributed

to the disappearance of industrial jobs, coupled with bragging about
his ability to bring jobs back, and even the occasional nod in the direction of needs like paid family leave, has come to little. He has nothing to offer but attacks for the vast swathes of the working class who
are not white men, and even his promises to those white men have
proven to be not worth the pixels in the misspelled tweets, as the over-
hyped deal to "save" the Carrier furnace plant in Indianapolis should
remind us. His meetings with high-profile building trades union leaders resulted in nothing but photo ops for the union leaders to take
home to their members as they explained that the new president who
claimed to care about working people was likely to shrug as the regulations that set prevailing wages for construction work are swept
away. And when United Steelworkers Local 1999 president Chuck
Jones pointed out the mass layoffs that would continue at Carrier,
Trump sent a frenzied series of tweet attacks aimed at Jones.

Settling for lip service is a relatively new state of being for white
male factory workers, who are largely not interested in moving into
the service jobs that are the fastest-growing part of the economy. After
all, lip service has historically been about all that service workers can
expect for their hard work—at Walmart, as historian Bethany More-
ton detailed in her book *To Serve God and Wal-Mart*, the women who
made Sam Walton's fortune for him were recruited specifically because
they were unlikely to demand higher wages or unions. Walton and
his managers skillfully played on the women's values in order to win
their loyalty while picking their pockets and passing them over for
promotions. (When pressed to show that he valued women, instead
of giving a raise to his existing employees, Walton recruited a local
attorney and then–First Lady of his home state to join his company's
board: Hillary Clinton.)

But Walmart remains the world's largest private-sector employer,
and the demands of its workers, like Venanzi Luna, should be central
to today's progressive movements if they intend to actually challenge

not just one individual bad boss in Donald Trump, but actually fight for a more equal world. Venanzi Luna lost her job when Walmart closed down the store where she worked, in Pico Rivera, California. The store had been the site of the first-ever strikes at a Walmart retail store back in the fall of 2012, and Luna had been one of the leaders in the store, which became a hotbed of activism. In the spring of 2015, I watched as Luna confronted Walmart's CEO Doug McMillon on the floor of the company's shareholder meeting, asking him to prove that she hadn't lost her job because of her strike leadership. McMillon oozed sympathy, but made no promises.

It is women like Venanzi Luna who are in the crosshairs in Donald Trump's America but were largely forgotten even in Barack Obama's and Bill Clinton's. The risks she took are the same risks that built the labor movement, which in turn created a stable American middle class for decades. Luna risked her job to walk out on strike; years later, in a very conscious echo of the famed Flint sit-down strikes that helped set the cornerstone of industrial union power, she sat down with tape over her mouth in the middle of a Walmart. Luna, whose job barely paid her enough to shop at the Walmart she worked in, much less Neiman Marcus, was willing to risk losing her job and being arrested to win decent wages and a reliable schedule. Venanzi Luna and her comrades remind us that those factory and construction and mining jobs Trump pledges to bring back were not "good" jobs because of some inherent characteristic of the work or the benevolence of bosses—they were good jobs because workers had fought, struck, and even died to organize unions.

It is to Luna's example that we should look if we want to talk about strikes and disruption to stop Trump. As many commentators have noted, Trump's presidency seems often designed as nothing more than an operation to siphon wealth to Donald Trump. This is more blatant than we are used to, but it is nothing new in American politics, which have become little more than a machine for creating inequality, stripping working people of our rights and the public goods that our taxes are supposed to fund while funneling that money instead into the hands of the already wealthy. To stop this machine, people will have to refuse any longer to grease it with their labor and in fact to put their bodies in its way.

We must become comfortable with the idea of risk, the way Venanzi Luna did.

This is not to say that resistance cannot be fun—indeed, disruption, as the Tea Party protesters discovered under Obama, can be tremendous fun. But it can also be dangerous, and not grappling with that fact—and not grappling with the fact that danger is not equally distributed—will spell disaster for the movement.

After the Women's March on January 21, some crowed at how peaceful the marches were, thanked police for support, and cheered women-led movements for avoiding arrest. Yet the protesters in Ferguson, Missouri, in the summer and fall of 2014 did not get the option to peacefully take to the streets and hug it out with the cops; their public mourning for teenage Michael Brown, shot dead in the street by one of those police officers, was interrupted by the National Guard—the same National Guard that Trump was rumored to want to send out to round up undocumented immigrants.

The violence around a movement, in other words, is not based on the movement's conscious decision or its gender makeup (the Ferguson movement and the broader Movement for Black Lives were led in large part by young black queer women), but on the perception of its participants by those in power. Young black people in the street chanting "Hands up, don't shoot!" heroically faced down police in armored vehicles aiming assault rifles at them. Today's resistance must prepare itself to do the same.

Direct action involves risk. The water protectors at Standing Rock locked themselves to construction equipment to stop an oil pipeline being drilled underneath their water source. In New Mexico, when Guadalupe Garcia de Rayos was loaded on a van to be deported by immigration officials, Maria Castro and seven others were arrested trying to physically block the van's departure. "The van literally pushed me at least 30 feet, hyperextending my knees, hurting some of my friends, knocking some of my fellow organizers down to the ground," she told me. "Another person started to hug the wheels and put his own life at risk, because this is just the beginning. This is the beginning of the militarized removal of our communities, of our families, and of our loved ones."

There has been some handwringing about the lines that consti-tute "peaceful" or "nonviolent" resistance; debates over everything from the punching of avowed white supremacist Richard Spencer to the blocking of Internet troll and Trump supporter Milo Yiannopou-lous from speaking have raged, with someone always bringing up the specter of "playing into their hands" by crossing some imagined lines. These actions get deeply gendered; a criticism of them is nearly always that they are "macho bullshit," signifying nothing.

There is some truth to this—Trump is not likely to be dethroned by a broken Starbucks window. And yet in considering what resis-tance looks like, I would caution against cheering for marches that win hugs from police and frowning at a thrown brick. Marsha P. Johnson's brick that (apocryphally) began the Stonewall Riots was an act of love for her community, not posturing, and the man who wrapped his arms around that car tire may have been dragged off to jail, but he, too, was expressing his love for Garcia de Rayos even as she was taken away.

With this understanding, a group of feminist organizers called for a women's strike on International Women's Day, March 8, 2017, to be a catalyst for building "a feminism of the 99 percent," one that puts violence into context with work.[9] In a piece also published in *The*

Guardian, Linda Martín Alcoff, Cinzia Arruzza, Tithi Bhattacharya, Nancy Fraser, Barbara Ransby, Keeanga-Yamahtta Taylor, Rasmea Yousef Odeh, and Angela Davis wrote, "The idea is to mobilize women, including trans women, and all who support them in an international day of struggle—a day of striking, marching, blocking roads, bridges, and squares, abstaining from domestic, care and sex work, boycotting, calling out misogynistic politicians and companies, striking in educational institutions. These actions are aimed at making visible the needs and aspirations of those whom lean-in feminism ignored: women in the formal labor market, women working in the sphere of social reproduction and care, and unemployed and precarious working women."

On March 8, women in red and their supporters took to the streets around the country to make this vision a reality. Three school districts, Alexandria city public schools in Virginia, Prince George's County public schools in Maryland, and the Chapel Hill–Carrboro school district in North Carolina, were closed down for the day because so many teachers—a profession, again, dominated heavily by women—stayed home from work. The women of the Walmart campaign joined hundreds of others in Washington, D.C., for a "Women Workers Rising" event alongside the women of the National Domestic Workers Alliance and other service workers, centering the gendered labor that women do. In New York, several women were arrested forming a human chain around Trump Tower, including Linda Sarsour and Tamika Mallory of the Women's March on Washington planning committee. They joined women around the world, including in Ireland, where abortion remains illegal; women shut down the center of Dublin to demand the repeal of the Eighth Amendment and the granting of the right to an abortion.

Debates around the strike hemmed and hawed around the issue of "privilege," but the women who turned out on March 8 were work-

ing women whose struggles in the workplace were intimately connected to their political struggles. For the decades of the early labor
movement, this was understood as basic fact, that strikes could be
used to win larger political goals as well as gains in individual workplaces. To move forward in the Trump era, such an understanding
will be necessary again, an understanding that draws on the bedrock
principle of the labor movement—solidarity. That solidarity does not
mean we are all the same, or that we all face the same challenges or
have the same levels of power. But it means that we understand our
struggles as connected and understand that a winning movement
must use the power and talents we all possess in order to bring about
justice.

It means that we are willing to take risks together, because our
liberation is bound up together.

---

1. Mike Isaac, "Uber C.E.O. to Leave Trump Advisory Council After Criticism,"
   New York Times, February 2, 2017. Accessed at https://www.nytimes.com/2017
   /02/02/technology/uber-ceo-travis-kalanick-trump-advisory-council.html?r=0.

2. Francine Prose, "Forget Protest. Trump's Actions Warrant a General National
   Strike," *The Guardian*, January 30, 2017. Accessed at https://www.theguardian
   .com/commentisfree/2017/jan/30/travel-ban-airport-protests-disruption (accessed
   June 6, 2017).

3. Rosa Luxemburg and Patrick Lavin, *The Mass Strike* (London: Bookmarks, 2005).

4. "The Growing Movement for $15," National Employment Law Project, No-
   vember 4, 2015. Accessed on June 6, 2017, at http://www.nelp.org/publication
   /growing-movement-15.

5. Reena Flores, "Andrew Puzder Expected to Withdraw from Labor Secretary
   Nomination, Source Says," CBS News, February 15, 2017. Accessed on
   June 6, 2017, at http://www.cbsnews.com/news/puzder-expected-to-withdraw
   -from-labor-secretary-nomination/.

6. Oliver Laughland and Lauren Gambino, "Restaurants Run by Labor Secretary Nominee Report Disturbing Rates of Sexual Harassment," *The Guardian*, January 10, 2017. Accessed on June 6, 2017, at https://www.theguardian.com/business/2017/jan/10/andrew-puzder-cke-sexual-harassment-labor-secretary.

7. Akiba Solomon, "Special Report: How to Get Away with Harassing, Firing or Never Even Hiring a Trans Worker of Color," *Colorlines*, February 23, 2017. Accessed on June 6, 2017, at http://www.colorlines.com/articles/special-report-how-get-away-harassing-firing-or-never-even-hiring-trans-worker-color.

8. Sarah Jaffe, "In GOP Country, a Small Labor Organization Offers a Model for Fighting Trumpism," *The Nation*, November 4, 2016. Accessed at https://www.thenation.com/article/in-gop-country-a-small-labor-organization-offers-a-model-for-fighting-trumpism.

9. Linda Martín Alcoff, Cinzia Arruzza, et al., "Women of America: We're Going on Strike. Join Us So Trump Will See Our Power," *The Guardian*, February 6, 2017. Accessed at https://www.theguardian.com/commentisfree/2017/feb/06/women-strike-trump-resistance-power.

WE'VE ALWAYS BEEN NASTY
Why the Feminist Movement Needs Trans Women and Gender-Nonconforming Femmes

Meredith Talusan

I WANTED TO BE SAD, but I was too angry. Over the weeks after Donald Trump's election, that anger steadily shifted toward alienation as I watched cisgender women across America find comfort in each other as they planned the Women's March in Washington, an event that over time grew to emphasize emotional relief over radical action. Being an immigrant trans woman of color, I'm used to adapting to the mood of the majority. But from both collective and personal experience, I'd learned that comfort and despair are emotions that must be deferred out of necessity in times of grave crisis, and to be wary of protests that don't engage in confrontation, because people in power have no motive to change their ways unless they feel threatened. While I've taken to writing in part because there are so few trans women of color like me who have overcome the systemic discrimination that pervades our lives, and recognize the need to amplify the voices of my trans siblings, I am keenly aware that it has been through directly confronting injustice that my communities have survived and persisted.

Trans women and gender-nonconforming femmes have always

been marginalized at best if not outright excluded from the American feminist movement. Even among cisgender women who don't believe that someone needs to be born with a vagina to be a woman, we continue to be seen not as potential leaders with unique knowledge, but either as victims or as tokens to include, as long as our opinions don't stray too far from the majority. Cisgender women who lead other women boldly are lauded; transgender women are accused of behaving like men, and those of us who are feminine but don't consider ourselves women are commonly excluded altogether. These exclusions are particularly glaring in light of Trump, as trans women and femmes who have a long collective and individual history of battling for our rights are relegated to the margins of discussions about how feminists should fight this unjust administration.

Ironically, trans women's position among feminists is analogous to Hillary Clinton's position among the American electorate, even other white, cisgender women like her. In both cases, it's not simply the assumption that women are inferior that's to blame, but more precisely a gender essentialism that dictates how men and women are supposed to behave to be deemed good and respectable. Clinton's loss, despite the fact that she was exceedingly better qualified than Trump, mirrors the way trans women and femmes are marginalized in post-Trump feminism, despite our significantly greater experience with fighting oppression, compared to the vast majority of white cisgender women.

In Clinton's case, the proof of this gender essentialism is that despite all the feminist movement has achieved, 53 percent of white women voted for a blatant misogynist in Trump, who repeatedly expressed disregard for women's bodies and hostility toward our minds. They did so because they agreed—at least implicitly—with Trump's assessment of Clinton in the third presidential debate as a "nasty woman."

According to gender norms that Trump espouses, a woman is

"nasty" simply for disagreeing with him, much less occupying the ultimate position of power as U.S. president. Despite decades of progress by the feminist movement to expand the reach of women's rights and abilities, there is still a deeply ingrained belief that a woman shouldn't be too loud, too smart, or too ambitious. This is why a large proportion of women persisted in seeing Clinton as ruthless and untrustworthy while granting Trump every excuse for behavior that was far more objectionable.

Now, as feminists organize to resist the Trump administration, I find myself deeply concerned that patriarchy continues to undermine feminist action. The same gender essentialism that contributed to Clinton's loss still plagues the movement, making it harder for feminists to adopt aggressive and confrontational strategies that challenge ingrained notions of what a woman is and how she's supposed to behave. This essentialism—and the fixed gender roles it assumes—undermines the very feminist movement we're attempting to enact for the benefit of all people, in a society that constantly pressures us into adopting rigid definitions of who we are and what we can be.

To find its way, the feminist movement needs guidance and inspiration from trans women and femmes. Cisgender white women are deemed nasty when they behave in a way that challenges gender norms. But trans women and femmes' very existence is rooted in rebellion against gender expectations: we defy the patriarchy's fundamental assumption that any person "born" male would never want to give up that privilege. In this era of crisis, feminists must turn to the example of transgender women and femmes, who have always been nasty.

We were nasty in August 1966, when Felicia Elizondo and other trans women and femmes rioted at the Compton's Cafeteria in San Francisco's Tenderloin district, where police attempted to remove them for cross-dressing, which was then illegal.

We were nasty when Marsha P. Johnson and other transgender

women and femmes of color were the first to spar with police during the 1969 Stonewall Riots in New York, sparking the modern LGBTQ movement.

We were nasty when Sylvia Rivera grabbed the mic at the Christopher Street Liberation Day in 1973, fighting to speak onstage after organizers tried to silence her and referred to her as a "man in women's clothing."

We were nasty in the 1980s, when the Sisters of Perpetual Indulgence in San Francisco and denizens of the drag ball and pageant scene in New York rallied and raised money to call attention to the AIDS epidemic.

We were nasty when Chelsea Manning leaked videos and documents in 2010 that showed the U.S. military and diplomats had intentionally killed Iraqi civilians, including women and children.

We were nasty when Jennicet Gutiérrez interrupted former president Barack Obama during a speech at the White House LGBT reception in 2015, calling for better treatment of trans and queer immigrants in immigration detention centers.

We were nasty when we acknowledged to ourselves that our gender did not fall into the binary.

We were nasty when we lived in defiance of gender expectations in spite of great personal and social cost.

FEMINISM'S GENDER PROBLEM

The Women's March on January 21, 2017—the largest one-day demonstration in U.S. history—has been post-Trump feminism's most visible manifestation, and a prime example of how the movement marginalizes trans women and femmes. The demonstration grew out of a call by fashion designer Bob Bland, who recruited a multiracial team of organizers—Tamika Mallory, Carmen Perez, and Linda Sarsour—to plan the event. The group included no trans women or gender-nonconforming femmes. While organizers made a late attempt to include trans women among the march's leadership, their efforts only further demonstrated the ways feminists fail to include transgender people. Even the march's name adheres to the strictures of binary gender, leaving no room for lives that exist between the lines.

"Although I'm glad to be here now, it's disheartening that women like me were an afterthought in the initial planning of this march," wrote Raquel Willis, one of the march's two transgender speakers, in a speech she prepared for the event. "Many of us had to stand a little taller to be heard and that exclusion is nothing new." As if to underscore the point, Willis was unable to say these words at the demonstration itself because organizers cut her off. The other trans speaker, Janet Mock, contributed the line "in solidarity with the sex workers' rights movement" to the march's platform, reflecting her own experience performing sex work to obtain gender-affirming surgery. The line was mysteriously revised to "those exploited for labor and sex" before Mock asked for it to be restored.

More sweepingly, trans marginalization in post-Trump feminism is embedded in the continued use of gender-essentialist rhetoric and symbols. Slogans such as "Pussy Power," "Pussy Grabs Back," and the ubiquitous pink pussy hats worn by a large proportion of women attending the march centered genitals as the primary symbol of womanhood. While designed to counter Trump's controversial remark that he routinely "grabs women by the pussy," these instances demonstrate ignorance of the long and ongoing history of trans-exclusion on the basis of genitals.

While it's important to discuss the specific oppressions associated with vaginas in matters ranging from abortion rights to sexual assault, to deploy the vagina as an overarching symbol for womanhood marginalizes trans women and GNC femmes. For many of us, the phrase "grab them by the pussy" does not just raise the specter of assault, as it does for cis women, but recalls threats and experiences of violence—even murder—at the hands of men who have grabbed our genitals only to discover that we're the "wrong gender." Pussy hats may empower cisgender women, but they are a painful reminder of the high price of admission to womanhood for trans women who want reassignment surgery and cannot afford it, as well as those of us who do not think surgery should be a necessary condition for acceptance into the feminist fold.

Rather than engage in dialogue or address the hats' unintended effects, Pussyhat Project co-founder Krista Suh could only offer a well-worn method for excusing oppression, which is to claim good intentions. "I never thought that by calling it the 'pussyhat' that it was saying that women's issues are predicated on the possession of the pussy," she said. To Suh and the leaders of the Pussyhat Project—who continue to promote pussy hats without any substantial change to the name or message—good intentions are enough because, like centuries of men oppressing women with similarly good intentions, they do things for our own benefit as long as we remain quiet.

Like so many other periods in feminist history—from the suffragette movement to second-wave feminism's emphasis on the right to work for middle-class white women—the current moment demonstrates how a feminism driven by cis, white values inherently marginalizes those of us who do not fall into the category.

DECENTER THE PUSSY

I don't engage in this difficult critique of a movement I want to embrace, involving many women I admire and a gender I have made many sacrifices to belong to, merely to rehash squabbles about who gets a seat at the table and why. I do so because it is my firm belief that a feminist movement that marginalizes, alienates, and excludes a people who have had no choice but to struggle for our legitimacy and existence is deeply wrongheaded, that the march unquestionably did so, and that a feminist future cannot afford to engage in such exclusion if it is to be at its most effective in fighting the Trump administration.

To refuse binary gender is not just to include trans women and femmes, but to deny the social construction that oppresses women in the first place. It opens the door for necessary collaboration across the multiple definitions of gender. I see the goal of the feminist movement not as a displacement of masculinity and men by women, but for all genders to have an equal chance to be represented in all spheres. This requires not just femininity but masculinity, not just women but also people who are not women, and ultimately men.

A successful feminist movement must include us not merely as token individuals but with our full selves and the revolutionary perspectives we represent. Trans women and femmes' acceptance into the feminist fold cannot be conditional on us needing to call ourselves women or on womanhood being symbolized by genitals. We cannot be truly included in the current movement if we are spoken of primarily as victims, occasionally as inspirations. To include representatives of a marginalized community only when they agree to the structures and frameworks set up by the majority is the definition of respectability and tokenist politics. This agenda is not only ineffective against Trump, but is rooted in the belief that women can get what they want if they only ask politely.

By our very nature, trans and gender-nonconforming people challenge the way gender is defined and policed. The litany of assumptions that come with the gender binary boil down to expectations about how women are supposed to behave. Women are conditioned not to take; they ask because it is men who take. Women aren't violent because it is men who are violent. Women don't use physical force because it is men who use physical force. These dynamics were continually reinforced during and after the Women's March, which was characterized by safety and nonconfrontation. Multiple news headlines like PEACE, POSITIVITY AS MASSIVE WOMEN'S MARCH MAKES VOICES HEARD IN D.C. and NO ARRESTS MADE AT PEACEFUL WOMEN'S MARCH emphasized this aspect of the event.

But as a number of critics subsequently noted, the reason the march was so safe is that white women are not considered dangerous. From a protest perspective, this should be cause for concern, as even a cursory historical examination shows how protesters are only taken seriously by unjust administrations when they disrupt and threaten the existing order.

Indeed, the dominant strategy of post-Trump feminism has been to call, send postcards, make requests of elected officials, engage in nonconfrontational protests, make speeches among sympathetic audiences. It only takes a glance to see how gendered these strategies are, especially compared to the large-scale and necessarily confrontational protests that have attended the LGBTQ and black civil rights movements, from Stonewall to ACT UP, Birmingham to Black Lives Matter.

Now is not the time to be conciliatory. Now is not the time to request or plead, but to demand. When faced with large-scale injustice, we must be prepared to rebel and disobey, to risk physical harm or imprisonment. To confront state power, we must be dangerous enough to foment actual resistance.

There is a mountain of evidence that Trump has committed impeachable offenses that may also involve other members of his administration, yet we have not used our bodies and selves to forcibly fight for his removal, whether by refusing to leave public spaces until officials agree to begin impeachment proceedings, entering spaces like congressional offices to confront officials who prop Trump up, or other actions that could lead to police confrontation, arrest, or imprisonment because we fight a state power we know to be unjust.

The history of transgender resistance in the United States can offer post-Trump feminists important tactical lessons. Here are a few:

We must interrupt, otherwise it's too easy for us to be ignored.

We must take the mic when other people exclude us.

We must take to the streets not merely to chant and make ourselves feel better, but to risk and anticipate confrontation.

We should not be afraid to throw a brick if a brick needs to be thrown. There are times when a single instance of violence is a justifiable response to pervasive and encompassing oppression by the state.

We must risk our safety, because it is only when we ourselves are unsafe that those in power can truly fear us.

We must risk imprisonment, because it is our unjust presence in prisons that stands a chance of demonstrating grave injustice.

If we want to address the oppression of women, we must assume the larger goal of abolishing a binary gender system that oppresses all of us. That can only be achieved by fully embracing the presence, example, and inspiration of trans and gender-nonconforming people as part of a broader feminist movement. Now is not the time to marginalize and tokenize us, to name us but not embody us, to represent us but not listen to us. Trans women and femmes have always been nasty. To resist, we must all be nasty together.

X CUNTRY
A Muslim-American Woman's Journey

Randa Jarrar

IN THE SUMMER of 2016, a sabbatical ahead of me, and my adult son now living away from home, I decided to drive across the country alone. Before I left, I went to Washington State to see one of my favorite lovers. When I arrived, he told me he was falling for a new woman. So I took a ferry to Vashon Island alone and stayed there for a week.

My friend, the poet M, came to the island to visit me. He has written books of poetry and works in tech and is Arab. He is one of my Others. You recognize these people: siblings you have never met. The siblings you would choose if you could choose siblings. Friends without benefits, as M would say. We are both fat and beautiful.

M says Seattle's dating scene is oppressive. When I ask how, he says everyone wants to hike, or ride bikes, or camp, or canoe. He wants to know why he can't just watch a movie with someone and fuck. I tell him Netflix and chill is a thing. He says it is not a thing in Seattle. M is older than me and the women he meets are all fighting against wrinkles and death. M says it's easier being a Christian in Cairo than it is being a couch potato in Seattle.

M and I terrify everyone at a brunch place on the island. We are the only people of color and he keeps saying the word "suicide." He is talking about his depression but the woman in fabric sandals and a crocheted tank top sitting next to us is shifting uncomfortably across from her salad. When we leave, we see two young black men sitting in chairs outside a storefront and we greet each other instantly, helping erase the memory of the uptight woman at brunch.

Afterward we walk to a marijuana clinic I'd driven past the day before and are told that we need a prescription. I get angry and I ask M in Arabic if we should tip the woman or bribe her to give us weed. I am joking but he looks at me seriously and says, "Maybe we should." I say no and we walk back to my rental car.

Except we walk past the rental car and past the two young men again. They are sharing a joint back and forth. I notice and M notices, too. We have to turn around because we walked past the car. We pass the young men again. They greet us again. We get in the car and as soon as I start it, M says, "We can't ask those guys for weed."

And I say, "Of course we can't."

"We can't get those guys in trouble," he says.

I agree with M. I tell him that yes, it's racist to ask the only two black people we have seen today on the island for weed.

M says we should go to Seattle and score legal weed. This involves taking a ferry, which is beautiful and romantic, even in a friends-without-benefits kind of way, and I agree, and we drive past the two guys as they continue to pass the joint between each other.

M wants to know why I plan to drive cross-country. I tell him that I want to commune with the land I live on; to see America during this deeply troubled and troubling election year. To look at the place that might elect a person like Trump.

I tell him I love the feeling of forward motion; that driving feels like home. And I tell him that I had read an essay by Edward Said about Tahia Carioca, an Egyptian actress and belly dancer who had driven cross-country in America twice in the 1960s.

"Twice!" I repeat to M. "She didn't even live here. She had a tendency to do things multiple times," I say.

M understands, and says, "Yes, she was married more than a dozen times."

"Every time she wanted to fuck someone, she had to marry them," I said.

M agrees. Then he tells me to watch the road.

There are no squirrels on the island, but there are deer. In the five days I stay here, I have to avoid three deer crossing the road. A deer crosses now, gorgeous and graceful.

"Tahia?" I yell after the deer. "Tahia! You are beautiful in this new form."

Arizona meant unattractive people, and when I tried to drive to Sedona, I realized halfway there that the terrain and view were replicas of King's Canyon, which is forty minutes from my house in California. But by then it was too late. I was behind a row of cars whose drivers were elderly, their feet fluttering constantly against their brakes. When we pulled into the resort area, I found a way to turn around, and began making my way to New Mexico.

My last stop in Flagstaff was the gas station; my dog Jojo hates the car so I took her with me to the restroom after I pumped gas. We squeezed into the restroom, which was busy with a matriarch and her daughter and her daughter's daughter, all Native Americans, all instantly kind to me and my dog. The stalls were full except one, and when I got out, the women were gone. Instead a white woman in a trucker uniform was washing her hands. I stood by her and washed my hands, too.

"This place is a shithole," she said.

"I think it's rather nice," I said.

"The bathrooms across the street are like a four-star hotel, but I can't go there," she said, "because I'm a truck driver, and we don't really choose where we stop."

She was wearing a pair of wraparound blue trucker shades.

"Some people just shit in their trucks and throw the bag out the window," she said.

"They do?" I said, amused.

"Yes, well, the people they got driving now, they're not from here. They're not American. They're Syrians. Might as well hire monkeys to drive trucks now."

"I'm glad they got out of Syria," I said, now that I understood that this woman had waited for all the brown people to leave the bathroom, and that as soon as she saw me, a light-skinned woman whom she assumed was white, she was able to be comfortable and vocal in her racism.

"Are ya?" she said, vaguely disgusted.

"Yes," I said. "They've been through hell. I'm Palestinian," I said, and for the first time realized I was taller than her.

She walked away and said, "Well, I hope you're okay with spending your tax dollars on them."

"I am," I said. "My tax dollars pay for my son's school, for the roads I drive on, and for bombs that kill Arabs, by the way."

She didn't say anything. I could have left, but I went after her. She had hidden in the convenience store's aisles. When I saw her, I said, "I'm not a monkey. You're a racist. You have no idea what it's like to be a refugee."

It has happened before; a person thinks I'm cool with their racism, or, more confusingly, when they find out I'm queer, with their sexism.

I got back to the car and held my dog and shook.

———

Woke up in Santa Fe to the news of fifty dead in Florida. Fifty gay people. Murdered.

A few minutes later: the shooter was Muslim.

A little while after that: he identified with ISIS.

A few hours after that: he was gay and went to the club often.

I drove from northern New Mexico to Truth or Consequences. Every few miles a sign would announce that I was leaving a reservation.

NOW LEAVING SANTO DOMINGO RESERVATION.

NOW LEAVING SAN FELIPE RESERVATION.

NOW LEAVING ISLETA RESERVATION.

Reservations all named after Spanish conquerors; genocidal.

The drive was less than four hours long. I arrived in Truth or Consequences in the hazy afternoon, the sun beating down and blanching the sidewalks, sending heat off the asphalt. I checked into my motel and the attendant told me that the room I was staying in had been floated, along with the rest of the row house, down from Elephant Butte Lake in the early twentieth century. After she left I washed my hands in the sink, and the walk from sink to bed was wobbly, as if the wood plank floors were still over water. I curled up with my dog on the bed and slept for a long time.

When I came to, I read a list of the dead in Orlando and wept. After I started weeping, I couldn't stop.

From New Mexico I drove to El Paso and from there I drove to Marfa. Border patrol checkpoint asked me if I was a citizen. I said yes. They let me through. In my bra, a half-smoked joint. My happy fat Arab heart.

———

I am on sabbatical, and I am expecting myself to write about domestic violence. To record the pain my body has been in. I don't want to. I want to take baths and swim and fuck and eat and walk and read and laugh. I don't want to relive the pain I hated living through the first time I lived through it.

My old friends from Austin come to visit me.

The Marfa thrift store. We walk in and there are three Confederate flags in a vase. I ask the cashier, an ex–New Yorker, why they have them. He says they were donated and that we can have them for free because he knows we will destroy them. We put them in the trunk, then take them to a field and break and trash them. We want to set them on fire but the desert is dry.

We each receive citations for drinking beer at a natural pool. Other people are drinking out of Koozies, or hiding their liquor in the cooler. We are drinking openly and Officer Teel does not like that. I argue with him for half an hour but he just gives me an additional note on my citation for language. He categorizes me as white. I tell him I'm not white. He asks what I am. I tell him. He puts me down as white anyway. The pool is full of small fish and catfish. We leave as soon as Officer Teel is gone.

At night, we make shadow puppets in front of the Catholic church in town and I ring the church bell and thank the nun for her service to Jesus. I piss on a fire hydrant. We disturb a man named Bill, a visual artist, and he lets us into his studio. We climb up to the roof, and climb back down.

I left Texas a week early. Loneliness. Aimlessness. An hour northeast
I passed a bar called I Don't Care Bar & Grill. In Wichita Falls a
woman at Whataburger befriended me and showed me pictures of
the son she birthed three months earlier, the son who was so prema-
ture he died. I could not say no to her; she wanted to unburden her
grief for just a few minutes and I was free to hold it for her.

I drove on to Oklahoma City and checked into an old hotel. I read
about Alton Sterling, a black man shot point-blank in the head by
police. I watched the video knowing that it would make me rageful.

White men with money sit across the hotel lobby from me on red
velvet sofas, under a painting of white men sitting on sofas. The real
white men talk about Donald Trump and the longer I look at them,
the longer their bodies seem to be surrounded with red blood.

My hotel was built in the 1800s by black people. There was a white
bartender complaining to another bartender, a woman, who had to
emotionally massage his pain. He said he'd been captured on film by
a news crew and that they'd asked his permission to use his likeness
and he'd said yes. But when he watched the news that night he'd been
cut out of the segment.

He was very upset telling the other bartender about this.

"I thought I was going to be on the news," he said, "but they cut
me out."

I got cut out of the news.

They cut me.

Out of the news.

Alton Sterling dying, being murdered, every minute on the news.
Over and over again. Palestinian children in white burial cloth. Black
and brown bodies wishing they weren't on the news. Mothers wishing they didn't live in an empire or under the thumb of one, an empire that depends on the myth of their resilience.

———————

Before breakfast I walk outside the hotel with my dog, and the valet wants to talk to us. He likes my dog. He reaches over to pet her and I notice he has a tattoo on his wrist. I ask him if it's a tattoo in Arabic. He says yes and shows it to me. It says *I love.* I tell him, "It says 'I love.'" He says, "It says *my* love." It says *I love.* But I nod. He says an Iraqi friend wrote it for him. An Iraqi guy, he said. He used to work here. I ask him if he heard of the bombing in Baghdad a few days ago. He nods, sadly. I say, "The Global North is fucked up for living in comfort at the expense of the Global South." He says yes, and we act like our lives are so hard. He shakes his head. I want to embrace him.

I drive through Bricktown. There's a Flaming Lips Lane. I drive past bars shut down because it's morning, and the fanciest Sonic I have ever seen—it's a brick building, not a drive-through.

I drive north and wind my way to the Alfred P. Murrah Federal Building, to the site of the 1995 bombing. It is no longer a bombed-out building at all. Years of living in the Middle East, of growing up around sites of trauma and war, make it difficult for me to process memorial sites.

The serenity, cleanliness, sterile slate-gray tile, water, life replacing horror.

This site has all of that. It is across the street from a church. There is a small painting of a Jesus who appears biracial; indigenous and white. He embraces the nineteen children who died in the bombing.

The site is windows on sky and an artificial and shallow lake where the building once stood. It reminds me of the Robert Irwin Project, a rebuilding of a World War I hospital in Marfa, Texas, at the Chinati Foundation. Both are updates on sites of death. Here, there is a tiny section of the original building left. It's beautiful. The top of it is devastated: cracked, burned, and bombed. It reaches up toward a tree and the sky.

The bombing was the deadliest act of "native" U.S. terrorism: 168

people died; hundreds were injured. The white perpetrators were sentenced to death (Timothy McVeigh) and life in prison (Terry Nichols). McVeigh was executed three months before 9/11.

DRIVE TO ST LOUIS.
Signs along the way:

LEAVING KIOWA-COMANCHE-APACHE RESERVATION
LEAVING SAC AND FOX NATION

No sign welcoming drivers to the nations and reservations, which I love. *You are not welcome here. We'll let you know when you're wanted, which is never.*

I'm remembering the story inside Leslie Marmon Silko's *Ceremony*. A group of indigenous American witches have a contest hundreds and hundreds of years ago about who can cast the best spell or create the best ceremony. And the one that does is the one that calls the white people over, the one that predicts colonizers. It's always been such a hair-raising and terrifying idea, one that places power back in the hands of the oppressed, as if to say, "We sent for you."

I get pulled over by a Missouri police officer for speeding. There is a larger SUV that was going the same exact speed as I was but I'm the one who gets pulled over and my hair is extra frizzy and big today. The cop approaches my car gingerly—he is slim, pale, and short, and wearing a wide-brim hat. As soon as he sees my face his body language changes. If I seemed like a light-skinned black woman from behind, I seem like a white woman from the front. My dog climbs up on the window frame and he asks if she is friendly. I say she is very friendly. He asks for my license and registration. I reach into my bag. I bring out my wallet. I lean over and give him my license. At no point does he seem threatened or pull a gun on me or kill me. I even ask if he can give me a warning. I was going eighty-six in a seventy. I understand my privilege and actually request a warning. He says I am receiving a citation because eighty-six is too high for a warning, but his inflection is apologetic. He gives me my ticket, which says I was going eighty-five. I go along my way, alive. In one piece.

It's raining in St Louis. I'm sitting across from an interracial old buddy duo.

The white one says *turbanhead*. The black one laughs.

Philando Castile was shot dead yesterday in a routine traffic stop. He'd been stopped forty-six times up until that point. He paid off every single citation. The police officer shot him anyway. I walk around Soulard and go to the farmers market. An elderly man wants me to sit with him to talk about my dog, so I do. On the way into St. Louis there are signs: PASS WITH CARE. My fat Arab body continues to pass for white.

Coup in Turkey. My friend M the poet had asked if he could contribute to my ticket to Istanbul two days earlier, and I had finally agreed. I find out at the Detroit Institute for the Arts. My friend K tells me to check the news. No gathering for us there. Fewer and fewer places to be safe.

Mid-July, and I'm drinking tea at an Arab queer coffee shop called The Bottom Line in Detroit. Later, K will take me to a jazz club and D will meet us there and tell us stories about her mother. We stop at a gas station for cigarettes and the Arab guy looks at all three of us and says, "Lebanese, Chaldean, Palestinian," pointing at K, D, and me. He's right but K isn't impressed; she says later that we should've gone to the hot-Arab-guy gas station two miles away. Detroit is full of white people. Where did they come from? They've bought houses and turned them into Airbnbs. The old train station has windows on it now. Glass, real windows. It no longer resembles the site of a bombing.

I've made it clear across the nation and am now in Connecticut, visiting my parents. My parents, who thought they'd be safe and sound if they moved to a place like Connecticut. My parents, who do not pass for white.

The neighbors on our left and our right are both voting for Trump. They have their flags and signs up. My parents don't want to put any signs up. They're afraid.

Hillary was officially nominated by the DNC last night. Everyone who spoke ahead of her these past few days, especially the people of color—the Khans, Astrid Silva, etc.—was so much more interesting than her. Why, I keep thinking, why would our next president be someone who is married to an ex-president? The ways power in our country remains in a fixed place angers me.

The morning after the last day of the convention, I try to tell my mother that the house is haunted. That my father chased me around that house with a knife once. The neighbors didn't call the police that day. I had to call them myself.

"Why do you remember these old things?" my mother says, annoyed. "There were so many other, happier memories in this house."

I can't help but laugh. My mother, the empath.

———————

My parents' neighbor next door keeps coming over to say hi. She's known me since I was fifteen. She never had children because she couldn't. The neighbor on the left says hi, too. She had her child via surrogate. I was so aware, as a young mother, of the perceived ease with which I conceived and had my son at the age of eighteen.

The neighbor on the left tells me that she's voting for Trump but that she knows Muslims aren't bad people. "Look at your family," she says. "You guys are just like everyone else. Hardworking and kind."

I don't want to talk to her at all, so I say, "Please don't act welcoming. This is my country."

Later, when Trump wins, I'll imagine, in a terrifying fever dream, she and the other neighbors watching as fascist police drag my father's Parkinson's-addled body out of his house, our house. I'll imagine my son and me back in the basement, where we used to live when he was a baby. This time, he's an adult, and I have to make-believe he's my servant to keep him alive.

I have crossed the entire country, and am nowhere near home.

TRUST BLACK WOMEN

Zerlina Maxwell

BLACK WOMEN TRIED to save you, America. You didn't want to be saved.

Ninety-four percent of black women voted for Hillary Clinton in the 2016 presidential election, if for no other reason than to keep Donald Trump out of the White House. We tried to save you, even though there were good reasons to have some skepticism that President Hillary Clinton would bring meaningful change to black lives. In many ways, the first woman to earn a major party nomination personifies the second-wave feminist movement of the 1960s and '70s, which didn't do enough to center the most marginalized women. Had she won, it would have been seen primarily as a victory for white, affluent feminists, who remain a narrow subset of the movement with outsize influence on public discourse. And yet, at the center of her campaign—in policy making, web design, communications, and strategy—were black women. From the most junior staffer up through senior advisers, we were involved in every single aspect of the campaign. Hillary may be the public face of white feminism, but nevertheless she attracts and empowers black women.

humanity, must declare our "magic" in the face of obstacles to progress at every level. The phrase "Black Girl Magic" stems from a
hashtag and online movement to uplift black women and to acknowledge their excellence in the face of white-supremacist structures that
perpetuate constant messages of inferiority. It's all about celebrating
our universal awesomeness even when the world writ large does not.
So, while cable news fed America's appetite for sensationalized
tragedy by airing seemingly endless images and videos of black
bodies being brutalized, the black women on Hillary's campaign
tried to keep the focus on our magic and our goal of electing the
first woman president. The act of getting up to go to work began to
feel like an act of resistance.

"We flocked to each other every time a new member of the Black
Girl Magic team joined the campaign," says Blandin. "We sought
each other out and created a community, from brunch to venting sessions; we always had each other's backs. [One of the most important
lessons I learned] is the importance and value of black sisterhood."

Erin Stevens, the campaign's New York political director, told me
that on the hardest days, Hillary's own example of how to handle ad-
versity was helpful. "I would reflect on how she persevered through
some of the most challenging moments—like being vilified for being
a career woman in her own right or daring to fight for universal health
care. And she still figured out ways to push through and move forward
and make things happen. And she would do it with grace. It's what
we do as black women *all the time*."

It's clear upon reflection that in many ways, black women connected more with Hillary's platform and message than the 53 percent
of white women who voted for Donald Trump. Maybe that's because
Hillary Clinton's political resilience is something that black women
are best positioned to understand. We know what it's like to be left
out of important conversations about issues that affect us directly,
as when people claim to discuss "women" but really mean "white

women." We know what it's like to see our suffering ignored; there were no "Million Hoodies" marches for Renisha McBride or many of the other black women slain by police or vigilantes in recent years. We know what it's like to be underestimated, hence #BlackGirlMagic. And we know what it's like to persevere anyway.

"I'm almost certain working on this campaign was the most important thing I will ever do," says Logan Anderson, who joined Team Hillary three days after her college graduation and spent the better part of two years trying to make history. "I've spent so much of my life fighting for justice—racial justice, reproductive justice, economic justice—and the campaign allowed me to fight for what I believe in on the highest level, in the most high-stakes environment possible. And while I can't understate how important fighting to elect the first woman president was to me, it was even more important for that woman to be Hillary Clinton."

This was a common sentiment inside the campaign. But even to black women who didn't naturally jump on board to support Hillary as a candidate, because of the perception that she wasn't centering our experiences in her policy proposals, the importance of voting for her in the general election was obvious. As director of African-American media Denise Horn told me, "These white women need to learn how to step outside of their white privilege and imagine the lives of those who are at risk under the Trump-Pence administration." Adds Blandin, "As usual, they will benefit from the fight and sacrifices of the other women, who will continue to march and push back against all of Trump's efforts."

Conversations between white women who voted for Donald Trump and black women who supported and worked for Hillary Clinton will not be easy, but that's why we need to begin having them, every day, at every opportunity, and with anyone open to having them. It's not until we confront these inequities among different types of women that we can move forward. Progress for one white woman *can* be part of progress for all women, but only if women of all colors play a role in making that progress a reality.

"I supported [Hillary] not just because she was the most qualified person to ever run for president but [because] I appreciated how she always elevated and supported black women throughout her career," says Blandin. "If she [had been] elected, I am more than confident that she would have made sure that we all had a seat at the table in her administration." The question remains why 53 percent of white women did not share the belief that Hillary's agenda would represent their interests well.

We tried to save you.

Upon realizing the reality of a President-elect Donald Trump, the first thought I had was, Did you really think you were going to get the first woman nominated and she was going to win? I suddenly felt naive for getting caught up in the history-making aspects of the 2016 campaign, without a full acknowledgment of the sexist structures that allowed forty-four men to be America's president, compared to zero women, over the course of 238 years. In that moment of loss, I was forced to admit that while America may be ready for a black president, it's not yet ready for a president who is not a man. And in light of that, it's definitely not ready for a black woman. Not yet.

As a black woman who has lived thirty-five years of life in America in my black-girl body, I know just how much better we have to be to get half as far as the white man standing next to us at the starting line. It still hurts to be reminded so starkly.

"Electing the first woman president is and will remain a priority for me until we can accomplish that goal," says campaign senior adviser Minyon Moore. "I think it is important, because we know that women are immensely qualified to run this country . . . [But] being the first at anything is always hard. There is no blueprint or roadmap.

You are making the blueprint as you blaze that trail. Black women know this."

The world may not always acknowledge our abilities and excellence, but Hillary's campaign put us all in a position to become our own biggest cheerleaders, advocating for each other's ideas and centering our communities in every single move we made. "I am still so impressed and proud of being part of a campaign where so many dynamic black women were in key positions across the campaign and in roles of leadership. It was amazing how we would come together and help support each other and lift each other up. We helped each other when we faced resistance to our ideas and when we voiced our opinions, and we also created opportunities for one another and celebrated each other's accomplishments and successes," says Stevens.

"I watched the same thing happen over and over to black women in every department of the campaign," says LaDavia Drane, the campaign's African-American outreach director. "When people trust us, great things happen." Or, as the young political newbie Logan Anderson puts it, "The biggest lesson I learned: the most important thing I can do is trust black women—including myself."

Hillary Clinton trusts black women. Her campaign employed and empowered black women, and the #BlackGirlMagic that filled the cubicles at the campaign's Brooklyn headquarters is certain to change the world in the coming decades, even as Trump occupies 1600 Pennsylvania Avenue. Future generations of black women can look up to the women like me who helped Hillary become the nominee of a major party for the first time in American history. We may not be at the center of the national political conversation or mainstream policy goals, but at the center of Hillary's campaign and agenda, black women made history in a different way.

HOW TO BUILD A MOVEMENT

Alicia Garza

I'VE BEEN GRAPPLING with how to challenge cynicism in a moment that requires all of us to show up differently.

On Saturday, I joined more than a million women in Washington, D.C., to register my opposition to the new regime. Participating in the Women's March—if you count satellite protests around the country, the largest one-day mobilization in the history of the United States—was both symbolic and challenging.

Like many other black women, I was conflicted about participating. That a group of white women had drawn clear inspiration from the 1963 March on Washington for Jobs and Freedom, yet failed to acknowledge the historical precedent, rubbed me the wrong way. Here they go again, I thought, adopting the work of black people while erasing us.

I'd had enough before it even began. Fifty-three percent of white women who voted in the 2016 presidential election did so for a man who aims to move society backward. Were white women now having buyer's remorse? I wondered. Where were all of these white people while our people were being killed in the streets, jobless, homeless, over-incarcerated, undereducated? Were they committed to freedom for everyone, or just themselves?

For weeks, I sat on the sidelines. I saw debates on Listservs about whether or not to attend the march, the shade on social media directed at the "white women's march." Unconvinced that white women would ever fight for the rights of all of us, many black women decided to sit the march out.

Yet as time went on and the reality of the incoming Donald Trump administration sank in, something began to gnaw at me. Did I believe that a mass movement was necessary to transform power in this country? Did I believe that this mass movement must be multiracial and multiclass? Did I believe that to build that mass movement, organizing beyond the choir was necessary? If I believed all of these things, how did we get there and what would my role be in making it happen?

I decided to challenge myself to be a part of something that wasn't perfect, that wouldn't articulate my values the way that I did, but that I'd still show up for, clear in my commitment, open and vulnerable to people who were new in their activism. I could be critical of white women and, at the same time, seek out and join with women, white and of color, who were awakening to the fact that all lives do not, in fact, matter, without compromising my dignity, my safety, and my radical politics.

In the end, I joined an estimated 1 million people who participated in the Washington, D.C., march and the estimated 3 million who marched around the world. I have participated in hundreds of demonstrations, but this was one of the first times where I didn't know or know of most of the people there.

Sandwiched between other protesters like a sardine in a can, I spoke with demonstrators in the crowd who said this was their first time participating in a mass mobilization. I saw people for whom this wasn't their first time at a demonstration, but who thought that the days of protesting for our rights were over. I asked them what brought them there. They said they wanted to stand up for all of us. They realized that they, too, were under attack. They wanted to live in a world where everyone was valued, safe, and taken care of. They were in awe of just how many people were there, just like them, to oppose the values of President Donald Trump's administration. They wanted to do something besides feel hopeless.

That evening, I participated in a town hall meeting that drew more than seven hundred people and had more than eleven hundred on the waiting list. Those gathered were mostly white, though there were also people of color present. About half the room said that the Women's March was the first time they'd participated in a mass mobilization. They were willing to learn about how change happens and how they could be involved. And that was just the beginning.

Checking my social media feed that evening, I read comment after comment dismissing the march—an experience that was transformative for hundreds of thousands of people. I wondered what would have happened if, instead of inviting people in, I'd told people to fuck off and go home. Would they have come back? Would it have mattered if they didn't?

Anger has an important place in transforming our political consciousness, and should be valued as such. But it's not enough. The white lady with the pink knitted pussy hat who came to the march was angry as hell when her future president talked about grabbing women by the pussy. Though she may have been sitting on the sidelines up until now, she decided that she was going to do something about it. Anger at the way America depends on immigrant labor yet forces undocumented immigrants to live in the shadows may lead others to join the movement. Black Americans mad as hell about the ways that this country strips us of our humanity might join the movement, even though they didn't before.

I agree with Solange Knowles when she says, "I got a lot to be mad about, and I have a right to be mad." But again, that anger is not enough. It is insufficient to build or take power. Anger will not change the fact that Republicans have taken control of all three branches of government and control both chambers of the legislature in thirty-two states. Anger will not stop vigilantes from terrorizing our communities, and anger will not change an economy that deems too many of us disposable.

More than a moral question, it is a practical one. Can we build a movement of millions with the people who may not grasp our black, queer, feminist, intersectional, anti-capitalist, anti-imperialist ideology but know that we deserve a better life and who are willing to fight for it and win?

If there was ever a time to activate our organizer superpowers, this is it. I'm not going to argue that black people or other people of color need to stop holding white people accountable. White people are not going anywhere, but neither are we if we don't start to think and do differently.

Hundreds of thousands of people are trying to figure out what it means to join a movement. If we demonstrate that to be a part of a movement, you must believe that people cannot change, that transformation is not possible, that it's more important to be right than to be connected and interdependent, we will not win.

If our movement is not serious about building power, then we are just engaged in a futile exercise of who can be the most radical.

This is a moment for all of us to remember who we were when we stepped into the movement—to remember the organizers who were patient with us, who disagreed with us and yet stayed connected, who smiled knowingly when our self-righteousness consumed us.

Building a movement requires reaching out beyond the people who agree with you.

I remember who I was before I gave my life to the movement. Someone was patient with me. Someone saw that I had something to contribute. Someone stuck with me. Someone did the work to increase my commitment. Someone taught me how to be accountable. Someone opened my eyes to the root causes of the problems we face. Someone pushed me to call forward my vision for the future. Someone trained me to bring other people who are looking for a movement into one.

No one is safe from the transition this country is undergoing. While many of us have faced hate, ignorance, and greed in our daily lives, the period that we have entered is unlike anything that any of us has ever seen before.

We can build a movement in the millions, across our differences. We will need to build a movement across divides of class, race, gender, age, documentation, religion, and disability. Building a movement requires reaching out beyond the people who agree with you. Simply said, we need each other, and we need leadership and strategy.

We can tell people a hundred times over that because they haven't been here, they have no right to be here now. But I promise that the only place that will get us is nowhere.

ALL-AMERICAN

Nicole Chung

WHEN I MADE an appointment to get my hair cut two weeks after the election, it was with a new stylist—a white woman in her thirties, with a streak of purple in her hair. She commented on the loose, rumpled waves that show up whenever my hair gets damp, and I explained that the slight curl appeared only after I had children. She welcomed the avenue for small talk: How many kids did I have; how old were they; did I have a photo? I pulled out my phone and showed her the picture on my home screen, my two girls at the beach.

"Oh," she said, visibly surprised. "Is their dad American?"

"Yes," I told her. "So am I."

She went on to ask "what" my children were, and whether I thought their coloring was "more olive, or more yellowish like yours?" Later, as she snipped away, she revealed that she and her father and her boyfriend had all voted for Donald Trump.

Though her comments about my kids were the most offensive, it's her assumption about my nationality that has stuck with me in the weeks since. She identified my husband as "American" when what she meant was "white," isolating and othering me in the process. There is nothing out of the ordinary about being taken for a foreigner when you're Asian American; by itself, without years of similar accumulated remarks, her slip might not have bothered me. But in the same month that Donald Trump was elected to our nation's highest office, this white woman's unthinking words served as a stinging reminder of just how many people in this country look at me and see not an American, not someone like them, but an outsider, intrinsically different.

I remember, at some young age, being at the grocery store with my parents when a white woman approached us and asked, "And where is *this* one from?" as though I were some curiosity acquired from a catalog. You can experience "harmless" racism like this as commonplace, week in and week out, and still understand that it is wrong. I hated the woman's phrasing, her strangely benevolent smile, her expectation that we would answer because the information was hers to demand.

No matter where you are from, when you are adopted and nonwhite you become, to many, a symbol of the magnanimity of white Americans. Your foreignness, real or perceived, is transformed into a far more palatable exoticism when propped up by ideals about "colorblind" love. A certain type of white liberal will see you with your white family and feel good about this country, about the open arms and big hearts that make race seem unimportant. Even those who rail against our porous borders will often have something nice to say about the generous people they know who saved some poor kid through adoption. International adoptees are immigrants, too, but the *best* kind, handpicked by white people.

I am not an immigrant, but my birth parents were. They made their way from Seoul to Washington State just a few years before I was born. Like many immigrant families, they ran a small business, where they worked from sunup to midnight. I was the first person in my family born on U.S. soil, and I don't know if I'd be an adoptee at all if my parents hadn't been such recent immigrants—for them, secrecy was paramount, and had they stayed in Korea it would have been difficult to manage the adoption placement without their families finding out. If I hadn't been born early, if they'd had relatives nearby to help, if they'd had good health care, if they hadn't been so isolated, if there had been less stress and strain in their lives, if they had been navigating medical and child welfare systems in their native language, if they hadn't been breaking their backs trying to build their American dream, if they'd remained where they were planted, their lives—and the choices they made about mine—might have been very different.

I have always been aware of the fact that I am here, and American, only by chance. My birthright made certain things easier for my adoptive family, who never had to travel abroad to adopt me, deal with foreign courts and bureaucracies, or take steps to acquire my new citizenship. I grew up being told that I was God's child, I was theirs, and I was American—and that all of these things were blessings. And I knew the quickest way out of awkward conversations with strangers was to answer them directly. "You just tell them you were born here," my parents said; "tell them you're an American, too." Though I didn't realize it at the time, I now understand they were teaching me how to assert my citizenship, my right to be here, from a young age. They were showing me how to live on the defensive with an identity that required constant defending.

Of course, to people for whom "American" means "white"—and Trump's election has only empowered, emboldened such people—it doesn't matter how loudly or how often you say who you are. When white kids called me names no doubt learned from their white parents and siblings, when white people told me to go back where I came from, they didn't care that my *where* had always been *here*. As a child I rarely gave voice to my fury and confusion when I was made to feel this wasn't my country; that it never would be. But every morning at school, standing beside my desk with my hand over my heart, I was conscious of reciting the Pledge of Allegiance clearly, reverently, just a fraction louder than everybody else, because I knew I was the only one in the room who had anything to prove.

A friend who I know does not support Trump recently asked if I thought we should teach our children to respect him "because he's the president." She seemed genuinely conflicted over the idea of "biasing" kids against him. The truth, I told her, is that I have long been obsessed with biasing everyone I know against Trump; I have no intention of teaching my eight-year-old (keenly interested in politics, still #withher all the way) or my five-year-old (oblivious to politics, for the time being) to respect him.

But I know my friend isn't alone in wondering whether she ought to discuss her political views frankly with her children; it's something I hear often from peers. My own parents rarely chose to discuss theirs with me when I was growing up. The first presidential election I can clearly recall is 1988, when I voted for Bush in our school mock election because I'd overheard kids in my carpool making fun of Dukakis. When I asked my parents who they voted for, they refused to tell me, insisting it was "personal." "Oh. Is it like asking someone's age?" I asked. "Worse," Mom said firmly.

Still, by the time I was a teenager, I'd overheard enough to grasp that my family did not trust the federal government. This confused me, as I'd long been hyperaware of the social safety net we had all, at various points, relied on. Even my dyed-in-the-wool-FDR-Democrat grandparents eventually began casting their votes for Republicans ("I can't vote for Hillary," my grandmother declared over the summer, "so I guess it'll have to be Trump"). Though my family is Christian, to me their politics seem to have less to do with religion and more to do with being independent, Libertarian-leaning white conservatives in a large Western state. The pre-election parade of "Trump country" profiles written by journalists traversing the country often made me think of my own origins—while my home state of Oregon is reliably blue, thanks to places like Portland, Salem, and Eugene, my home county in southern Oregon went to Trump.

When I go back, it's hard not to wonder if my family is right about politicians in Portland and Salem, let alone D.C., neither considering nor caring much about the people who live four, five, six hours from the only city in Oregon most people outside it can name. I don't know if my hometown is "dying" or "forgotten," but no matter how long I'm away, it never seems to change: there are the same peaceful mountain views, the same dueling local coffee chains, the same lack of jobs, and the same overwhelmingly white population. "We only saw one black person and two Asian people on our whole trip," my eight-year-old announced to me after our last visit, "not counting us, of course." At first I was horrified that she'd kept a tally, but then I remembered: I used to do the same thing when I was a child. Every time I land at my one-room hometown airport it hits me anew, that cold prickle of awareness somewhere between my shoulder blades—*my kids and I are the only nonwhite people in sight*—and I have to brace myself against the urge to grab my family and flee.

I've spent so long living in progressive, diverse pockets of the East Coast that sometimes it's difficult for me to understand how my white relatives can stand the lack of diversity, the slow-changing nature of the place. When I listen to their conversations, however, I'm reminded that any change back home is greeted not with relief, but with suspicion. "The Mexicans are really moving in on the other side of town," a family friend announced when I was there over the summer, "and they're bringing a lot of crime."

I looked around my parents' living room and saw heads nodding. My older daughter, sitting next to me on the sofa, had lifted her eyes from her book. "I don't think that's true," I said, more for her benefit than anyone else's. "People move here for the same reason anyone moves anywhere—to try and find work and support their families."

This led my mother to ask what I thought about "all the Asians coming over and having babies so they can stay." As I tried to think of a response, my mind leapt back to the last time I'd been made to feel so uncomfortable at a family gathering: several months earlier, during a holiday dinner at my in-laws' house, the relative of a family friend had informed me that I look like "everyone" on the television show *Fresh off the Boat*. In that moment, facing a rude stranger with no meaningful support and scrambling to think of an answer that wouldn't ruin the party for everyone, I honestly hadn't known if the woman was trying to single me out—perhaps because I'd unknowingly offended her—or if her remark had been made in total ignorance, without the intention to wound. With strangers, I find it's often difficult to be sure.

My mother, on the other hand, didn't mean to hurt me, and I knew it. I imagine she felt comfortable voicing her question about Asian immigrants because she *doesn't* think of me as an Asian American— at least, not first and foremost. To her, I'm just her child, and she genuinely wanted to know what I thought about Asian families attempting to put down roots in America in a way my white relatives seem to view as fundamentally unfair. If my mother felt a flicker of regret or embarrassment in asking this of me—a child she would never have adopted had my Korean parents not moved here prior to my birth—it was impossible for me to tell.

As I scrolled through my Twitter feed on November 9, unable to look away from the endless march of postmortems—on Clinton's campaign mistakes, the "forgotten" white working class, and who was *really* to blame—one point, for me, seemed raised above the rest: white

people hadn't done enough to prevent this. Sixty-three percent of
white men voted for Trump. Fifty-three percent of white women.
White people didn't try hard enough, didn't confront their white
families, didn't convince their white friends that Trump would be a
singular disaster for immigrants and Muslims and people of color.
White people had once again put their social comfort before the survival of everyone else.

I nodded as I read these pieces, knowing the charge was also laid
upon me: I, too, have white Trump supporters in my family. I have a
measure of privilege that comes with being East Asian American—a
more "acceptable" minority nowadays, though who knows how long
it will last. I have still more privilege as a transracial adoptee with even
closer proximity to whiteness, and this is a proximity I must use. Still,
I can't say I relish the unsolicited role of race counselor and explainer
to my adoptive relatives, a position I've assumed by virtue of being the
only person of color in the family. And I don't know how effectively
I can act in this role, as I don't think I have much more credibility
with them than any person of color has in any large, friendly group
of white people. I've been called "brainwashed" more times than I
can count. While my family certainly sees me as no threat, in their
eyes I have become yet another angry minority.

For all our political battles over the years—as I have crept further
to the left of anyone the Democratic Party would actually nominate,
and my relatives have moved in the opposite direction—2016 was the
first year I even attempted to sway my parents' presidential votes. In
my otherwise brutally honest, filterless family, one's vote is still seen
as a private, almost hallowed decision, and some residual conditioning from childhood had always prompted me to stop just short of saying, "This is who you should vote for," or "Please don't vote for that
person." But this election felt different. I knew I had to try and
convince them not to vote for Trump, even if they resented me for it.

You have a daughter who isn't white, I reminded them, a daughter in an interracial marriage. Trump is racist, and he's supported and influenced by white nationalists. He's stoking the fears of other people who hold racist views. He's talked about a Muslim ban, a registry, building a border wall, ending birthright citizenship. His supporters don't just want to slow immigration; they want to *end* it. I'm your daughter, and I am a child of immigrants.

So do you think we shouldn't even *have* borders? my father asked.

Another time, I tried appealing to them as grandparents. You have an autistic grandchild, I said. You've seen what a nonstop fight it is for us to advocate for our five-year-old, for her rights and her education. Trump has mocked a disabled reporter and a deaf actress. He's promoted the false claim that vaccines cause autism. There's no way he cares about the education of kids like mine, or the rights of disabled adults. Hillary Clinton's platform on disability rights is not a magic bullet, but it could be a real step forward.

Well, I guess it's good that she's thinking about that, my mother said. But there's no way I'm voting for her.

If they cannot see hatred and bigotry in the rise of Donald Trump, I often think to myself, how will they recognize it anywhere else? But I also know that I have no choice but to try and be a bridge between my white family and all the people like me who are terrified to be living and raising children in Trump's America.

To have a hope of success, I must convince them to acknowledge my racial reality in the first place, a task with which my white relatives have always struggled. Then I need them to recognize that my race *does* have an impact on how I'm perceived, how others speak to me, how I experience the world. Finally, I have to explain why my children and I require their solidarity, whether they like it or not, and

what that means in a country so divided. For all my efforts with
the people who have loved me longest, I fail at reaching them more
than I succeed. It's too easy for them to say "of course," and absorb
the stories without actually seeing the scars.

But I know it's our duty to talk to our people if they chose this.
And these *are* my people, because they chose me. My parents still like
to talk about this fact as though it makes us superior to other families. Other parents are stuck with their kids, they've told me countless times, but we *chose* you.

I've long known this to be an oversimplification, a line reeled off
to make us all feel better. Yet when I consider their politics, which
baffle me as much as mine do them, I can't help but think that "choosing" me was never meant to be a onetime event, sequestered in the
past. They thought my adoption was their happy ending. It was only
the beginning, I want to tell them. If you chose me then, why not
choose me *now*? Why not listen when I tell you how afraid I am for
my children? Why not take my side, even if you can't yet see how
important this is?

Ever since Trump took office, I've been sending my family carefully
composed emails about his unconstitutional executive orders, his various petty and authoritarian statements, his bigoted and unqualified
appointees. Perhaps there are still soft spots, I tell myself, issues on
which they might be more inclined to listen. I always include clear,
concise commentary and links to several credible sources. Then I offer a suggestion: "You can call and tell your senators that you oppose
this [action] [executive order] [nomination] because [it's wrong] [it's
illegal] [you have an autistic grandchild]." These missives have a great
deal in common with similar posts I leave all over social media, encouraging friends to call their senators and representatives. But when
I write these words to loved ones, or call and try to discuss these is-

sues with them, it's a far more loaded request: I know I'll be more upset if they disagree.

This election and its aftermath have changed how I think about allyship, how much it matters to me. Trump's election has made me wonder if it's possible to have honest, sustainable relationships with those who look at him and want to see politics as usual; who look at the widespread resistance to his policies and see mere partisanship. On November 9, after I spoke with my kids about the alarming outcome I had previously sworn wouldn't happen, I scrolled through my social media feeds noting who was outraged and who was silent, feeling something heavier, angrier, but still akin to what I felt when I left home for college and wiped the dust of my hometown from my feet. It seemed this was a moment for evaluating my existing relationships, a time to choose sides and close ranks—not out of spite, but sheer self-preservation. How many people were expecting to remain in my life, I wondered, after choosing to vote against me, against my family, against my children's futures?

Still, there exist family ties I can't and don't wish to escape. So I email my relatives back home, and while this is far from the only thing I do to combat Trumpism, for me it feels like an important if also unwanted assignment—something I have to do if we are going to continue to have a relationship. I email because it's often the easiest way for me to organize facts, sources, and assorted action items into clear bullet points. I email so they can't interrupt or debate me in real time, because my heart can't take it.

It occurs to me that my family could read all of this as patronizing; that it might, in fact, *be* patronizing, or at least hopelessly quixotic. Still, I can't seem to stop writing. I remind them that even if they support some of what this administration is doing, they can try and hold Trump accountable for the rest. When my emails go unanswered, I ponder what their silence means and why I've asked them to take action at all. My relatives may be opinionated, but they aren't

activists; they are busy, with many cares and burdens of their own.
Do I really expect them to join the resistance just because I've asked
them to? I asked them to vote against Trump, too.

It finally occurs to me, while composing my second or third mis-
sive about our disastrously unqualified secretary of education, Betsy
DeVos, that what I am really doing is offering them a chance to take
responsibility for their votes. To try and make amends for their tacit
support of this administration. What does it mean, I wonder, that I
now think about our relationship in terms of *atonement*? And if they
choose to do nothing, where do we go from here?

After weeks of seesawing between anxiety and disgust, swearing while
I read the news, and calling my senators several times a week, I go to
the Women's March on Washington with my friend Rita and two
friends visiting from North Carolina, Marissa and John. My eight-
year-old wants to come with us ("I'll wear one of my Hillary shirts!"),
but I know we'll be on our feet all day and I'm anxious about bringing
her into the huge crowds. I promise to bring the sign she made for
me, her big block letters embellished with colorful Crayola-marker
designs: BLACK LIVES MATTER on one side, and on the other YES WE
CAN. Talking with my daughter about my activism makes me think
about my own parents—I never told them I'd be marching today.
What will they say when they see the photos online? I find myself
anticipating their comments, rallying my arguments.

In the city, the turnout is even bigger than anticipated. We have
to stop well short of Independence and Third. At least a hundred
people I know are out there, somewhere, in the throng, yet I see
no familiar faces except the ones who came with me. I unroll my
daughter's handmade sign and, eventually, after hours of waiting, we
are on the move.

I find I'm emotional, a little choked up, as we are swept up along

with hundreds of thousands of other marchers, chanting and singing, smiling and shouting encouragement at one another. I think
about the millions rising up on every continent, and for the first time
since the election I am flooded with the wild, defiant hope that good
people might yet outnumber the rest. It is the most buoyant—maybe
the most *American*—I have felt in months. This country is no more
mine than an immigrant's, no more mine than anyone's, but it *is* my
country, and in this crowd I have nothing to prove.

When we get home, exhausted but happy, to eat the dinner my
husband prepared and regale him and the kids with stories from the
march, I'm surprised to see a new email from my mother. I had nearly
given up after weeks of silence. She already knows where her Democratic senators stand on the Trump administration's plans for education, she tells me, but she has called her representative to ask him to
support the education of "our special needs children" and make sure
their rights are protected.

It's the first time in years my mother has contacted one of her
elected officials. She didn't do it because she relished the opportunity
to take action or call a stranger, I am sure of it—she must have called
for me. For my kids.

It's a short email. She doesn't ask me for any more action items.
Maybe she even hopes I won't respond. In my head, though, I'm
already composing my response. *Thanks, Mom. That's great. Here's what
you can do next.*

ABOUT THE CONTRIBUTORS

MELISSA ARJONA is an adjunct English professor and activist living in south Texas. She is an avid reader of fiction and women's history, and records her literary musings on her book blog, "The Feminist Texican [Reads]." She also contributes to *PostBourgie*.

KERA BOLONIK is the executive editor of *DAME* magazine and an essayist and critic whose work has appeared in *New York* magazine, *Glamour, Elle, The New York Times Book Review*, the *Village Voice, The Nation, Slate,* and *Salon,* among many other publications and anthologies. She lives in New York City with her family.

CARINA CHOCANO's writing has appeared in *The New York Times Magazine, Elle, The California Sunday, Vulture, The Cut, GOOD, Texas Monthly, Wired, The New Yorker*, and others. She has been a film and TV critic at *The Los Angeles Times, Entertainment Weekly*, and *Salon*. Her second book is *You Play the Girl*, published in August 2017. She lives in Los Angeles.

NICOLE CHUNG is an editor at *Catapult* and the former managing editor of *The Toast*. Her essays and articles have appeared in *The New York Times*, *The New York Times Magazine*, *The Atlantic*, *BuzzFeed*, *Hazlitt*, and other publications. Her first book, a memoir about adoption, is forthcoming in 2018.

SADY DOYLE is the author of *Trainwreck: The Women We Love to Hate, Mock, and Fear . . . and Why*, a book on how the media build up and tear down "badly behaved" women. She founded the feminist blog "Tiger Beatdown" in 2008, and received the Women's Media Center Social Media Award for online activism in 2011. Her work has appeared in *Elle*, *The Guardian*, *Rookie* magazine, *In These Times,* and just about anywhere you can imagine across the wide, wonderful Internet.

JILL FILIPOVIC is a journalist based in Nairobi and New York City, and a contributing opinion writer for *The New York Times* and a columnist for Cosmopolitan.com. She is also an attorney, and her work on law, politics, gender, and foreign affairs has appeared in *The New York Times*, *The Washington Post*, *Time*, *The Nation*, *Foreign Policy*, and others.

ALICIA GARZA is an activist and writer who lives in Oakland, California. She has organized around the issues of health, student services and rights, rights for domestic workers, ending police brutality, anti-racism, and violence against trans and gender-nonconforming people of color. Her writing has appeared in *The Guardian*, *The Nation*, *The Feminist Wire*, *Rolling Stone*, *Huffington Post*, and truthout.org. She currently directs special projects at the National Domestic Workers Alliance. She also co-founded the Black Lives Matter movement.

KATE HARDING is the author of *Asking for It: The Alarming Rise of Rape Culture—and What We Can Do About It,* a finalist for the 2016 Minnesota Book Award in General Nonfiction. She's given lectures on rape culture and body image at colleges around the country, and in spring 2017, she was the Distinguished Visiting Writer at Cornell College. She is feminist as fuck.

SARAH HEPOLA is the author of the memoir *Blackout: Remembering the Things I Drank to Forget.* Her essays have appeared in *The New York Times Magazine, The Guardian, Elle, Glamour, Slate,* and *Salon,* and she is a contributor to NPR's "Fresh Air." She is currently working on a collection of essays about traveling alone.

SARAH MICHAEL HOLLENBECK has published personal essays in *Dogwood* and *TriQuarterly.* Her essay "A Goldmine" was nominated for a Pushcart and received a Notable Mention in *Best American Essays 2014.* She often shares her writing aloud at Live Lit shows around Chicago. Sarah is in the early stages of writing and compiling a collection of essays exploring the experiences of women living with invisible and visible disabilities. But she's been a little distracted from her writing since becoming the co-owner of Women & Children First, one of the last remaining feminist bookstores in the country. As a bookstore owner, she has been featured in *New City*'s Lit50 and in *Publishers Weekly* Star Watch, which honors forty young people who are making a difference in the U.S. publishing industry.

SAMANTHA IRBY is the author of the books *We Are Never Meeting in Real Life* and *Meaty,* as well as a blog called "Bitches Gotta Eat."

SARAH JAFFE is a Nation Institute fellow and an independent journalist covering labor, economic justice, social movements, politics, gender, and pop culture. Her work has appeared in *The Nation, Salon, The Week, The American Prospect, The Washington Post, The Atlantic,* and many other publications. She is the co-host, with Michelle Chen, of *Dissent* magazine's "Belabored" podcast, as well as an editorial board member at *Dissent* and a columnist at *New Labor Forum.* She is the author of *Necessary Trouble: Americans in Revolt.*

RANDA JARRAR's work has appeared in *The New York Times Magazine, Utne Reader, Salon, Guernica, The Rumpus, Oxford American, Ploughshares, The Sun,* and others. Her first book, the Arab-American coming-of-age novel *A*

Map of Home, is now on many college syllabi. It was published in half a dozen languages and won a Hopwood Award, an Arab-American Book Award, and was named one of the best novels of 2008 by the Barnes & Noble *Review*. Her new book, *Him, Me, Muhammad Ali*, was named one of the Most Anticipated Books of 2016 by The Millions, a Key Collection for Fall 2016 by *Library Journal*, and one of *Electric Literature*'s twenty-five best collections of the year, and has recently won the Story Prize's Spotlight Award. She has received fellowships from the Civitella Ranieri Foundation, the Lannan Foundation, Hedgebrook, and others, and in 2010 was named one of the most gifted writers of Arab origin under the age of forty. She runs RAWI (the Radius of Arab-American Writers).

ZERLINA MAXWELL is the director of progressive programming for Sirius XM Satellite Radio. She was formerly the director of progressive media for Hillary Clinton's presidential campaign. Zerlina has hosted live political and celebrity interviews for the *Huffington Post* and her writing has appeared in the New York *Daily News, The Washington Post, Jet* magazine, *Marie Claire*, on theGrio.com, BET.com, Feministing.com, CNN.com, and in other mainstream media outlets. She has a law degree from Rutgers Law School Newark and a BA in international relations from Tufts University.

COLLIER MEYERSON is a contributor to *The Nation*. She has an Emmy for Outstanding News Discussion and Analysis (*All In with Chris Hayes*) and an award from the National Association of Black Journalists for her commentary. She lives in Brooklyn.

SAMHITA MUKHOPADHYAY is a writer, editor, and speaker. She is currently the senior editorial director of Culture and Identities at *Mic*. She is the former executive editor of the award-winning blog "Feministing.com" and the author of *Outdated: Why Dating Is Ruining Your Love Life*. Her work has appeared in *Al Jazeera, The Guardian, New York* magazine, *Medium, Talking Points Memo*, and *Jezebel*.

MARY KATHRYN NAGLE is an enrolled citizen of the Cherokee Nation. She currently serves as the executive director of the Yale Indigenous Performing Arts Program. She is also a partner at Pipestem Law, P.C., where she works to protect tribal sovereignty and the inherent right of Indian Nations to protect their women and children from domestic violence and sexual assault. Nagle has authored numerous briefs in federal appellate courts, including the United States Supreme Court. As a playwright she has received commissions from Arena Stage (*Sovereignty*), the Rose Theater (Omaha, Nebraska), Portland Center Stage, and Denver Center for the Performing Arts. Her other plays include *Manahatta, Diamonds, Waaxe's Law, Sliver of a Full Moon, My Father's Bones, Miss Lead,* and *Fairly Traceable.*

KATHA POLLITT, the author of *Pro: Reclaiming Abortion Rights, Virginity or Death!* and *Learning to Drive,* is a poet, essayist, and columnist for *The Nation.* She has won many prizes and awards for her work, including the National Book Critics Circle Award for her first collection of poems, *Antarctic Traveller,* and two National Magazine Awards for essays and criticism. She lives in New York City.

REBECCA SOLNIT is the author of eighteen or so books on feminism, Western and indigenous history, popular power, social change and insurrection, wandering and walking, hope and disaster, including the books *Men Explain Things to Me* and *Hope in the Dark;* a trilogy of atlases of American cities; *The Faraway Nearby; A Paradise Built in Hell: The Extraordinary Communities That Arise in Disaster; A Field Guide to Getting Lost; Wanderlust: A History of Walking;* and *River of Shadows: Eadweard Muybridge and the Technological Wild West* (for which she received a Guggenheim, the National Book Critics Circle Award in criticism, and the Lannan Literary Award). A product of the California public education system from kindergarten to graduate school, she is a columnist at *Harper's* and a regular contributor to *The Guardian.*

CHERYL STRAYED is the author of the number one *New York Times* bestselling memoir *Wild*, the bestselling advice essay collection *Tiny Beautiful Things*, the novel *Torch*, and the quotes collection *Brave Enough*. Her books have been translated into forty languages. Strayed's essays have been published in *The Best American Essays*, *The New York Times*, *The Washington Post Magazine*, *Vogue*, *Salon*, *The Sun*, *Tin House*, and elsewhere. Strayed is the co-host, along with Steve Almond, of the WBUR podcast "Dear Sugar Radio," which originated with her popular "Dear Sugar" advice column on *The Rumpus*. She lives in Portland, Oregon.

MEREDITH TALUSAN has written numerous features, essays, and opinion pieces for publications like *The Guardian*, *The Atlantic*, *Vice Magazine*, *Matter*, *BuzzFeed News*, *The Nation*, *The American Prospect*, *Mic*, and many others. She divides her time between New York City and the Philippines.

JESSICA VALENTI is a columnist for *The Guardian*, where she writes about gender and politics. In 2004 she founded the award-winning Feministing.com. Her work has appeared in *The New York Times*, *The Washington Post*, *The Nation*, and *Ms*. She is the author of several books, including *The New York Times* bestseller *Sex Object*, and the national bestseller *Full Frontal Feminism*. Jessica lives in Brooklyn with her husband and daughter.

JAMIA WILSON is a leading voice on feminist and women's rights issues whose work and words have appeared in and on *The New York Times*, *New York* magazine, the *Today* show, CNN, *Elle*, *Refinery29*, *HuffPost Live*, *The Washington Post*, and more. She's a staff writer for *Rookie* magazine and has contributed to several books such as *Madonna and Me: Women Writers on the Queen of Pop*, *The V Word*, *Slut: The Play*, *When Grace Meets Power*, and *I Still Believe Anita Hill*.